How to Weave a Navajo Rug and Other Lessons from Spider Woman

LYNDA TELLER PETE AND BARBARA TELLER ORNELAS

ILLUSTRATIONS BY MYCHAL YELLOWMAN

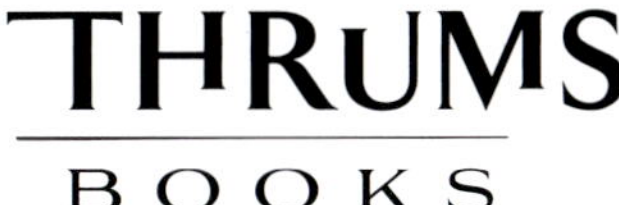

An Imprint of Schiffer Publishing
4880 Lower Valley Rd., Atglen, PA 19310 USA

Library of Congress Control Number: 2020933745

Publisher: Linda Ligon
Associate Publisher: Karen Brock
Technical Editor: Velma Kee Craig
Copyeditor: Kathryn Bright
Design: Launie Parry

ISBN: 978-1-7344217-0-5
Printed in China

Published by Thrums Books
An Imprint of Schiffer Publishing, Ltd.
4880 Lower Valley Road
Atglen, PA 19310
Phone: (610) 593-1777; Fax: (610) 593-2002
E-mail: Info@schifferbooks.com
Web: www.schifferbooks.com

For our complete selection of fine books on this and related subjects, please visit our website at www.schifferbooks.com. You may also write for a free catalog.

Schiffer Publishing's titles are available at special discounts for bulk purchases for sales promotions or premiums. Special editions, including personalized covers, corporate imprints, and excerpts, can be created in large quantities for special needs. For more information, contact the publisher.

We are always looking for people to write books on new and related subjects. If you have an idea for a book, please contact us at proposals@schifferbooks.com.

DEDICATION

Barbara and I dedicate this book to the Diné weavers who survived "The Long Walk." Their perilous and courageous journey to bring weaving back to our homeland within our sacred mountains ensured that our family and countless other Diné weavers could continue our weaving traditions and teaching of Navajo weaving to our future generations.

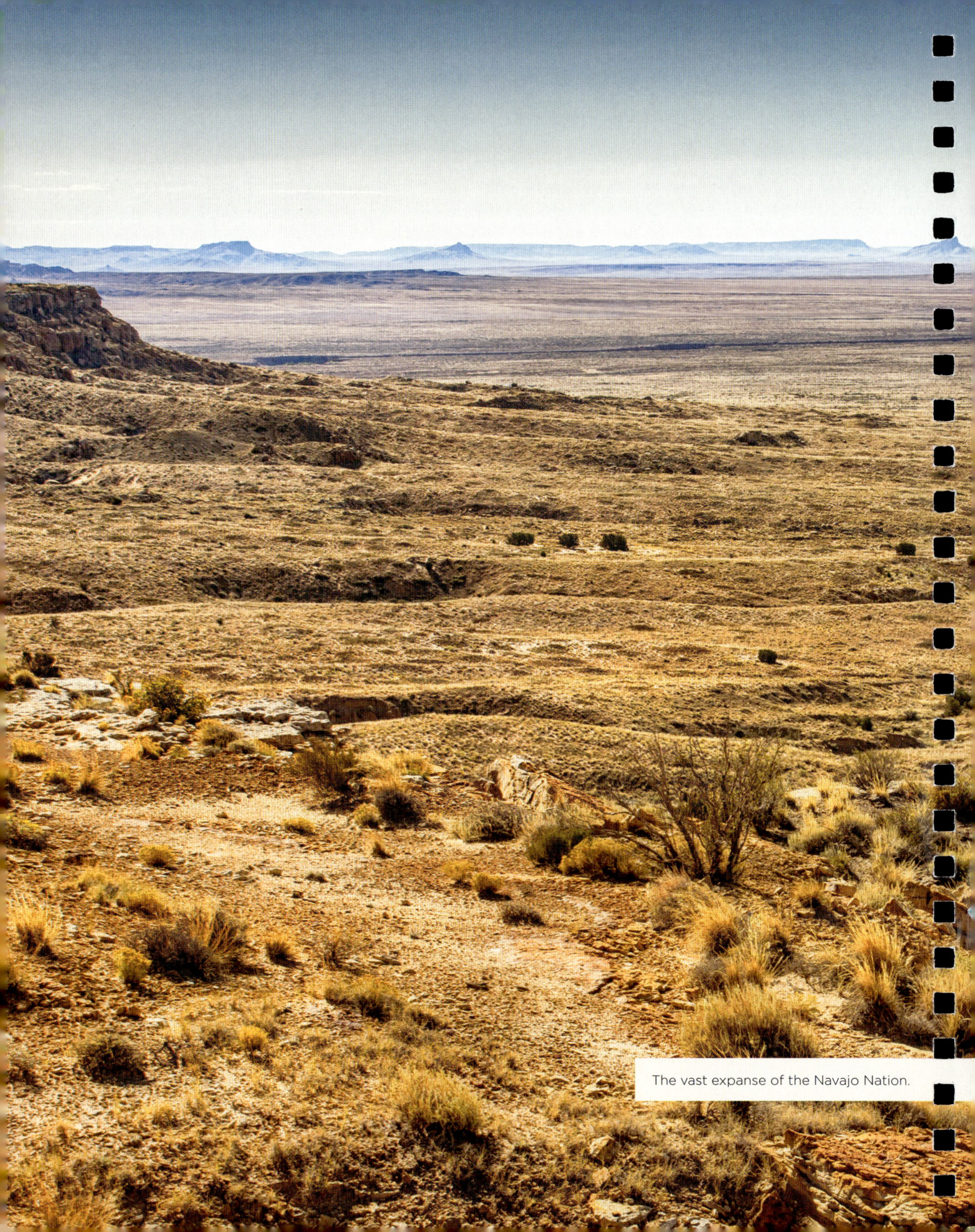

The vast expanse of the Navajo Nation.

ACKNOWLEDGMENTS

Barbara and I would like to acknowledge many family, friends, colleagues, students, book contributors, museums, guilds, and universities. Please be patient; the list is long.

We begin with our parents, Sam and Ruth Teller. Our father built our first looms and tools, and we learned how to weave from our mother. Without our older sister, Rosann Teller Lee, we would be, at best, mediocre weavers and certainly not teachers. Her firm resolve often reduced us to tears, but we live by her motto "You are only as good as your last weaving," meaning that with every weaving project, we take no shortcuts, and we cannot rest on our laurels, award ribbons, and prize money; we have to improve with each weaving and weave challenging designs.

We acknowledge our paternal grandparents, Paul and Nellie Teller, who gave us the traditional teachings of weaving. Every family member is contributing to our weaving lives: our aunts, uncles, brothers, nephews, nieces, numerous cousins, and grandchildren. Every single family member has to contribute for a weaver or a family of Diné weavers to be successful. We are grateful that Paul's father, our great grandfather, survived the prison camp at Bosque Redondo and came home to Canyon de Chelly; we recite his weaving songs and prayers today.

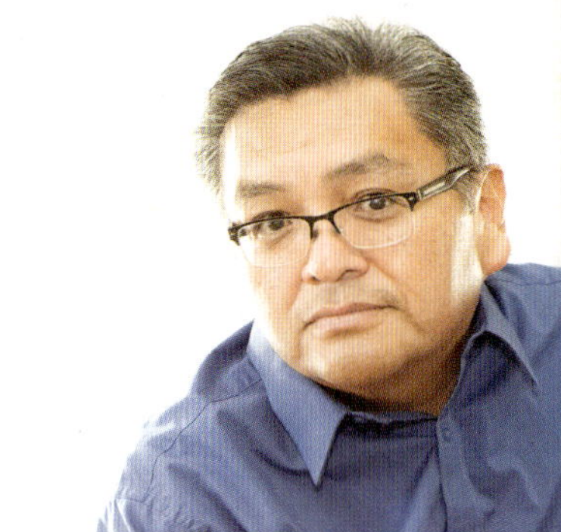

Belvin E. Pete

Barbara's husband, David, has been instrumental in documentation and led us to our weaving history in print and photos. My husband, Belvin E. Pete, also from a Diné weaving family, has brought his engineering and "Injun-uity" to our weaving and has elevated us into embracing innovation. He has passed on his knowledge of toolmaking to Terry Lee.

Our nephew Terry Lee, our sister Rosann's son, kept us in weaving tools for many years and often surprised us with specialty tools when weaving students had physical challenges. Barbara's children, sixth-generation weavers Sierra and Michael, have inspired us to weave beyond our "Trading Post style" of Two Grey Hills tapestry weaving. We still weave Two Grey Hills tapestries, but we are branching into other styles, period styles from the mid to late 1800s and some modern abstracts. It's a little nerve wracking at times but keeps our weaving acumen sharp. We are extremely proud that our seventh generation of grandchildren, Roxanne Rose Lee and Javier Teller Ornelas O'Mara, will be representing the Teller line of weavers for our future. A large circle of family keeps us humble when we need it, encourages us when we need it, elevates us when we need it, and douses us with humor when we need it. Ultimately, it's the genuine love of family and tradition that keeps us weaving.

We have two groups of student weavers, Diné students and non-Navajo students, all of whom have been instrumental to this book. Barbara started teaching in 1997, and I joined her in 2000 at Idyllwild School of Arts in Idyllwild, California. We gave our class a one-page handout in 2001, and our handouts have grown in nineteen years, culminating in this book. After every class, at least one student will highlight an error, ask for clarification on a process, or address a weaving issue gone awry. Sometimes in my haste, I make a correction on my smartphone, but since I do not have squirrel fingers, I make more errors. It is the peril of being a teacher.

We acknowledge the Diné students who contributed their Diné family's weaving traditions and teachings in classes and have enriched our own traditional knowledge.

We acknowledge a special group of students who have become close friends and have been instrumental in building our weaving classes: Leslie Thompson Chatwin, Leeanna McNeilley, Ercil Howard-Wroth, Rocky Gaines, Bill and Carole Greene. And we send a huge thank-you to Pamela Bliss, a floor-loom weaving teacher, colleague, and friend who connected us with weaving guilds.

We acknowledge the museums, curators, and personnel who invited us to collaborate on all things Diné weaving: the Heard Museum, Phoenix, Arizona; the Denver Museum of Nature and Science, Denver, Colorado; University of Colorado Museum of Natural History, Boulder, Colorado; the National Museum of the American Indian at the Smithsonian Institution, Washington, DC; the Amerind Foundation and Museum, Dragoon, Arizona; the Colorado Springs Fine Arts Center, Colorado Springs, Colorado; Museum of Texas Tech University, Lubbock, Texas; Mariposa Museum, Peterborough, New Hampshire; Mount Holyoke College Art Museum, South Hadley, Massachusetts; Museum of Indian Arts and Culture, Santa Fe, New Mexico; Arizona State Museum, Tucson, Arizona; American Museum of Natural History, New York, New York; and the Bard Graduate Center, New York, New York.

We acknowledge the many weaving guilds, fiber art centers, universities, art schools, wool mills, and a lot of small private groups that provided an opportunity for us to teach Navajo weaving, cultivating a diverse student population.

We acknowledge the three Diné cultural contributors to our book: Freddie Johnson, Cheron Nez Johnson, and Lyle Harvey. Freddie Johnson and his wife, Cheron Nez Johnson, along with their family of six children, moved to Tempe, Arizona, for employment and education opportunities; they are dedicated to teaching the Diné language and cultural protocols, and they are mentors to those seeking a linkage to their Diné heritage. Freddie and Cheron come from a long line of Diné weavers. We acknowledge Diné educator extraordinaire Lyle Harvey, resident of Rock Point, Arizona, and grandson of Diné weavers and four Diné medicine men. Using his family's knowledge, he provides cultural stories for Diné youth at various schools on the Diné Nation.

We acknowledge our new weaving student Sarah Rosalena Brady, assistant professor of art at the University of California, Santa Barbara, who generously shared with us an overlooked fact—that a mathematician named Ada Lovelace used her knowledge of a Jacquard weaving loom to invent computer coding, thereby developing the idea of computer software. That invention is huge, considering that everyone, anyone who uses design graphics for any type of art, has to thank Ms. Lovelace and the team of six women who programmed the first punch cards using weaving knowledge.

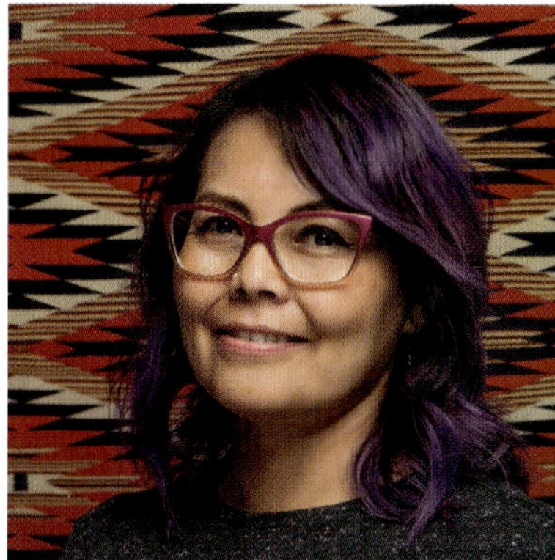

Velma Kee Craig

We acknowledge our Diné weaving student Velma Kee Craig, whom we encouraged to be a weaving teacher. We respect her as a colleague and value her friendship. She patiently combed through our weaving and warping instructions with a technical editorial eye, and her collaboration has been monumental in organizing the step-by-step instructions.

We would like to acknowledge our dear friend Myke Yellowman who allowed us to experiment on his wedding attire. Barbara and I collaborated and wove a Two Grey Hills tapestry for his kilt apron. The tapestry was sent to Scotland to Myke's fiancée's kilt maker, Stuart Shephard. The kilt maker was very excited to work with a Diné tapestry. We exchanged this labor of love for Myke's illustrations; as Diné, we still barter weaving skills even if we are far from our homeland.

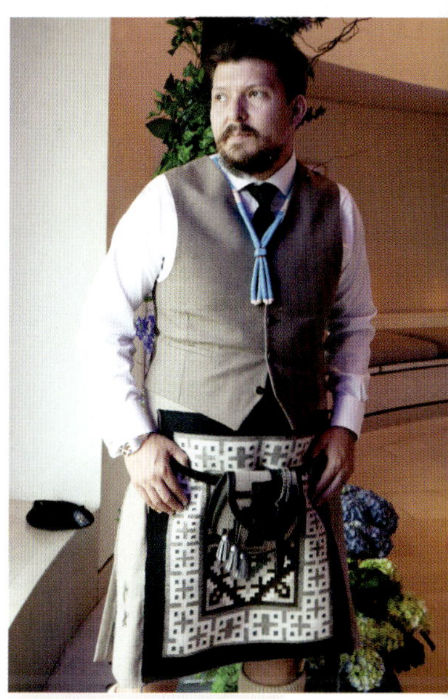

Myke Yellowman

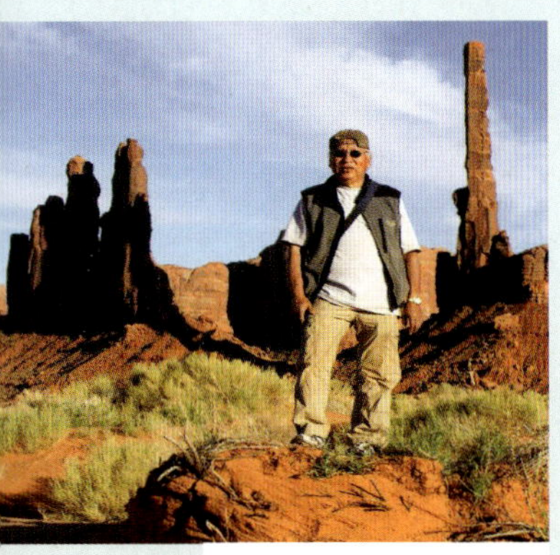
Dr. Charles Cambridge

We acknowledge our friend Dr. Charles Cambridge who contributed to our Diné history. We acknowledge our dear friend Ercil Howard-Wroth who graciously provided her perspective as a non-Diné weaver and supplemented the chapter on spinning. We acknowledge our Diné weaving student Verdenas Brown, originally from Chinle, Arizona, who undauntingly sat for hours as we used her hands for our step-by-step weaving photos. We acknowledge Thrums Books for this opportunity: Linda Ligon, Thrums Books director and publisher; Joe Coca, photographer; and Karen Brock, associate publisher. They have graciously extended their "Long Threads" of support and kindness to us. Their commitment to indigenous weaving communities worldwide, letting us tell our stories, is making a big impact on how our indigenous weaving art is being viewed and honored. *Ahxéhee'* (Thank you).

We hope you enjoy the book.

TABLE OF CONTENTS

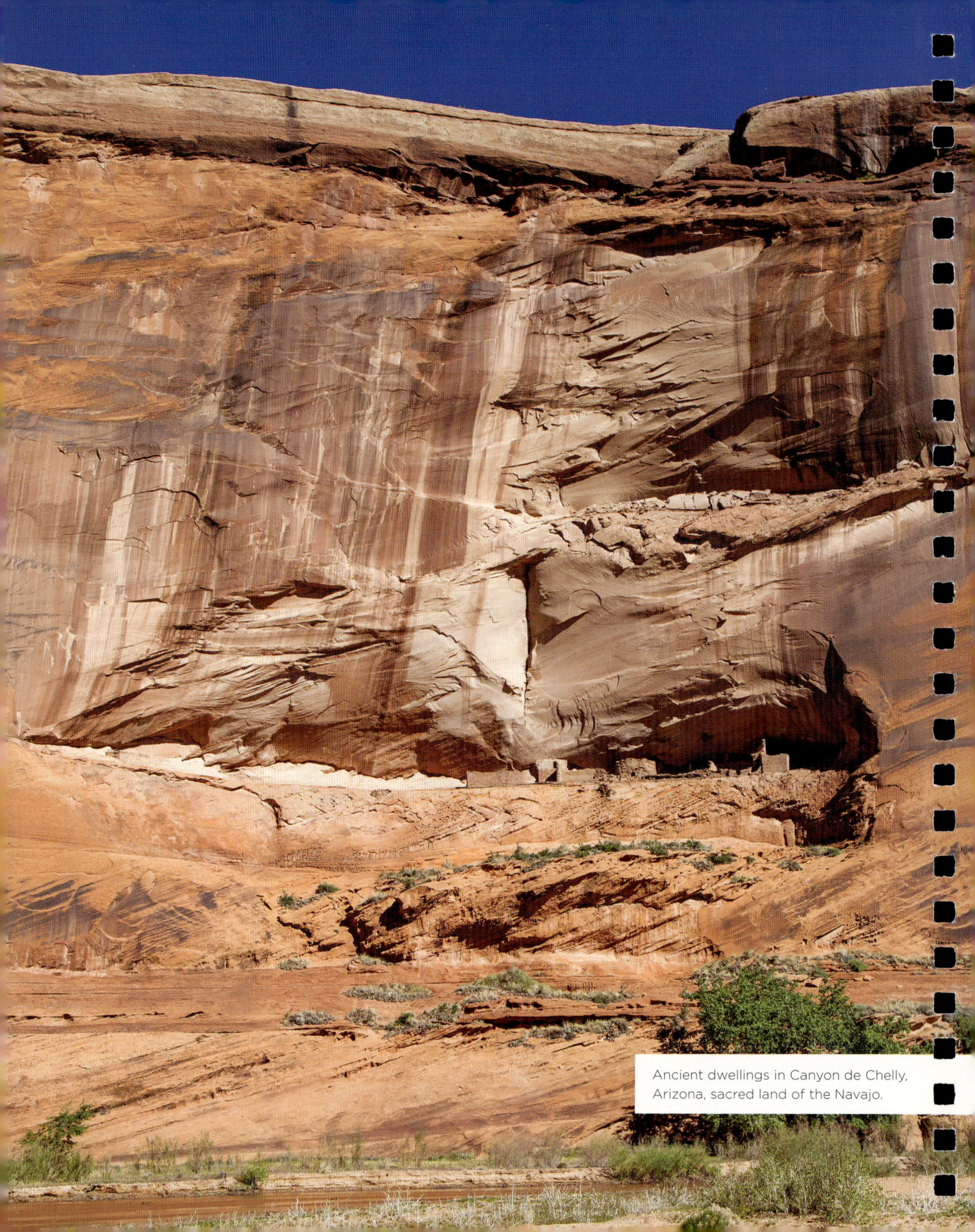

Ancient dwellings in Canyon de Chelly, Arizona, sacred land of the Navajo.

INTRODUCTION

Niizhóní dóó yá'át'ééh dóó ahxéhee' (Greetings in beauty and thank you). We are fifth-generation Diné weavers from the Two Grey Hills and Newcomb, New Mexico, area of the *Diné Bikéyah* (Navajo Nation). We greet you and extend our weaving hands to you in friendship. Our proper kinship greeting is a handshake. Our thumbs with our spiral print represent us as individuals; our index fingers are our maternal clans, representing our mother, Ruth Begay Teller, Born to the Water's Edge Clan, *Tábąąhá;* our middle fingers are our paternal clans, representing our father, Sam K. Teller, Born for the Water-Flows-Together Clan, *Tó'aheedlíinii*; our ring fingers are our maternal grandfather's clan, representing our mother's father, James Shorty Begay, Born for Red Bottom People, *Tł'ááshchí'í*; our pinkie fingers are our paternal grandfather's clan, representing our father's father, Paul K. Teller, One-Walks-Around Clan, *Honágháahnii*. We recite our clans to establish kinship. We recite our mother's clan first because the Diné is a matrilineal society. We speak in our *Diné Bizaad* (Navajo language) because this brings power to our words. This is how we are Diné women, how we are Diné weavers.

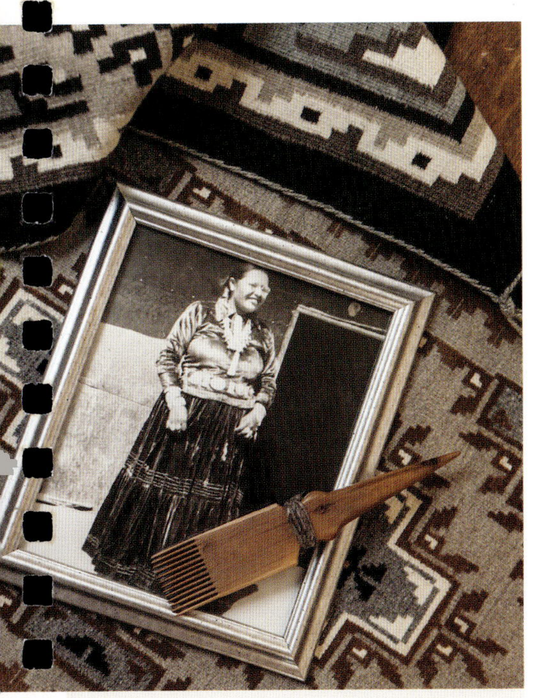

A photo of the authors' mother, Ruth Teller.

Hózhó is our way of life and it empowers us every day. Hózhó means seeking, making wise choices, and performing positive deeds daily. It is the guiding principal that encompasses all Diné philosophical ideals and spirituality and helps us achieve balanced harmony. Hózhó encourages us to walk in beauty, to be grateful for the gifts of life, good health, and our connection to nature, and to employ the concept of *k'é,* which refers to showing love, compassion, friendliness, understanding, and generosity to our kinships.

We sincerely hope that our reflection to the world is expressed through our weaving and our vocation of teaching weaving. We try to live our lives in balance each day. At age six, we learned how to weave from our mother, Ruth. In our teenage years, our older sister, Rosann Teller Lee, taught us the finer details of weaving including intricate design construction using math, color balance, and art theory. We followed the example of the traditional Diné weaving of our paternal grandmother, Nellie Peshlakai Teller, and we have incorporated the traditional teachings and protocols of proper Diné weaving etiquette into our daily lives. Through our songs and prayers, we acknowledge our relationship to the universe, the elements, the animals, our close and extended kinships, and inanimate objects. During our prayers, we touch the spirals on the tops of our heads. The spiral pattern, unique to each of us, appeared when we were born and our *Diyin Dine'é* (Holy People) breathed life into us. We wear turquoise daily to let our Diyin Dine'é recognize us as *Nihikaa Dine'h bi' la ishdlii* (the five-fingered Holy Earth surface people). We voice our gratitude that we are able to weave another day, for when we weave, we are answering our ancestors' prayers by being self-reliant; we are resilient; we are warriors; we extend kindness; and we pass on our weaving knowledge.

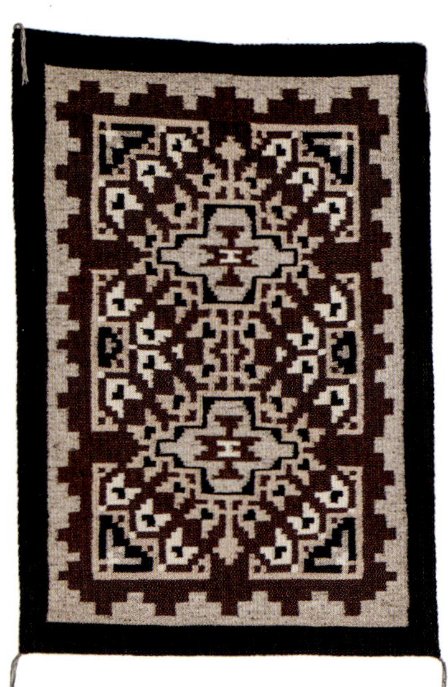

A Two Grey Hills rug by Ruth Teller.

There are different styles of teaching Navajo weaving, Navajo warping, and how to prepare weaving materials. This book is our way of providing instructions, and we do not claim that the instructions here represent all Navajo weaving. We take responsibility for all errors. We encourage all of our students to study under other Diné teachers and to embrace their lessons.

To our Diné readers, our style of weaving is by no means the only way to weave; we hope some of the warping and weaving techniques will encourage you to explore new weaving paths and will inspire you to seek out more weaving knowledge from extended kinships. The ability to pass on your Diné weaving knowledge to your children and grandchildren is decolonizing and paramount to our ancestors' way of teaching. "*Táá hwó ají t'éego*" means "Persevere by your own efforts." Diné teaching says that each of us is responsible for doing what is necessary to provide a good life for ourselves.

To our non-Navajo readers, we give you a glimpse into our Diné weaving world. We encourage you to apply these weaving techniques to expand your own weaving styles and enhance your weaving techniques. Attempts to understand each other's culture and way of life, strengthened by friendship in creating art together, make our unique fiber community a kind world.

Diné Hózhóji

BLESSING WAY PRAYER

Shitsiji' hózhǫ́ǫ dooleeł
Beauty before me

Shikéédęę' hózhǫ́ǫ dooleeł
Beauty behind me

Shiyaagi hózhǫ́ǫ dooleeł
Beauty below me

Shik'igi hózhǫ́ǫ dooleeł
Beauty above me

Shinaadę́ę' hózhǫ́ǫ dooleeł
Beauty all around me

Shizaad hahóózhǫǫd dooleeł
Beauty in our words

Si'ąh Naghéíí Bik'eh
Hózhóon nísísdlįį'
Beauty in our words is repeating, restoring and increasing

Hózhǫ́ náhádlįį. Hózhǫ́ náhádlįį. Hózhǫ́ náhádlįį. Hózhǫ́ náhádlįį'
Beauty is restored

ABOUT THIS BOOK

For many years, we have been teaching weaving classes to both Navajo and non-Navajo people. Our mission is to ensure the future of the art, and to spread an appreciation of its beauty and meaning to as many people as possible. For this teaching, we take a practical approach.

We have devised a loom that is portable and comfortable to use. It may not be as picturesque as the ones our ancestors used, but it works. We have collected a "kit" of tools, many of which were not available to our grandmothers, that make the process smooth and the results successful. We have devised a beginning project that teaches all the important skills, but on a small, manageable scale. The heart of this book is to use those tools, that know-how, and that practice to create a well-made small weaving that honors the weaver's efforts and expresses her creativity.

We've included a lot of Navajo history and cultural lore because the weaving springs from that heart. We've included a lot of family stories, too, not because we think our family knows the only way, but because we want to share the warm, nurturing experience of having grown up in a weaving culture.

LANGUAGE CHALLENGES

The instructional material in this book was derived partly from the handouts we give our students, and partly from experiences we've had teaching over that past years. Many of our students have been Navajo, but many have not. Some classes have been of mixed ethnicity, some have not. Adjusting our language, the words we use to describe different parts of the weaving process, has been a challenge!

The best example we can think of has to do with the term "warp." To a non-Navajo weaver, "warp" might mean a whole set of single threads, or it might mean a single thread. To a Navajo weaver, warps occur in pairs—male and female. We don't always say "pair of warps;" sometimes we say "double warp," and sometimes just "warp." Sometimes the male and female warps act together, and sometimes separately. If you're accustomed to very precise, consistent language, please have faith and look at the pictures. They should make everything clear.

Or selvage. That's another term that can seem tricky, especially if you come from a floor-loom weaving background. Navajo weaving has four selvages: one on each side, one at each end. We call them selvage cords, because they're made of heavier, multi-plied yarn. Sometimes we just call them side cords and end cords. Again, following the photographs and illustrations will make everything clear.

You'll find other examples as you work through the text. Is it a pole, a rod, or a dowel? Female heddle rod, male shed rod? As you learn by doing, the words will come naturally. And learning by doing is the point of this book. Traditional Navajo weavers learn as much by watching as by being told. They learn from mistakes and from successes. Weaving well is a lifelong journey, and we're happy that you're traveling with us on that road.

We hope you use this book in whatever way best suits your needs and interests: to create your own Navajo-style weaving, to appreciate its heritage and future, and to find commonalities between cultures. *Hózhǫ́ǫ.*

The Diné philosophy of *Si'ąh Naghéíí Bik'eh Hózhóon* and its related components, *Nitsáhákees* (Thinking), *Nahat'á* (Planning), *Iiná* (Living), and *Sihasin* (Achievement), are employed in each word of this book by us and by our Diné contributors.

—Lynda Teller Pete and Barbara Teller OrnelasLynda Teller Pete and Barara Teller Ornelas

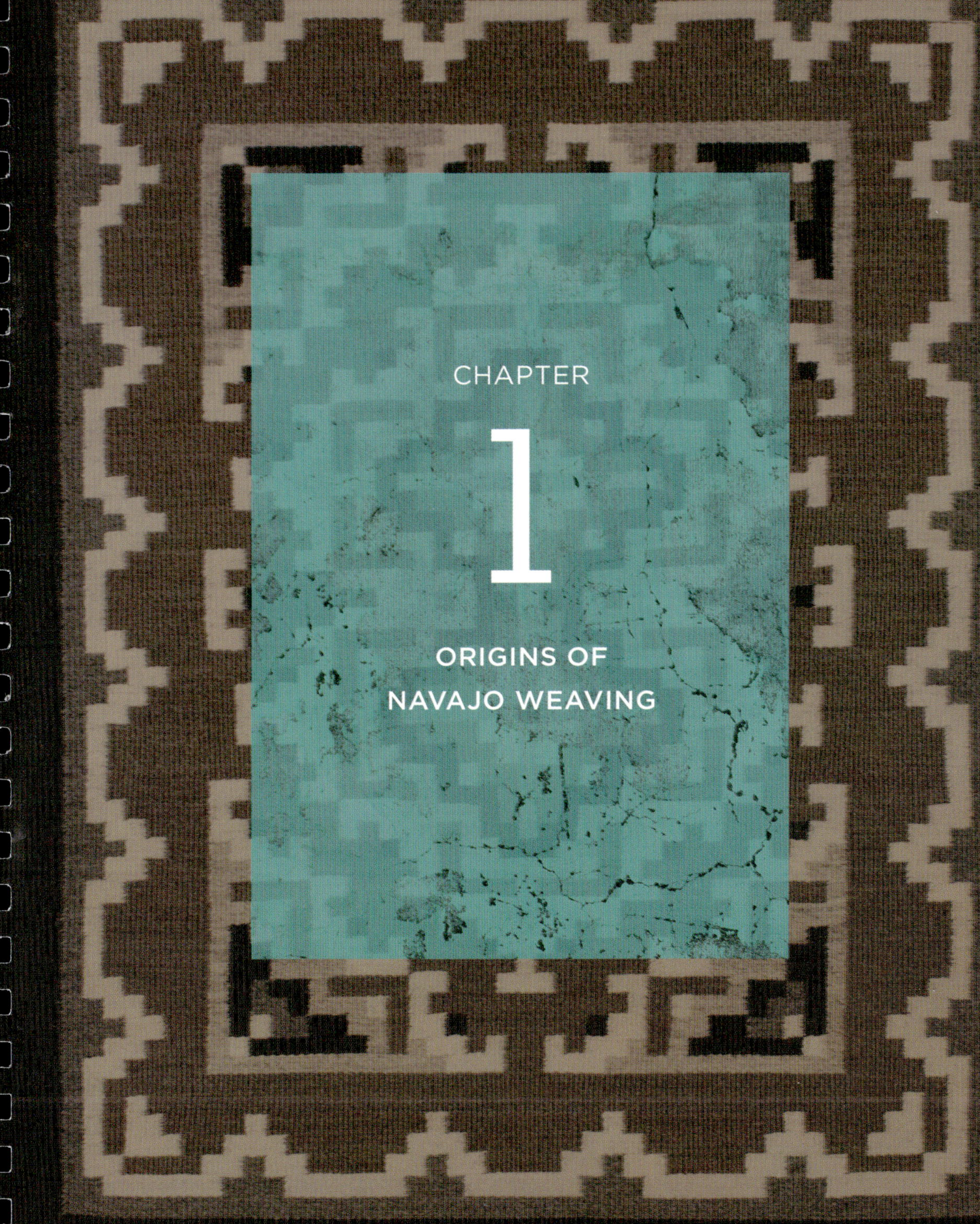

CHAPTER

1

ORIGINS OF NAVAJO WEAVING

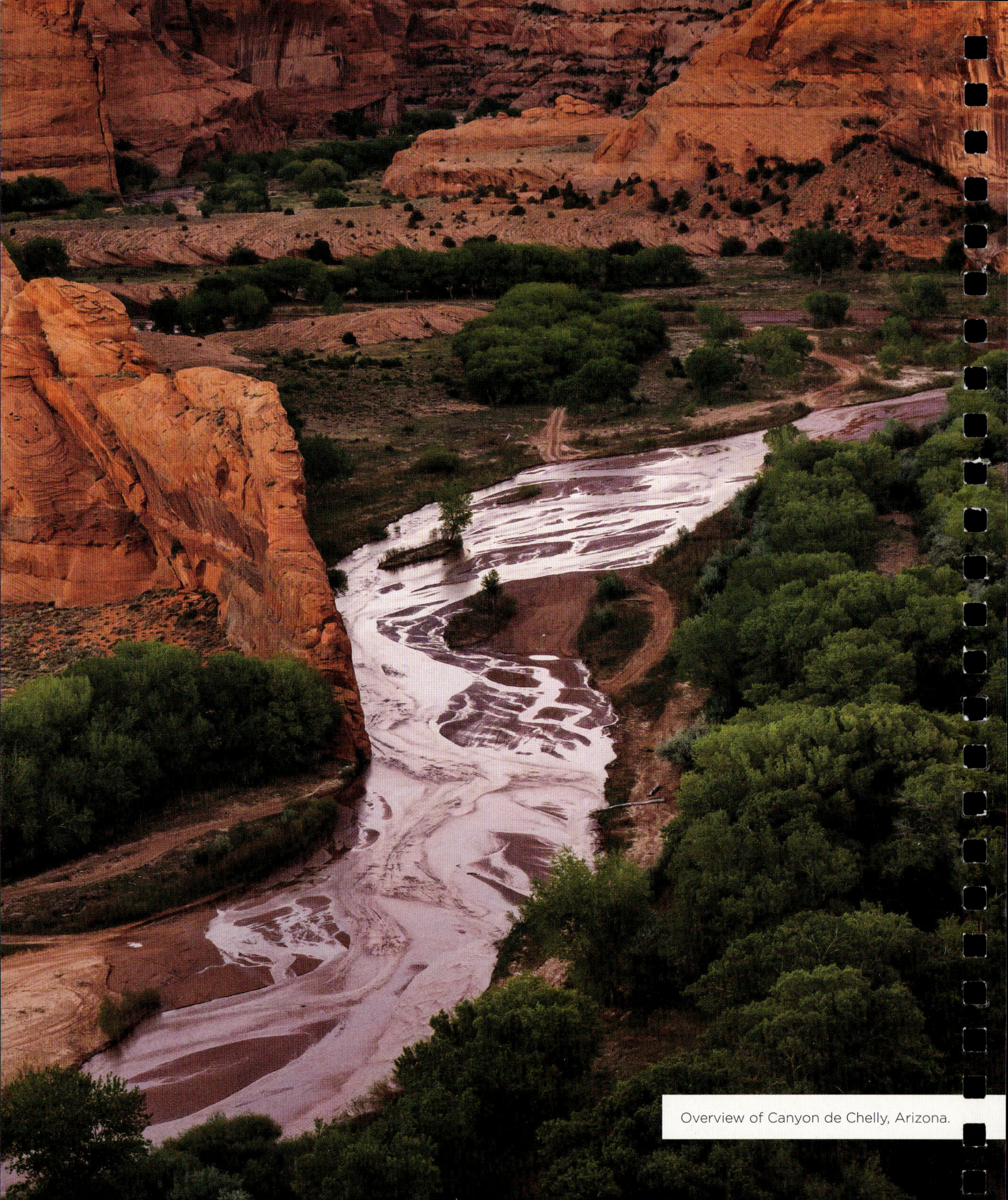

Overview of Canyon de Chelly, Arizona.

ORIGINS of NAVAJO WEAVING

She's weaving faster than a speeding bullet. More powerful than a trading post. Able to leap tall corrals in a single bound. Look! Up in the sky! It's a bird! It's a plane! It's Spider Woman!

Is it a myth? Is it a fabled tale? How, when, and from whom did Navajos learn to weave? Did Navajos borrow their culture?

While working on *How to Weave a Navajo Rug*, I researched several books about Navajo weaving at the Museum of Indian Arts and Culture/Laboratory of Anthropology in Santa Fe, New Mexico. The librarian stacked piles of books on three 8-foot tables and was kind to let me keep them there for the duration of my study. All the books were written by non-Navajo anthropologists and ethnographers. I read the forewords and searched out paragraphs about how and when Navajos learned to weave. Some believe we learned from the Pueblo Indians when we arrived in the Southwest in the twelfth century. Still others believe we learned from the Spanish in the sixteenth century.

Skimming through these books left me bewildered and exasperated. Since then, I have had a series of discussions about the arguments presented in these books with established Navajo weavers, beginning Navajo weavers, and weavers in my own family. We have all puzzled over the claims and statements about how Navajos came to the Southwest and learned how to weave from the Pueblos. We are confused when the Navajo are referred to as "cultural borrowers." We are befuddled by the language of "myths" and "tales" to describe our history, our way of life.

What I know to be true is what we learned from our grandparents about Navajo history, economics, worldview, politics, environmental issues, social issues, animal husbandry, planting and harvesting seasons, language, spirituality, culture, tradition, and weaving. My siblings and I grew up listening to our paternal grandfather, Paul Teller, tell stories about the Navajos'

Long Walk, grafting fruit trees, breaking horses, and—our favorite story—about when he met our grandmother. Throughout history, many events have impacted or changed the course of life for the Diné. These events allowed for variations in our creation stories. This version has been in our family and was told to us each time we visited our paternal grandparents in Canyon de Chelly, Arizona.

The Diné emerged out of five worlds and we now live in the Glittering World. (Some debate that we have emerged out of four worlds and that the fifth is still coming; for simplicity, I have combined the fourth and fifth worlds.) The first world, the *Ni' Hodiłhił* (Black World), is where only water, air, insects, and the Air Spirit People lived. First Woman was born from the black cloud and First Man was created from the white cloud. Coyote was formed in the water. The second world was the *Ni' Hodootł'izh* (Blue World). It was composed of blue birds, blue furred land mammals, air, and water. The third world was the *Ni' Hałtsooí* (Yellow World), where grasshoppers and more of our Holy People were living—Talking God, Black God, Water Sprinkler, and House God—and they traveled by rainbows. The Holy People also gave life to *Na'ashjé'ii Asdzáá* (Spider Woman) and *Na'ashjé'ii Hastį́į* (Spider Man) in the third world. The fourth world is the *Ni'halgai* (White World) or *Ni' Hodisxǫs* (Glittering World). In the fourth world, the sun and moon were created as well as the four sacred mountains to protect our *Diné Bikéyah* (Navajo land). *Yoołgaii Asdzą́ą́* (White Shell), the first human, was born in the fourth world. She matured into *Asdzą́ą́ Nádleehé* (Changing Woman) and in turn gave birth to the Hero Twins *Naayéé' Neizghání* (Monster-Slayer) and *Tóbájíshchíni* (Child-Born-of-Water).

Spider Woman gave Diné the gift of weaving. Our Holy People instructed her to weave her pattern of the universe and teach the Diné to weave *Hózhó* (beauty) to bring harmony and beauty to their lives. She had no knowledge of how to do it, but Spider Woman was observant; she watched everything in her environment, and her curiosity focused on a spider weaving a web. This became her plan for how she would weave the universe. When she felt comfortable with her experimental weaving, she returned home and presented it to her husband, Spider Man. With just this basic concept of weaving, the Holy People instructed Spider Woman so that her skills would be further enhanced by prayer, songs, and ceremonial duties.

Spider Woman was told to go to our four sacred mountains to gather specific items to further advance her weaving: Blanca Peak, the sacred mountain of the east, *Sisnaajiní*, "the dawn" or "white shell mountain"; Mount Taylor, the sacred mountain of the south, *Tsoodził*, "turquoise mountain" or "blue bead"; San Francisco Peak, the sacred mountain of

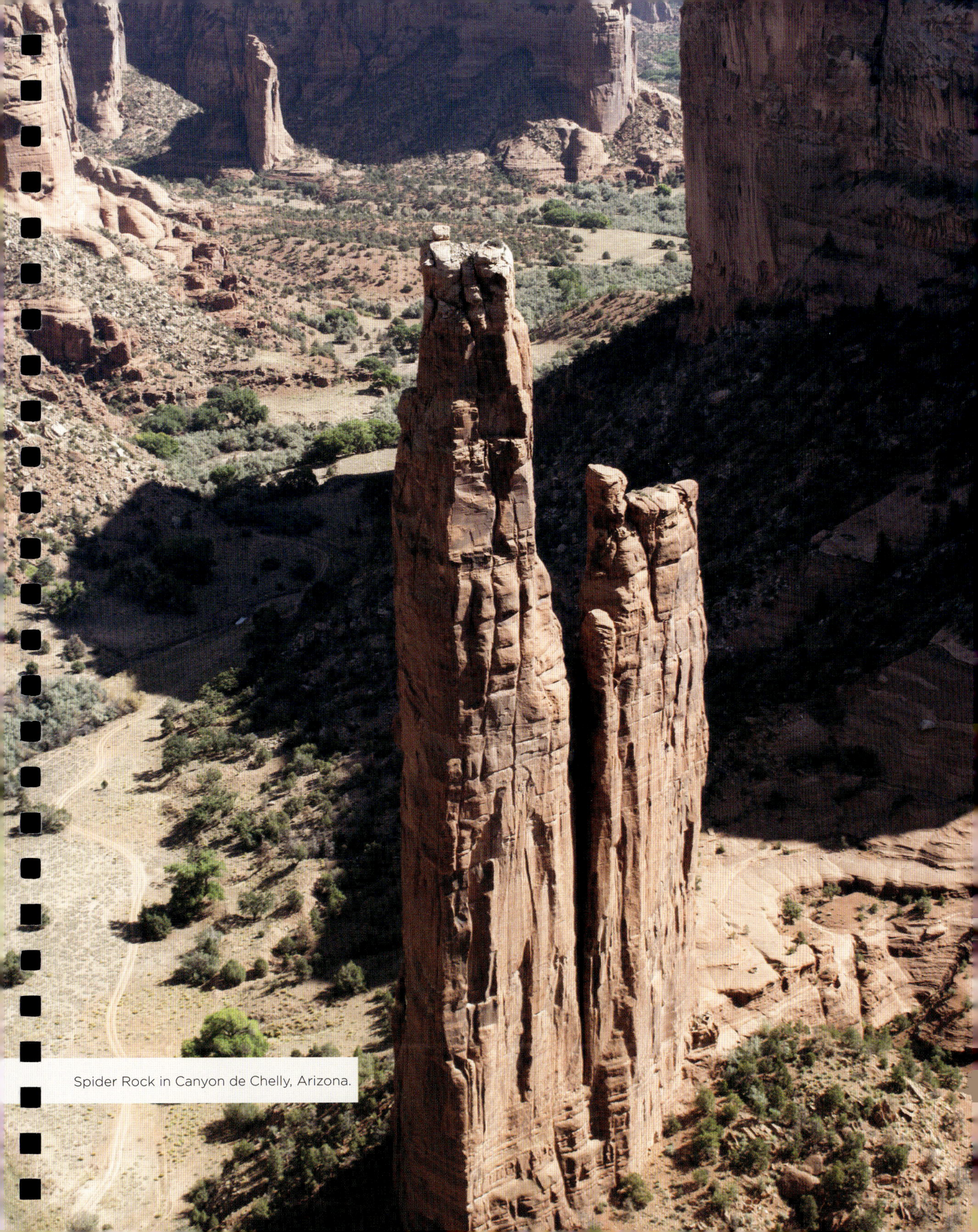

Spider Rock in Canyon de Chelly, Arizona.

the west, *Dook'o'oosłííd*, "the summit which never melts" or "abalone shell mountain"; and Hesperus Mountain, the sacred mountain of the north, *Dibé Nitsaa*, "big sheep." From the first mountain, she got wood for Spider Man to make the loom. From the second mountain, she harvested plants for vegetal colors for her wool. From the third mountain, she got patterns from the thunder gods, from whom she asked permission to use the patterns in her weaving. They granted her permission and told her to learn and teach the patterns so that other weavers could use them. From the last mountain, she got prayers and songs that are associated with all stages of weaving.

Spider Woman began weaving and increased her talents and knowledge about weaving. The Holy People visited her, and with the wood that was gathered, they instructed Spider Man on how to make a weaving loom and how to create the Navajo weaving tools. The top and bottom wood beams were made of sky and earth cords, the tension rods that hold the warps were made of sunrays, the inside heddle and shed rods (we refer to these rods as female and male) were made of rock crystal and sheet lightning. The wood batten was a sun halo to separate the female and male rain warps. The wood weaving comb was made of white shell. There were four spindles: the first spindle of zigzag lightning with a whorl of jet; the second spindle of flash lightning with a whorl of turquoise; the third spindle of sheet lightning with a whorl of abalone; and the fourth spindle a rain streamer with a whorl of white shell.

Later, with our final emergence into Glittering World, the twin sons of Changing Woman went on their journey to find their father, *Jóhonaa'éí* (the Sun). They were near the Spider Rock formation in present-day Canyon de Chelly when they noticed a hole in the ground. The Hero Twins climbed down and found Spider Woman weaving. By now, Spider woman was fully immersed in weaving, in prayer, and in song; she was ready to pass on her gift of weaving. The twins climbed out of the hole, and with the help of *Haashch'éé łti'í* (Talking God), they took the knowledge of weaving out into the world.

We know this creation story to be our history, as much so as the more commonly known set of events presented here by anthropologist Charles Cambridge:

> Nestled within the southwest desert of the United States are the Diné, a people otherwise known as the Navajo. Today, the Diné has a population of nearly 400,000 who live on their Four Corners reservation of 27,413 square miles. Their vast lands lie within a high desert region of the American Southwest

containing sand dunes, mesas, canyon lands, sagebrush country, and high mountain forest lands. This is the "Land of Enchantment" with unending vistas of magic and beauty, surrounded by the four sacred mountains in four different directions: *Sisnaajiní*, Mt. Blanca to the east; *Tsoodził*, Mt. Taylor to the south; *Dook'o'oosłiid*, San Francisco Peak to the west; and *Dibé Nitsaa*, Mt. Hesperus to the north. Within these lands, the Diné people maintain their traditional culture and language after centuries of abuse and destruction at the hands of the Spanish and Americans. The social goal of the Diné was never to assimilate to these alien cultures but to maintain their traditional culture and religion. Protecting their traditional language and culture are paramount to the Diné people.

After the military defeat of the Diné by Kit Carson in 1863, the U.S. military forced them to undertake their forced removal from their lands. This is known as the famous Long Walk of the Diné people. Other Diné hid from American forces in the canyons and mountains of the Southwest, but the vast majority were forced to Fort Sumner located in today's eastern New Mexico. At Fort Sumner, the Diné endured concentration camp conditions and starvation for a four-year period. Many Diné died on the Long Walk and in the American concentration camp. The United States Army and Mexicans wanted to slaughter the captive Diné while others wanted their removal to Indian Territory in Oklahoma. Eventually, after signing a treaty in 1868, the United States allowed the Diné people to return to their homeland between the four sacred mountains.

Originally, Europeans were not convinced that tribal people of the Western Hemisphere were humans. The effort was supported by the religious intellect declaring Indians as animals since there wasn't a mention of Indians in the Christian Bible. Indians were not offspring of Adam nor of Noah and thereby they were not human. Throughout the Western Hemisphere, gold and land drove the Europeans to conquer and destroy the animals. Animals did not have rights and therefore they could be eliminated. This legal decision began a unique form of racism toward American Indians that exists to this day. In 1537, Pope Paul III issued a papal encyclical, *Sublimis Deus*, declaring the Indians were fully rational human beings who have rights to freedom and private property, even if they are heathen. However, this did not end the killing of Indians for wealth, gold, and land nor the racism of Europeans toward Indians.

In 1537 when Indians became human, the church ordered all the rulers of European countries to care for and Christianize the heathen Indian.

Centuries later, the United States applied a guardianship policy to the Diné people by becoming the Trustee of Navajo land and the Guardian to protect them. Also, Diné became wards of the U.S. government. Each of these concepts has a long legal history of application to the Diné people.

As the Diné were placed on their reservation, the expressed policy of the United States was to educate, Christianize, and civilize the Diné. Christian missionaries flooded the Navajo lands, interfering with Diné traditional life. Christian missionaries have a beloved belief of the heathen Diné needing to be converted for their salvation. The civilizing process forced Diné parents to place their children into boarding schools far from their reservation. Each of these governmental policies and others took a toll on Diné language, culture, and traditional beliefs, which resulted in the loss or suppression of traditional arts, including weaving.

The Diné cultural salvation was that their tribal lands were vast and that they lived in physical isolation from their non-Navajo neighbors. It took tremendous physical and financial efforts for Christian missionaries and U.S. government officials to attempt to assimilate the Diné people. But, the Diné isolation tended to reinforce and strengthen the Diné culture and religion. Throughout this time, Diné could pick and choose from American culture what would make their lives easier in their vast lands. The cast iron and steel ax became prize possessions since they enhance the survival of Diné culture. Through decades of time, Diné decided on their own terms what to use from the American culture, and they added a Diné flavor to all of these items. Through this process, Diné people were not assimilating to the non-Navajo culture but created a culture based on their tradition and language while using what they needed from the non-Navajo culture.

It is with this knowledge of my people's history that I carried out my research about the origins of Navajo weaving. During that same Santa Fe study trip, I picked up two books by Navajo authors in the museum's gift shop. The first was *Reclaiming Diné History: The Legacies of Navajo Chief Manuelito and Juanita* by Jennifer Nez Denetdale. Denetdale explains how from the 1930s to the 1950s, Diné Bikéyah (Navajo land) became a prime study for anthropologists including Clyde Kluckhohn, Alexander and Dorothy Leighton, Ruth Underhill, Mary Shepardson, and Gladys Reichard, among others. Their studies remain the foundation from which budding scholars of Navajos begin their research. Denetdale goes on to cite contemporary feminist scholars like Kathy M'Closkey who have raised questions about how "classification of Navajo women's knowledge as secular (as opposed to sacred) has contributed to a devaluation of women's knowledge and labor." M'Closkey's studies reveal the degree to which colonizers use and benefit from the appropriation of "colonized people's resources, labor, knowledge, and traditions." M'Closkey goes on to argue that weaving has been categorized outside of a Navajo context and as such, Navajos have been classified "as primarily cultural borrowers who arrived late in the Southwest, a claim that contradicts Navajo understandings of their own past and origins."

The second book I discovered was *Spider Woman's Gift: Nineteenth Century Diné Textiles* edited by Shelby J. Tisdale. This excerpt from Joyce Begay-Foss's essay "Spider Woman's Gift: From a Weaver's Perspective" draws on an understanding of our creation story as our history in ways that perhaps only a Diné weaver could.

> The Diné do not believe that the Pueblo Indians taught them to weave, as proposed in the scholarly literature. Instead, they believe they were taught by Spider Woman, Na'ashjéii Asdzáá. The Diné and the Pueblo weave on the same type of vertical loom, yet their design elements are distinctive. The Diné have become proficient and diversified in their expertise in tapestry weaving, utilizing two-shed and four-shed applications. Diné oral history does not credit the Spanish with introducing sheep to the Southwest in the late 1500s, as scholars propose. Instead, the Diné believe that sheep were also a gift from Spider Woman, and from Changing Woman, Asdzą́ą́ Nádleehé. Changing Woman was responsible for forming and molding all the animals, including the first sheep.

Diné anthropologist Dr. Charles Cambridge shared this perspective:

> Navajo weaving existed long before Europeans entered the Southwest. This fact is lost upon scholars, anthropologists, and ethnographers who claim the

Diné obtained weaving skills from the Spanish or the Pueblo Indians. Navajo weaving is an ancient tradition existing before Spanish or Pueblo appearance in the Southwest. Previously, in the Great North, Diné took fur strips, rawhide, and natural fibers such as grasses, roots, and bark to transform them into woven clothing, shoes, and blankets.

Traditionally, young Diné become sensitized to the sacred landscape through our oral tradition. They reach awareness through a blending of the consciousness and unconsciousness of the sacred landscape until they become part of a different reality. This sacred reality is the beginning point of Diné weavers as they place their soul, sacred songs, and prayers into the weaving of a blanket, rug, or tapestry. This applies not only to the elements of the warp, yarn, wool, pattern, or loom and weaving tools, it also means integrating the sacred reality into the weaving process and into the weaving product itself."

Denetdale, Begay-Foss, and Cambridge are only a few Diné authors who have addressed the notion that Navajos are not cultural borrowers and that we have had weaving since our beginning of time. I am certain there are more works available by Navajo authors, and I encourage you to seek them out for authentic information. Diné weavers continue their weaving traditions passed down from generations of cultural torchbearers and teach their children and grandchildren. We know our history. We know how Navajo weaving began. We live humbly through the teachings of weaving.

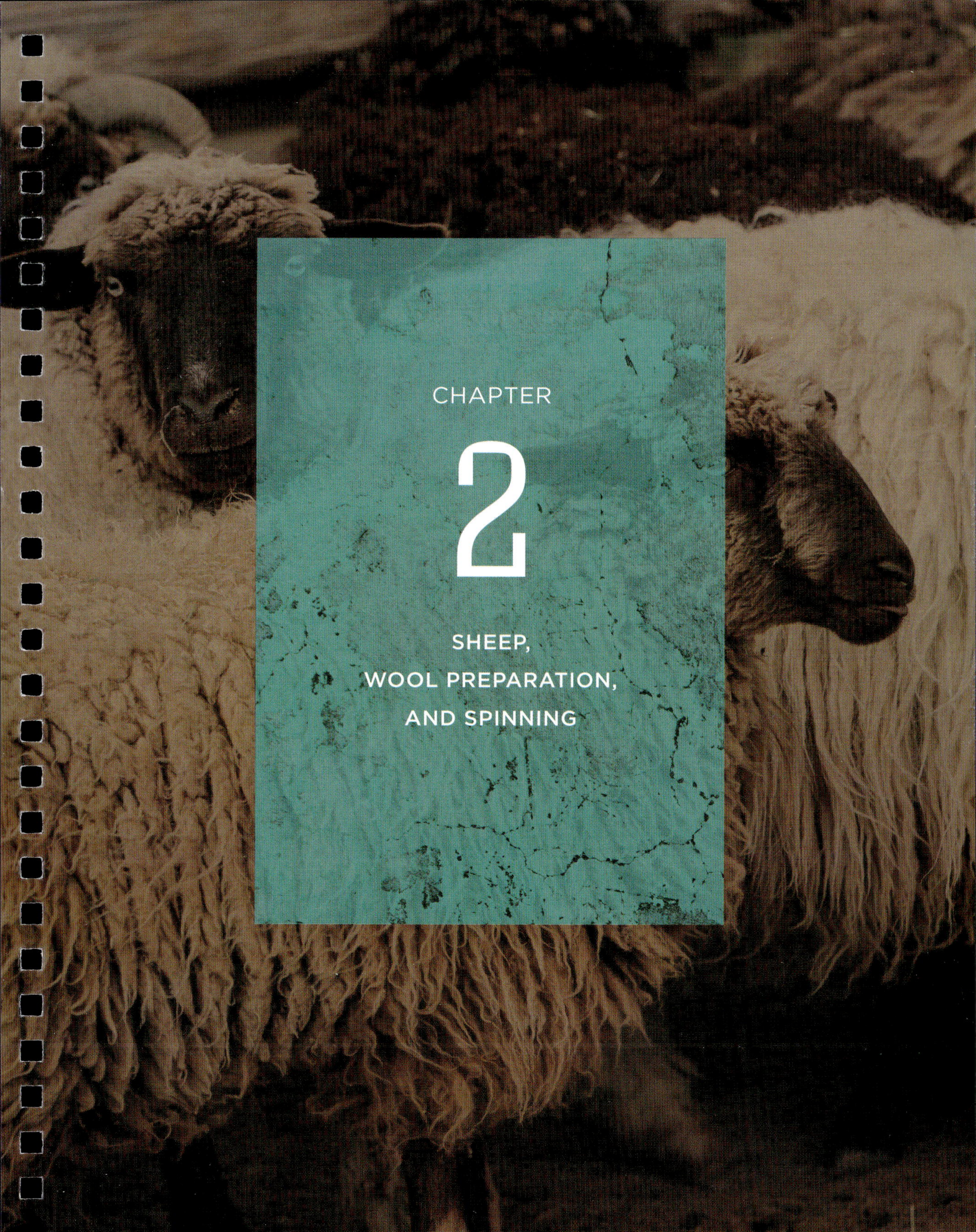

CHAPTER

2

SHEEP, WOOL PREPARATION, AND SPINNING

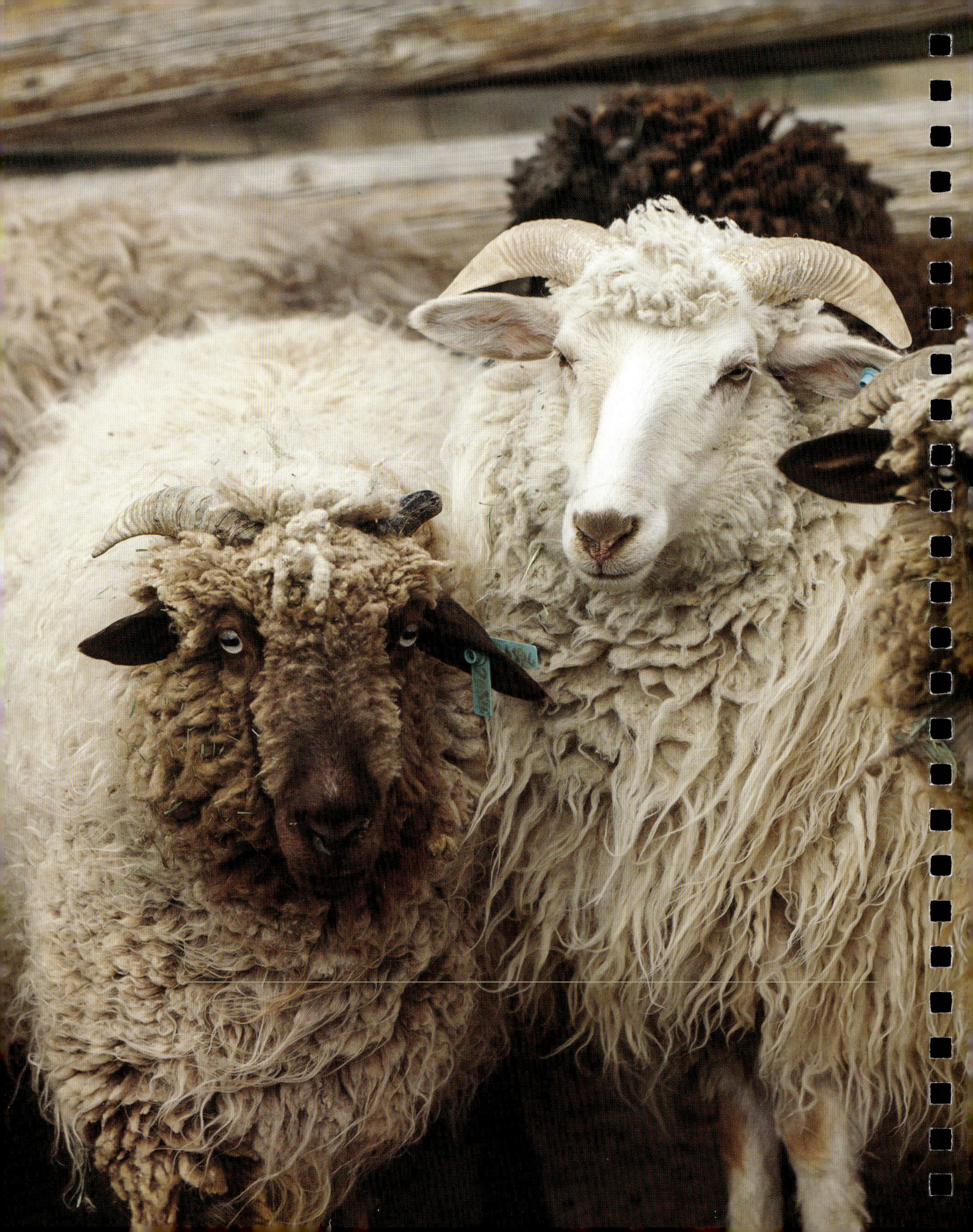

SHEEP IS LIFE—HÓZHÓ: HARMONY AND BALANCE

"As a child, I was taught by many elders that we weave for moisture, we raise sheep for moisture. These sacred animals have a connection to the Universe.

Their hooves awaken Mother Earth's energy. Their calls awaken Father Sky.

We must recite our prayers. Sing to and for your sheep, sing as you weave, sing to bring harmony. Do this proudly, so you're heard by the Holy People.

Collect the sacred plants as you're out with the sheep, use those plants with your prayers. And smoke their tobacco, let the smoke carry your prayers into the beyond.

Show the Universe that as a five-fingered being, you appreciate the moisture, you appreciate the sheep."

Nikyle Wes, Navajo weaver, Navajo shepherdess, Ganado, Arizona

SHEEP, WOOL PREPARATION, and SPINNING

Sheep have always been an integral part of the traditional Navajo lifestyle. We are a self-sufficient people, and the sheep have been a sacred link in our tradition of Hózhó, living balanced, harmonious lives. We care for them and they give to us—wool so we can weave, their bodies for food, and their hides for many uses. Without wool for weaving, we would not have survived The Long Walk, we would not have survived the return to our lands five years later, and we would not have survived through such difficult struggles over the many years. Wool, a gift from our sheep, and weaving have been the keys to our spiritual and physical survival.

Information about sheep husbandry, wool preparation, carding, and spinning are beyond the scope of this book. Today, we teach weaving to beginners using mill-spun yarn, and sometimes we even use mill-spun yarn in our own work. But we still have deep memories of the whole process of creating yarn, going back to our earliest childhood. It's an important part of Navajo life and culture, and the finest weavings still use handspun wool.

BREAKING A FEW SHEEPY STEREOTYPES

There seems to be a popular notion that all Navajos have sheep, but the reality is that while there are many who do, there are even more who don't. The tens of thousands of Navajos living in cities certainly can't keep sheep, and many weavers living in the Navajo nation lack the land, or the energy, or the time, or the inherited know-how to keep sheep. Not so long ago, Navajos weren't allowed to leave the Nation; now many take jobs in surrounding areas or make other choices that leave sheep raising out of the question. We love the sheep and honor them for their gifts to us. They are integral to our lives, even if we choose not to raise them.

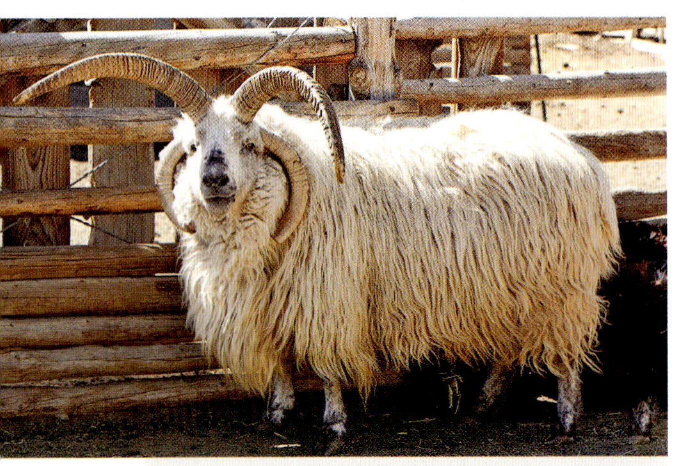

A Churro sheep with characteristic four horns.

Another stereotypical notion is that all the sheep in the Navajo Nation are the native Churro. That's just not the case. For one thing, during the 1930s, the federal government killed off most of the Churros, claiming that they were overgrazing the land. Today, thanks to the Navajo Sheep Project, founded and driven by Lyle McNeal in the 1970s and continuing to the present, this sturdy, historic breed is making a comeback. But because the Churro is a double-coated breed (coarse outer coat, fine undercoat), its wool is quite suitable for blankets and heavier rugs but not so much for fine tapestries. Because our work has very high weft counts, we need yarn that will spin to a finer grist than Churro. Our aunt Margaret Yazzie, in her younger years, had a Rambouillet/Merino mixed flock with very fine, long wool, and others have their own mixed-breed sheep.

SHEARING TIME

When we were growing up in Two Grey Hills, there was always a lot of laughter while the sheep were being shorn, lots of gossip. The flocks belonged to our grandmother, uncles, and aunts, and we always had access to the wool. We all worked together as a family. Barbara and I remember how these wool events would be a time to gather, eat, laugh, and listen to weavers discuss their future projects and how much wool would be needed and how it would get divided. Our sister Rosann would walk around handing out coffee, food that she prepared, and encouraging words. Along with our cousins and sisters, we had to help catch the sheep, and we would end up laughing so much we would get too weak to hold onto them. When shearing, we used old-fashioned hand-operated sheep shears. Many families in the Navajo Nation still use them today. Sheep are caught in the corral and laid down on a tarp or board, and their feet are held or tied together. Then they are shorn by hand. It is a very efficient method of shearing because the sheep don't struggle. Soon after, they are off to scratch their backs and graze with the other sheep.

As children, our main job was to cut all the thistles and burrs off the fleece. Later our mother and her sisters would do a final skirting on the fleeces, removing the stained and matted areas, and then decide how to divide it up by color. A crescendo of oohs and ahs would be heard when the red-brown wool was uncovered. Every weaver in my family cherished this color of wool, which we use for the main inside-field color in our weaving. They would put the divided fleece onto big screens that our dad made using two-by-fours. Some of these screens would be placed out in the sun and others under a shade house for a few days so that the lanolin in the wool would dry out and the wind could knock the dirt out. Wool placed on the screens in the sun might bleach lighter, and likewise wool kept in the shade would not fade. Since at that time Two Grey Hills tapestries were all naturally colored wools, color consideration was extremely important throughout every step of the processing. Major discussions were held about the blending of the wool into a variety of hues of grays, tans, and browns. The darkest wool would be set aside to be dyed black. The lightest shade of wool would later be soaked in gypsum clay, which whitened it.

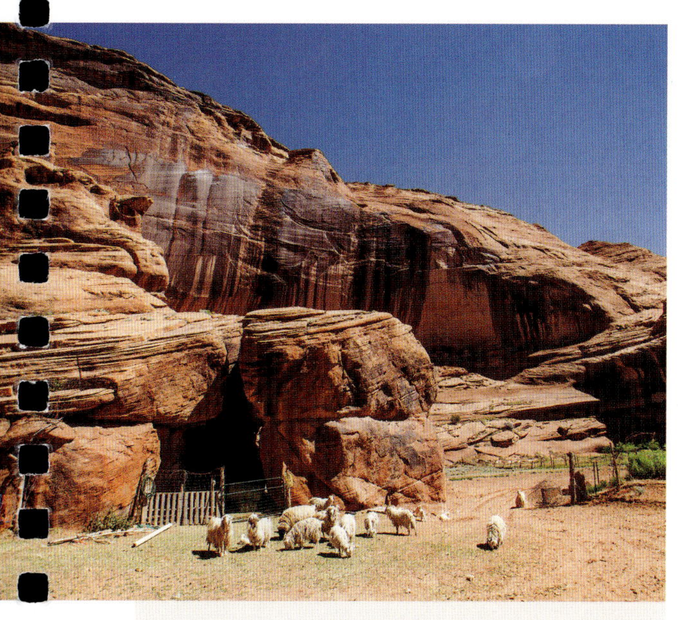

A flock of mixed-breed sheep in Canyon de Chelly.

After the lanolin had dried for a few days, we would wash the wool using two huge tubs. One held dish soap and boiling water for washing and the other held rinse water. After washing,

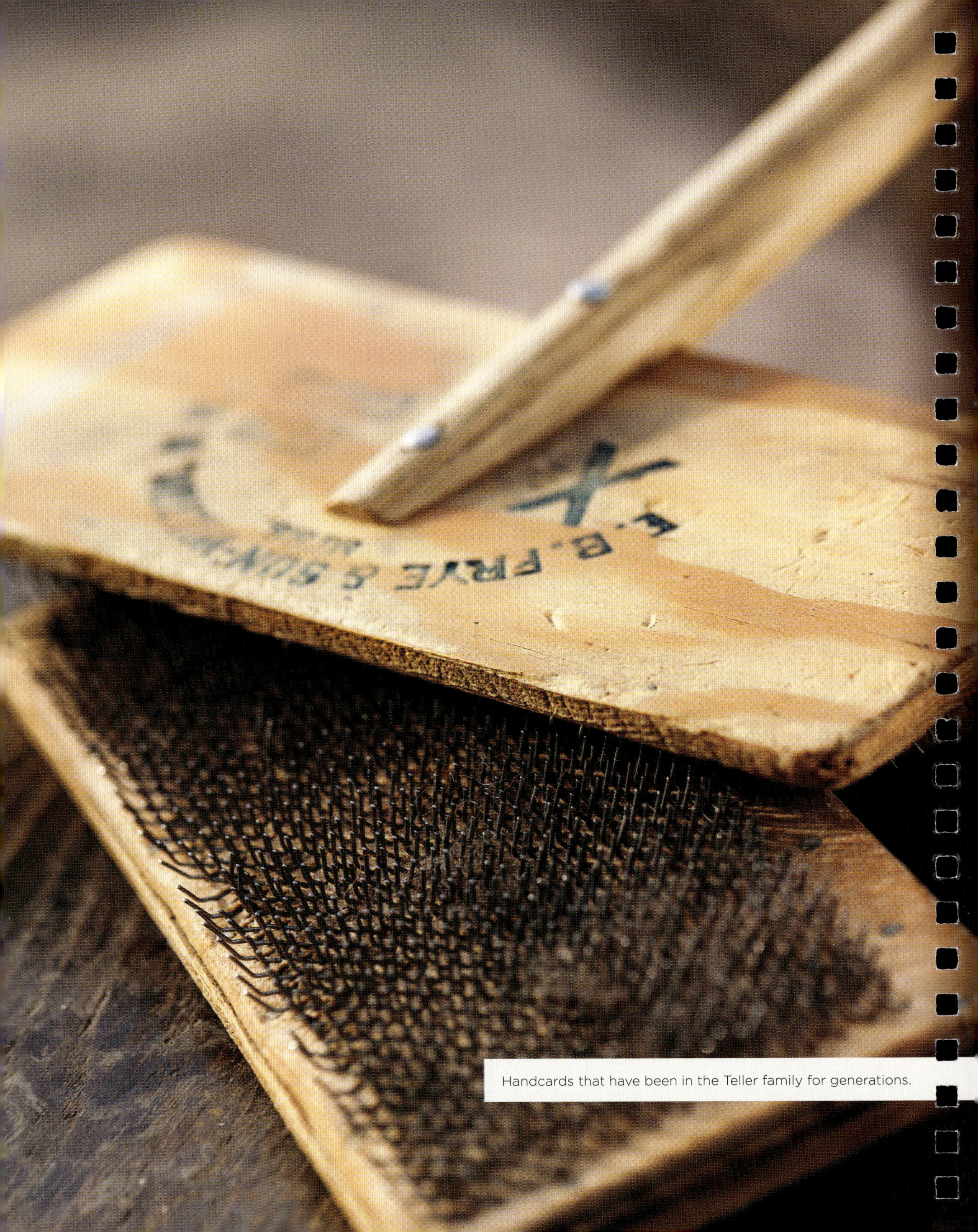

Handcards that have been in the Teller family for generations.

the wool was spread again onto the screens, and put in the sun or shade, depending on the color. When it was dried, it was the job of my sisters and me to fluff the locks by pulling them apart with our hands so that the wool wouldn't felt. Then the fluffed wool was sorted into boxes for immediate carding or put into gunnysacks for storage. It was advisable to use the fluffed fleece within the following few months so it wouldn't clump up or felt in storage. Then it would be time to card the wool.

CARDING THE WOOL

Our weaving tools are passed down for generations. The cards used at home belonged to our mother and her mother before her and were probably purchased in the 1950s. We call the cards *Bee'ha'nilchaadi*. *Bee'* means "thing you use" and *ha'nilchad* means "fluffing things up, combing it." These cards are well worn, know the wool, and know how to work it to make the kind of rolags we like to spin from. A rolag is essentially a cigar-shaped roll of wool that is light and airy, and good ones are very important in making the spinning of yarn smoother and easier.

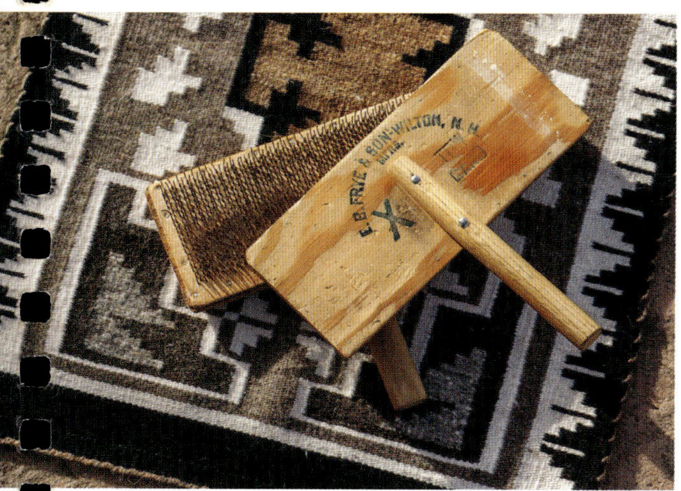

Carding is not just about creating rolags to spin, though. The Two Grey Hills tradition of carding is also about blending different colors of wool together to create a greater range of hues. Our mother, our aunts, and our older sister, Rosann, were master color blenders. They blended wool like artists mix paint. Rosann took this process to another level when she started weighing the amounts of each color of wool. She would get the same shade every time, even in different batches. Probably under a microscope, different batches of the same color might have been a little off, but it was so close that there was no color striping in our weaving.

It is worth the time to not rush through the process. Carding was a time for family and community for us, just like spinning. It was work that needed doing, but we would work on things together. Because our maternal aunt Margaret, the last family member to have a flock, is of advanced age and no longer has sheep, we no longer have access to family wool. We now generally spin from purchased merino roving, which we can blend or reprocess to suit our needs.

Spinning is traditionally part of Navajo weaving, not a separate process. We call the spindle *Bee'adizí*. *Bee'* means "thing you use" and *adiz* means "to spin." The spindle whorls are made of elements representing the four sacred mountains. The spindle shafts symbolize different forms of lightning and rain from the thunder gods and represent aspects of the male, the female, and energy.

Weaving embodies our quest for beauty around us, a balance of energy, harmony, and acceptance of the beauty of the circle of life. Spinning, part of traditional weaving, does the same. It encompasses the honoring of female and male, their equality, and the balance of beauty, energy, and harmony; that is Hózhó, our Beauty Way. Our spinning cannot be separated from traditional weaving. They exist together in symbiosis.

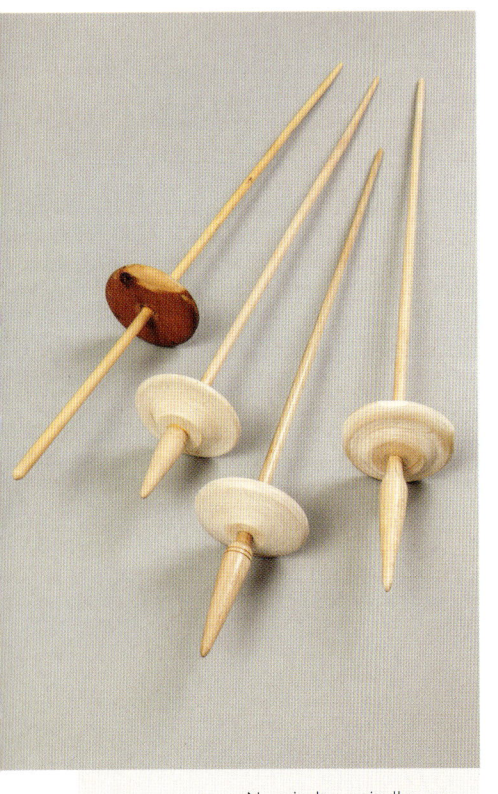

Navajo lap spindles are custom-sized for the user.

Some of our terminology is different from that of the North American spinning community at large. For instance, we refer to our spindle as a lap spindle, even though it is rested on the ground and spun off the side of the thigh. Rolags are rolags, but "pencil roving" is something special for us and not the same as industrially produced commercial pencil roving, as you'll see later. We also use the terms *yarn* and *wool* differently. We grew up calling our weft "wool" because we processed it from the fleece to be spun into weft. Commercially processed fiber and warp in stores was referred to as yarn. When people in and around the Navajo Nation speak of yarn, they usually mean commercially spun wool yarn rather than handspun wool yarn. The latter is generally just called wool, never yarn. To make it easier for the reader, though, I will refer to wool as yarn, whether handspun or commercial.

Even within a family, spinning methods can differ as each person finds what works for them. Across the Navajo nation there are many, many weavers and they all have their own ways of spinning and producing yarn. Always be respectful. A different method is not necessarily wrong. Listen and learn what is different and new to your eyes.

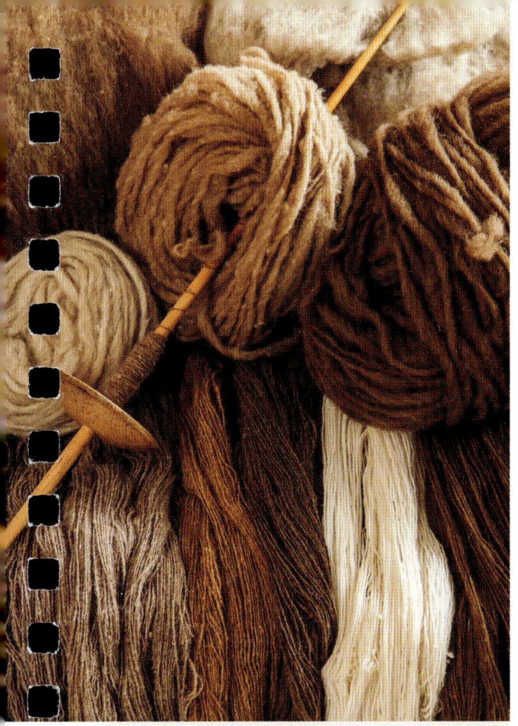
Pencil roving ready to be spun.

The spindle we use is essentially a supported spindle. It is long and reaches from the floor to above the thigh (or lap). The bottom tip is supported by the ground, and the upper shaft is spun off the side of the thigh or twirled upright, depending on the spinner. Whorls and shafts can be of different sizes, and as any spinner knows, your spindle and whorl weight and size make a difference in the type of yarn that is produced. For instance, because we spin a fine laceweight yarn, we use a lightweight wood such as cedar.

The shaft of the spindle has to be fairly thin and easy to twirl. If the diameter of the shaft is too big, your hand will cramp up and the process of spinning and twirling will become tiresome. If the length of the spindle is too long or too short, it impedes your spinning. The whorl has to be light for a finer spin and heavy for a heavier spin. From a seated position, the shaft of your spindle should be between 4″ and 9″ above your lap (the top of your thigh). This will vary depending on your height and the size of your hand. If the shaft is too long, the weft will tend to bunch up at the top of the shaft and not be properly spun, thus causing it to break.

Here are two examples of spindle sizing: Barbara's height is 5′1″, and the palm of her hand measures 3″ wide. When seated, the height from her lap to the floor is 19.5″. Her spindle length is 26.5″, the diameter of the whorl is 3.5″, and it is ½″ thick. The diameter of the shaft is ½″ and tapers to ¼″ at the tip.

Lynda's height is 5′4″, the palm of her hand measures 3″. When seated, floor to lap is 23″. Spindle length is 29.5″, the diameter of the whorl is 3.5″, and it is ⅜″ thick. The diameter of the shaft is ⅜″ in diameter and tapers to ¼″ at the tip.

THE PROCESS OF SPINNING

You may have heard the term *predrafting*. This involves lengthening rolags by gently pulling on them to create longer spans of fibers that are closer to the diameter of the yarn you plan to spin. You may also have heard the term *double drafting*, which refers to another way of achieving the same thing, but it is accomplished as you are spinning. That is, you pull out a

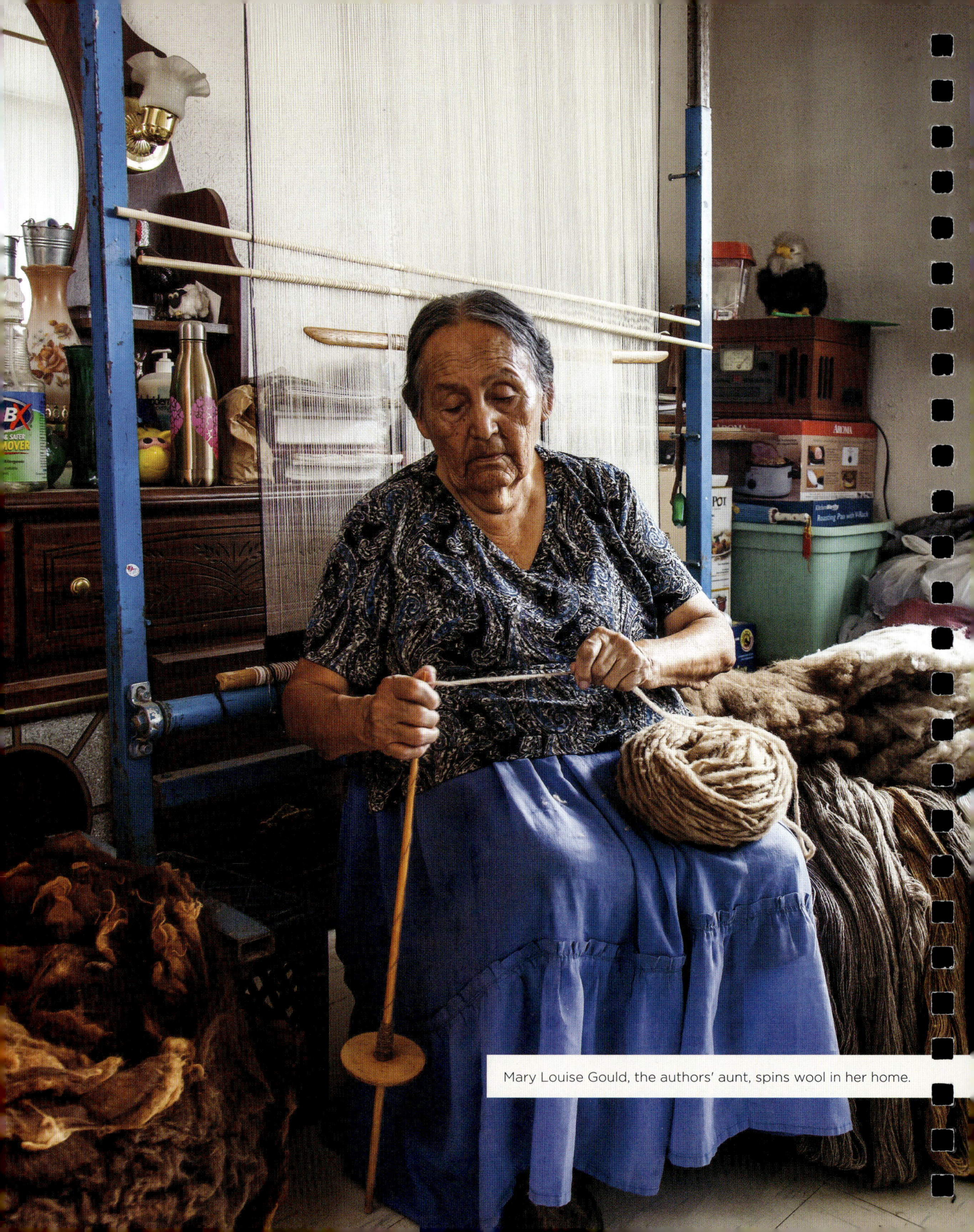

Mary Louise Gould, the authors' aunt, spins wool in her home.

thin length of wool from your rolag, let it twist a little bit, then pull it out a little more until it is the diameter of the yarn you want before twisting it into yarn. These terms and these ways of working are common in the North American spinning community.

You've probably also heard the term *pencil roving*. Among other North American spinners, this generally refers to a commercially produced fiber preparation that is about as thin as a skinny pencil and is ready to be spun into yarn.

We Navajo spinners make our own pencil roving, which we use in preparing what we call *twice-spun* yarn. It's a simple process of roughly drafting out lengths of wool from rolags, giving it a minimal amount of twist—just enough that it holds together—and winding it into balls to be spun into finished yarn later. Sometimes I see elder spinners with balls of pencil rovings at their feet or in a basket waiting to be spun. In the second spinning, this pencil roving will be refined into strong, consistent weft. Sometimes a third spin is done, but only if the yarn from the second spinning is not smooth or strong enough so that more twist is needed.

To confuse matters, there is another way to achieve a second spin besides preparing a pencil roving and spinning it again. In this method, the spinner drafts out an arm's length of wool, drops it, picks it up closer to the shaft, and begins to refine and do the second spin on this relatively short length. Once the drafted length of rolag has been spun the second time and is fully refined, it is rolled onto the lower part of the shaft, down by the whorl. This is what other North American spinners might call double drafting.

Our Grandma Susie and our Grandma Teller both loved to spin rolags into pencil roving. Our mom didn't like to make pencil rovings, so she went from rolags straight to the final spin. I spin the same as our mother. For me, it takes out extra work. Barbara spins both ways.

But wait…there's more. We often will respin commercial yarn for warp for our classes. What is commercially available is not spun tightly enough for our weaving techniques. Many Navajo weavers will respin yarn if it loses twist or if they are using a commercial yarn instead of spinning their own.

Warp yarns must be tight and strong, and usually are respun two or three times. They are then stretched taut and sprayed with water to set the twist. When dry, the warp yarn is wrapped tightly in a ball. For selvage cords, two, three, or four single yarns are plied together, depending on the size of the finished textiles. We use two plies for miniatures, three plies for textiles up to 2′ by 3′, and four plies for larger textiles.

BLANKETS, RUGS, AND TAPESTRY: WHAT ARE THE DIFFERENCES?

In Navajo weaving, there are differences between what is labeled a blanket, a rug, and a tapestry, and they are distinguished by their weft count. This is the number of weft yarns woven selvage to selvage in a 1″ woven height. This number is referred to as wefts per inch, or picks per inch (ppi). How close or far apart the warp yarns are (referred to as warp ends per inch, or epi) will affect how many wefts can be packed down in an inch. Determining weft counts can get complicated if you are weaving a pattern with many different yarns from selvage to selvage. Some weft yarns pack down more than others, so that in their space, the weft count is higher. To account for this difference, you basically count the ppi in each section of the design and take an average. It can get complicated.

For a simple example, say we are using commercial worsted-weight yarn for weft, and commercial warp spaced at 8 warp ends per inch. The weft count of one color of this weft woven in 1″ is 32 ppi. So, if the whole rug were woven with a yarn that packs down that same amount, the weft count would be 32 ppi.

Textiles woven with bulky-weight yarn with a weft count of 13 to 29 are referred to as blankets. Textiles woven with yarns with a weft count of 30 to 79 are referred to as rugs. Textiles woven with a weft count of 80 and above are referred to as tapestries. (Our family's typical weft counts hover around 108 to 122 ppi). This way of categorizing weaving according to weft counts is used for contemporary textiles and doesn't apply to historic ones.

Textiles woven by Navajo weavers using commercial warp and weft are no less authentic than those that are handcarded and handspun. We do, however, recommend that Diné weavers declare their materials when entering art shows or when marketing their textiles.

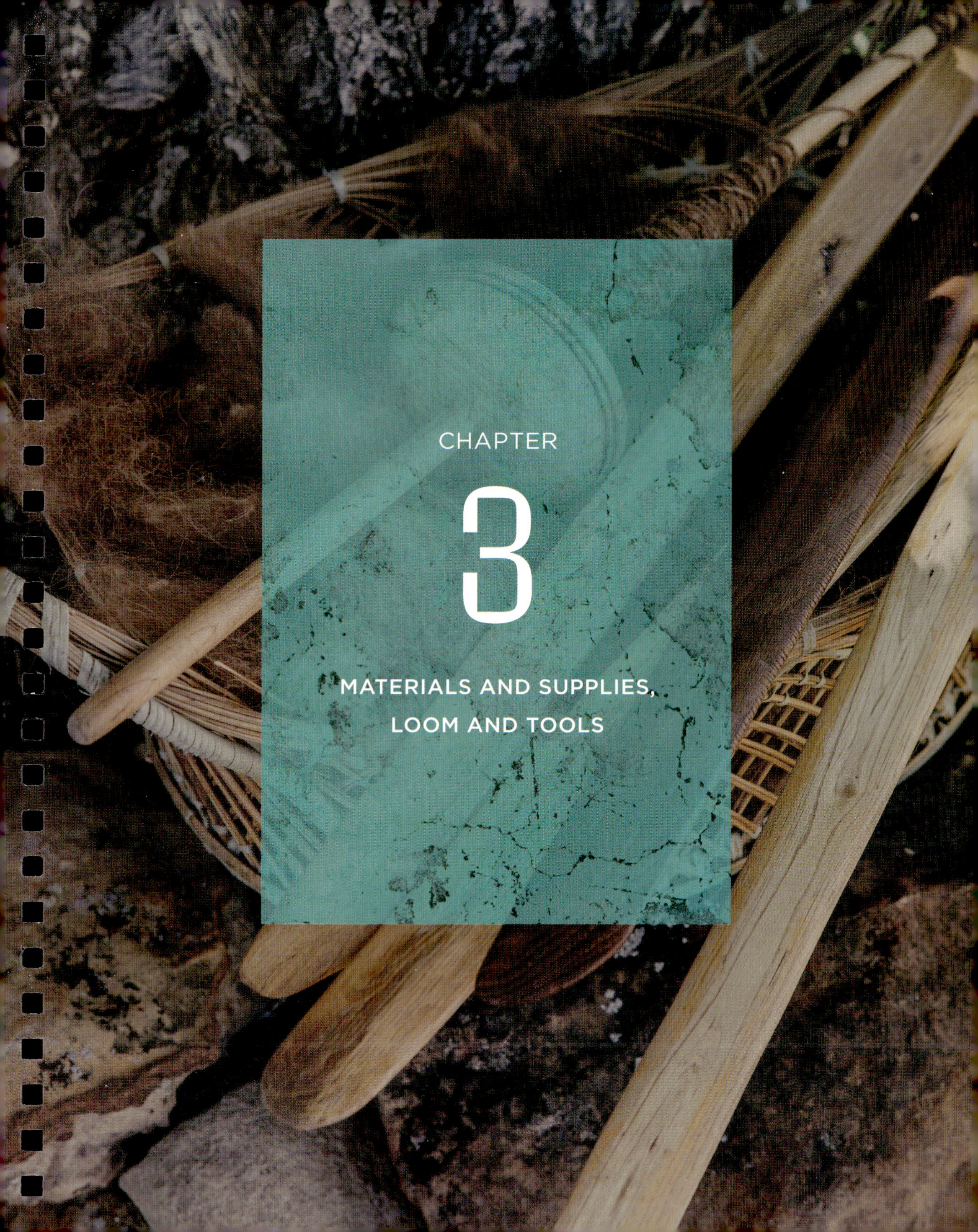

CHAPTER

3

MATERIALS AND SUPPLIES, LOOM AND TOOLS

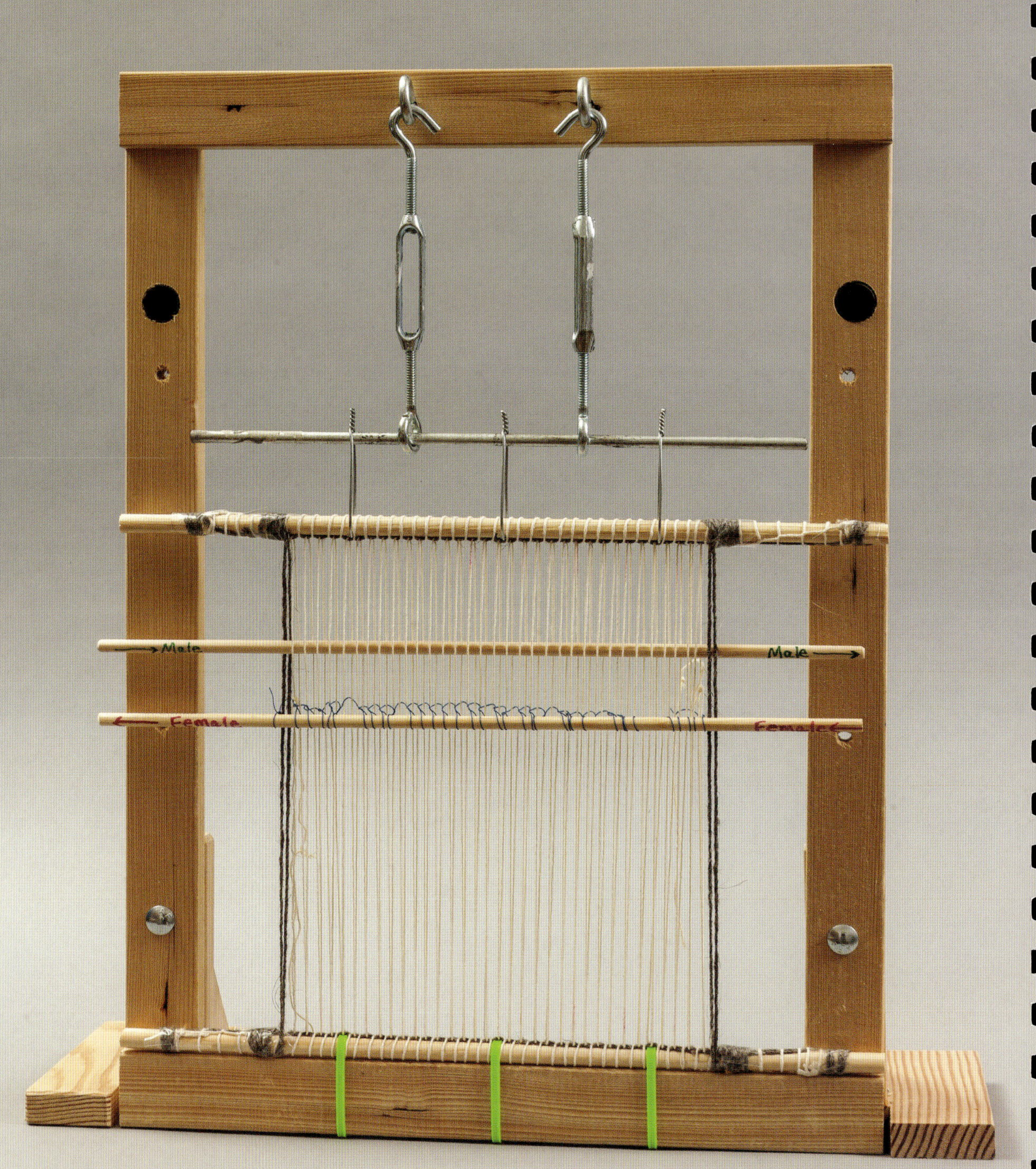

A table-top loom, warped and ready for weaving.

A LESSON IN EVERY STEP

Spider Woman instructed the Diné people about how to make the warp string using a Bee'adizí (Navajo lap spindle) and taught the Diné people how to weave. With the help of Spider Man, she taught them how to set up the loom, giving names that represented the natural elements and the higher powers of the universe. Together they brought the weaving art and the many lessons attached to every step of the process to our Diné people so they could sustain a good life. The very act of weaving protects us from laziness, poverty, hunger, and sickness. A finished blanket, rug, or tapestry in a home will provide an abundance of blessings.

Navajo weaving is a complex art form, and to Diné weavers, it is a living art form that dwells in our families through songs, prayers, and traditions. Every step in the weaving process is a lesson. We prepare our weaving materials: shearing sheep, cleaning the fleece, drying out the lanolin, using the sun to fade the color or shading the fleece to keep the colors dark, carding, spindling, and sometimes dyeing with vegetal or coal-tar-based aniline dyes. We warp our looms with songs and prayers and maintain our weaving tools. Family members search for trees that will become our weaving tools. Weaving encompasses our ability to acknowledge all forms of life, including duality, as we honor females and males and the equality of assigned roles. Weaving instills in us a quest for beauty, a balance of energy, harmony, and acceptance of our current state from birth to old age—the beauty of the circle of life.

MATERIALS and SUPPLIES, LOOM and TOOLS

In our instructions, we will concentrate on warping, weaving, designing, troubleshooting, and finishing an 8.5″ wide by 10.5″ high rug with respun commercial warp by Brown Sheep Company placed at 4 doubled ends per inch. For teaching, we use commercially spun, dyed, single-ply, worsted-weight yarn that measures about 50 yards per ounce. Our choice is Lamb's Pride by Brown Sheep Company, which is readily available in the Navajo Nation as well as at yarn shops all over the country. Four warps to an inch will be doubled, thus counting as 8. The inside measurements of the medium loom shown here are 19″ wide by 27″ high; the outside measurements are 24″ wide by 30″ high.

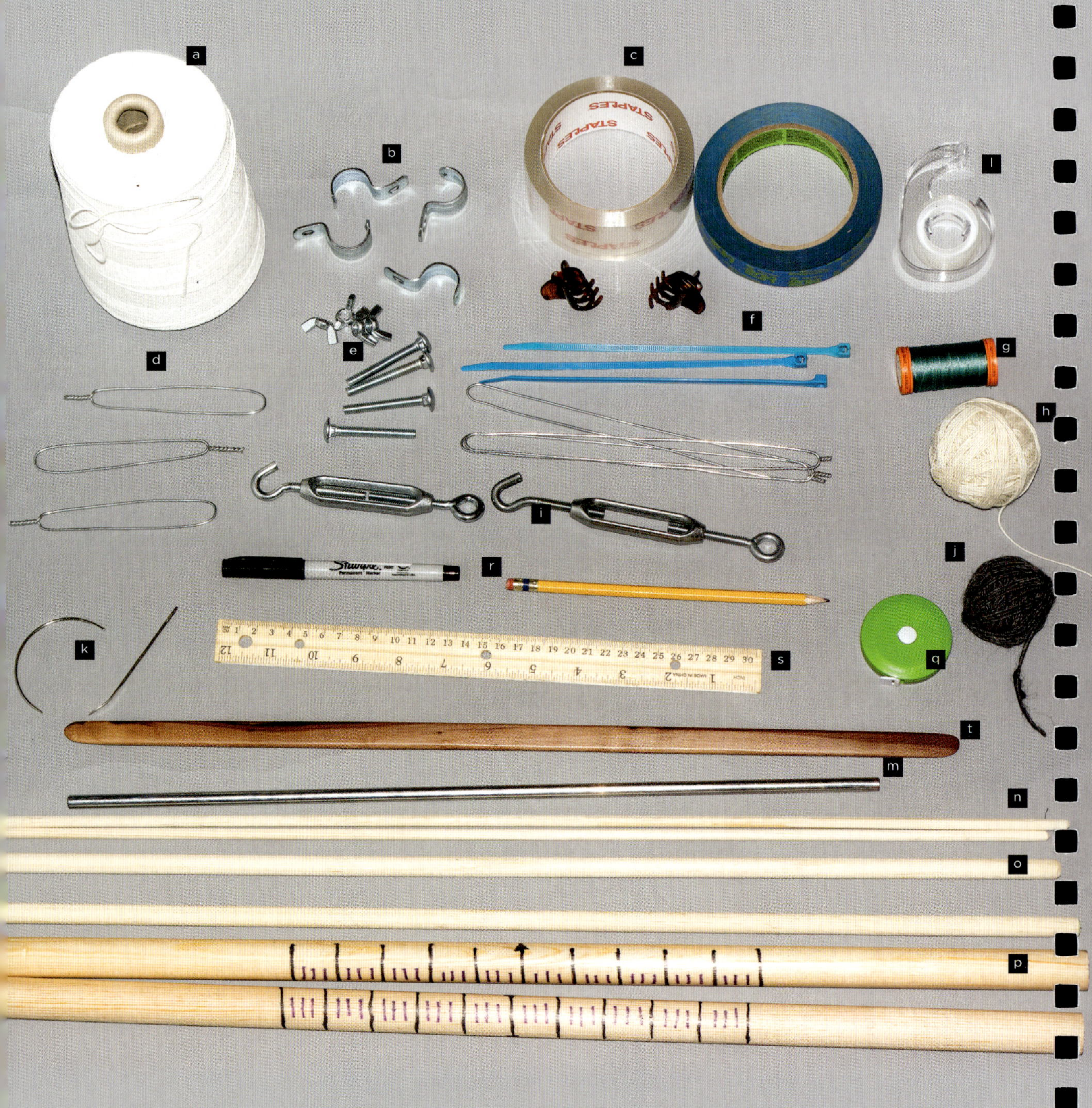
a
b
c
STAPLES
l
d
e
f
g
h
i
j
Sharpie
r
k
s
q
t
m
n
o
p

MATERIALS LIST FOR WARPING

A Navajo loom. (The one shown on page 28 is the one we use in our classes.)

20 yards of respun commercial wool warp h. Commercial warp is a single-ply mill-spun warp by Brown Sheep Company. We buy skeins of 4 ounces, 190 yards; the yarn will shrink after the skein is respun and stretched. We use a Navajo lap spindle to give it an extra twist and are careful not to overtwist. For our sample project, we will need only 20 yards of the respun commercial warp.

4.5 yards of selvage cords made from two wool yarns plied together j.

Four one-hole steel clamps, ¾″ diameter b.

Two ¾″ diameter wooden dowels, 24″ in length (warping poles) p.

Two ½″ diameter wooden dowels, 24″ in length (length-tension dowels) o.

Two ¼″ diameter wooden dowels, 24″ in length (female/heddle and male/shed dowels) n.

Two ¼″ turnbuckles with a metal hook on one end and an eye on the other end l.

One ¼″ diameter metal rod to fit through the turnbuckle eyelets, 18″ in length m.

Three 10″ premade wire loops identical in size, 16-gauge wire d. We make the ones that we provide to our students using a jig to ensure that they are all exactly the same size. This is critical! If you make your own, be sure the lengths of wire are exactly the same, and that the loops are exactly the same size after you've twisted the ends of the wire very firmly together.

A sacking needle or a curved upholstery needle k.

7 yards of cotton twine cut in half a.

Eight 6″ strips of clear transparent tape with ends folded down onto the sticky part of the tape to allow for easy handling i.

Four 6″ strips of 2″ wide packing tape with ends folded down, as above c.

Hardware: 4 bolts, 4 wingnuts e.

Three zip ties or cable ties f.

Fabric measuring tape q.

Sharpie and pencil r.

Ruler s.

Batten t.

Upholstery thread for female needle g.

MATERIALS LIST FOR WEAVING

Single-ply worsted-weight wool yarn in various colors a.

Navajo weaving tools including a regular-sized comb b and wooden battens of various widths c. A batten is a slender, flat, tapered piece of wood used to keep warp sets apart while a weft is inserted.

Navajo finishing tools including wire battens, sacking needles, and curved upholstery needles d.

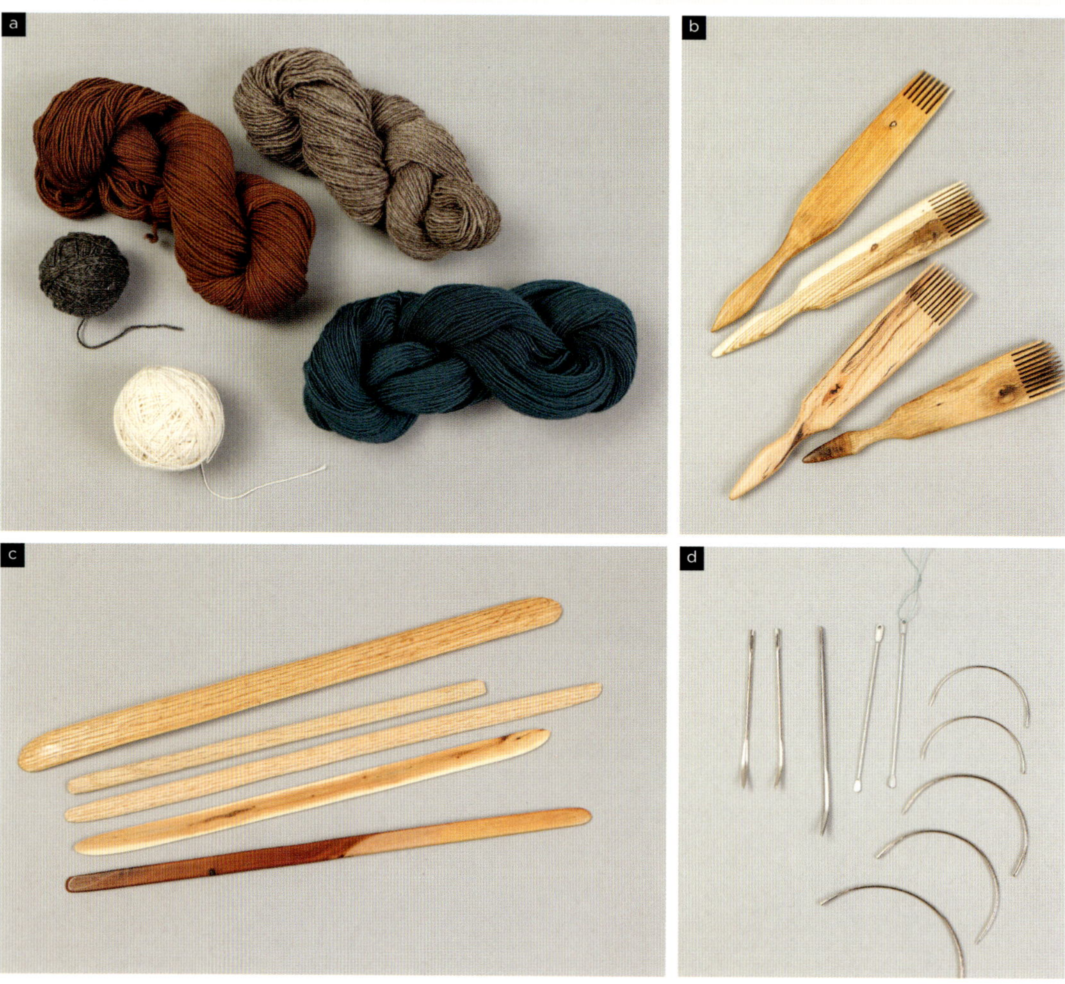

A WEAVING BOX WITH SUGGESTED ITEMS TO HAVE NEARBY

- A **knitting counter** to keep track of turnarounds.
- A **measuring gauge** to allow for the precise measurement of design blocks.
- **Fray Check**, in case your warp begins to fray. Put a small dot of it on your finger and gently smooth it onto the frayed portion of the warp string in one direction. Allow it to dry.
- One or more **magnets** glued to your loom to hold needles and small metal implements during the finishing process.
- **Small hair clips** to keep the female heddle rod from falling into the work area.
- **Plain dark cloth** to place behind the warp to block out the visual background.
- **Tweezers** to pull unwanted weft fibers out of areas of nearby color blocks.
- A **sweater or fabric shaver** to lightly trim accumulated wool fuzz off the finished textile to give added crispness to the design blocks.
- **Bumper guards** for padding the ends of rods at points that extend over the sides of the loom frame to minimize clanging when tamping down weft with a weaving comb.
- **Sandpaper or emery boards** for smoothing chipped or splintering areas of weaving tools.
- **Band-Aids**.
- **Office supplies** such as scissors, Scotch tape or painter's tape, and graph paper.
- **Writing instruments** such as colored Sharpie pens and plain or colored pencils.
- **Measuring instruments** including a ruler, a yardstick, and a metal or cloth tape measure.

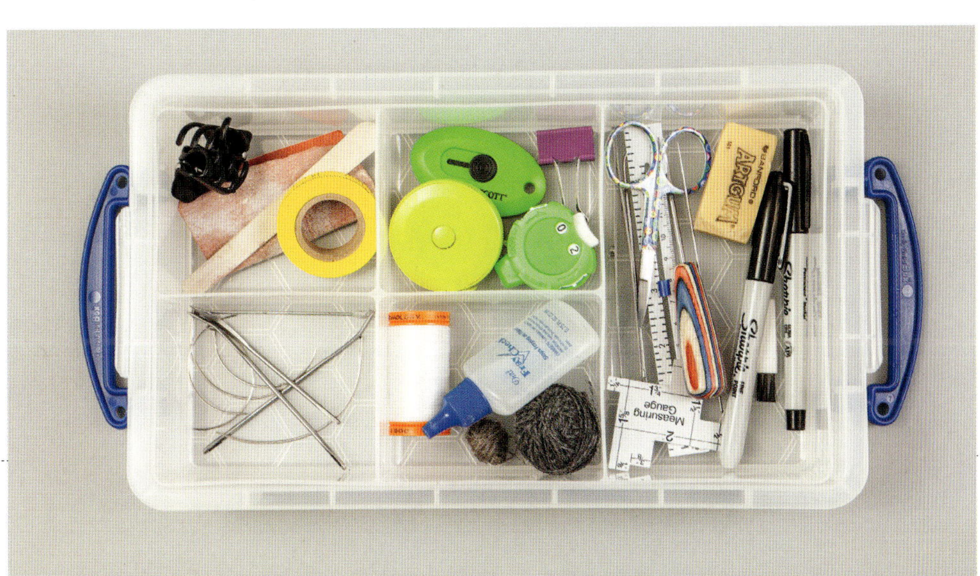

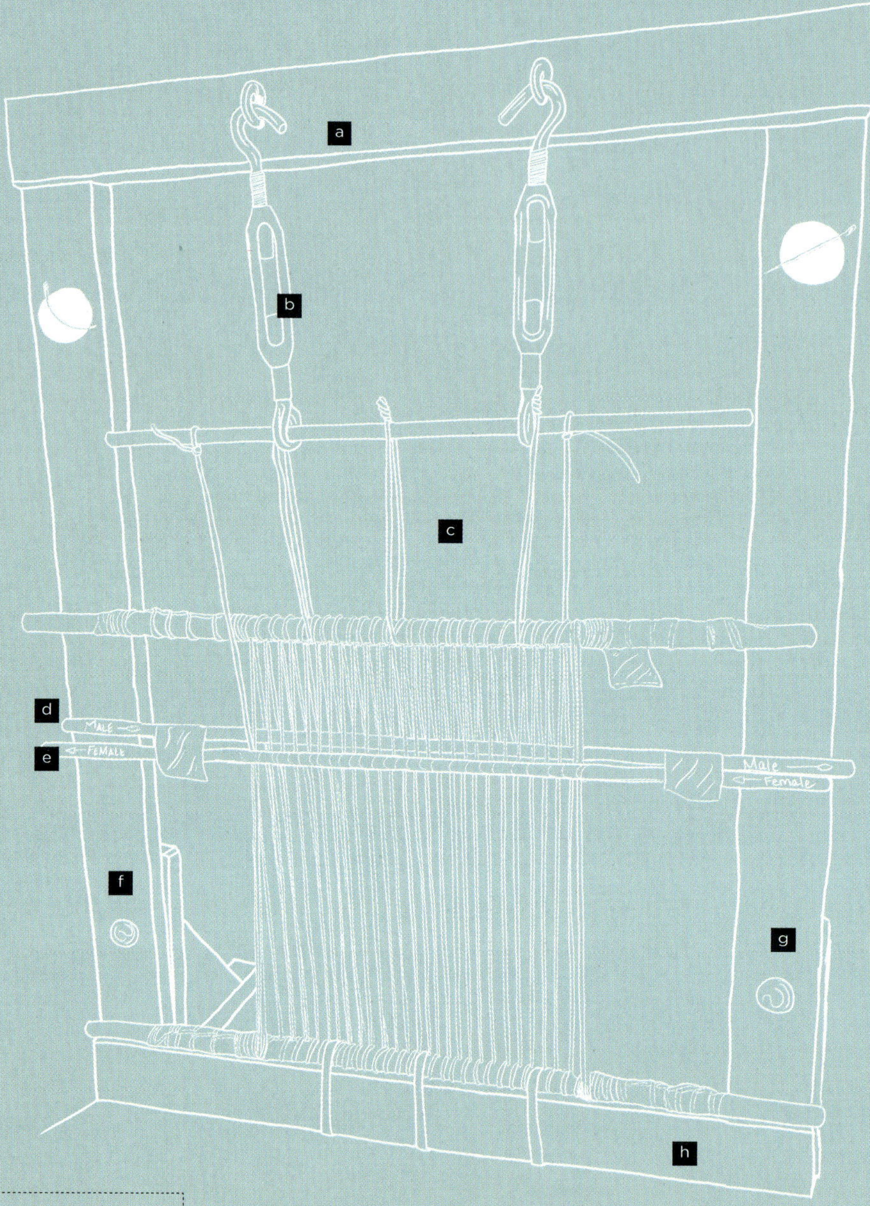

LOOM KEY

- **a** Sky Beam (top beam)
- **b** Male and Female Lightning (tension device)
- **c** The Clouds (space between the tension bar and the loom bar)
- **d** Male Rain (shed rod)
- **e** Female Rain (heddle rod)
- **f** Female Gravity (left vertical post)
- **g** Male Gravity (right vertical post)
- **h** Earth Beam (bottom beam)

THE NAVAJO LOOM

Spider Man made the first loom from sky and earth, from sunrays, rock crystal, and sheet lightning. The Navajo loom contains the natural elements and powers found in nature. It contains male and female qualities; these counterparts create equal representation of Iiná, *Life. The loom breathes the prayers and songs of the Holy People and is, therefore, a living entity. It has movement, and it has direction. It is sacred, as it provides blessings and protection for the home and family of the weaver. The loom frame consists of four main beams or poles representing the four sacred stones of* Yoołgaii, *or whiteshell (bottom),* Dootł'izhii, *or turquoise (left),* Diichiłí, *or abalone (top), and* Bááshzhinii, *or black jet obsidian (right). The bottom beam is the earth beam (female) and the top is the sky beam (male). The right side of the loom represents the night (male) and the left side represents daylight (female). Everything exists between the earth and sky.*

Within the loom, the warp yarns symbolize male and female rain. The upper part of the warp is dominated by the male, and the lower part of the warp is dominated by the female. The upper shed rod is the male rainbow, and the bottom heddle rod is the female rainbow. These rods represent our thoughts and our creative process. With both rods, there is balance to our way of thinking and to our creative process that allows balanced composition. Just as the Earth (mother) and the Sky (father) act as companions to balance the essence of Nature (family), the same principle applies to the loom and its setup. The loom is set up with good thoughts, songs and prayers, and the understanding that every energy you put into your project is a part of you.

The Bee'adzooí *(weaving comb) as the* Nááts'íilid *(rainbow) and the Bee'* Ak'í'níltłishí *(batten) as the* Nááts'íilid agodí *(short rainbow) create the designs through replicating the sound of* Ii'ni' *(thunder). When all these natural elements come together, the result is beautiful growth that nourishes life just as the loom and the tools create beautiful textile creations to nourish a family. Because the loom incorporates many of nature's elements, anything related to weaving is ceased in the presence of rain, thunder, and lightning. These are the teachings of our deity Spider Woman with the help of Spider Man.*

The Navajo wood loom is a rectangular frame that is built large enough for the project's warp to be stretched onto it tightly. Slight variations in modern looms are made to accommodate the weaver's comfort as the textile is woven.

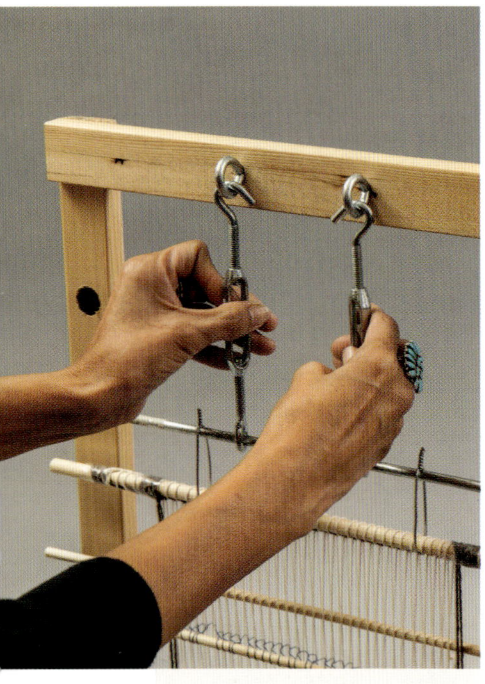

Both tensioning turnbuckles should be turned at once.

The kind of loom that our family usually weaves on today, which we also use with our students, is a tabletop loom. Made to be portable, it has a detachable stand secured to the frame with carriage bolts, washers, and wing nuts. The holes on the side beams of the loom allow the weaver to raise or lower it so that the part of the project being woven can remain at eye level.

At the top of the loom frame, two metal eyelets anchor the metal turnbuckles that adjust the tension of the warp and are used in place of the more common rope tensioning cords. It is important that both turnbuckles are turned at the same time to either stretch or loosen the warps. Turning one first and then the other risks torquing the warp and causing it to become uneven.

When the warps are stretched to the perfect tautness for weaving, they make a nice sound like harpstrings when you strum your fingers across them. It takes some experience to hear what the loom sounds like when its warps are at the perfect tension for weaving. A higher-pitched tone means the warps are tight; an inserted batten will quickly snap shut, indicating the warps are too tightly tensioned. A dull or lower-pitched tone means they are too loose for weaving; an inserted batten will drop down if the warps are too loose.

NAVAJO WEAVING TOOLS

Weaving tools have significant value to a Navajo weaver and must be treated with care. They should be maintained by sanding lightly and oiling after a few weaving sessions. With respect and careful forethought, weavers protect their tools, especially by not hitting another life-form with them or carelessly throwing them in frustration or anger. Most likely, the tools will be handed down to younger family members, so the tools should have good energy.

Many types of trees and shrubbery are used to make looms and tools. Traditionally, piñon, a hardwood and representative of males, and cedar, a softwood and representative of females, were the two types of wood used. Diné toolmakers search for fallen branches, trees, and stumps, but only during certain seasons, and they are careful not to harvest anything still green and living. Wood that has been struck by lightning is carefully avoided. Wood harvesting is paired with songs and prayers, and offerings are made; only then is the wood selected for various projects.

The teeth of weaving combs come in odd numbers, whether the combs are heavy for starting the weaving, of medium heft for midway through the weaving, or light for finishing the weaving. When you place a comb in your hand, your hand has five fingers; the comb, with an odd number of teeth, should be an extension of your hand.

Diné also use weaving tools in Kinaaldá, *a female puberty ceremony. There are puberty ceremonies for young men as well, and both ceremonies can last a day or will be conducted for four days depending on lifestyle, family, education, employment obligations, and how much money is available to spend on the ceremony. The male puberty ceremony takes place inside a* tá'cheeh, *a sweat lodge. The medicine man talks to the young man about his journey in life, having respect for all forms of life, his kinfolks, strength, endurance, and other lessons. The puberty ceremony for young ladies occurs at the onset of menstruation. A ceremonial corn cake is made to represent her mind, her body, and her transition to womanhood. She wears a traditional woven dress, moccasins, leggings, sash belt, and jewelry, and her hair is tied with buckskin strings. Everything she wears represents her physical and social growth. In addition to her personal items, she will also have a traditional hairbrush, seven stirring sticks to use during the making of the corn cake, a grinding stone, a batten, a weaving comb, the male and female dowels, and a spindle. These items help her to understand her new role as a woman. Each day of the ceremony, she must run toward the east at sunrise so she can have a healthy and strong body. A female matriarch brushes the young lady's hair to give her wisdom and massages her with the weaving tools. These actions will mold her into an industrious woman so that she will fulfill her responsibilities to her family and in her homelife; appreciate the elements of air, water, fire, and earth; and practice* k'é *for a harmonious lifestyle.*

WEAVING COMBS in different sizes and shapes are made from various types of wood a. They are used to tamp down the wefts as they are laid into the web of the weave. There are heavier ones to start the weaving and smaller, fine-toothed ones to use during the finishing process. The pointed end of the weaving comb handle is used to lift or reposition the weft yarns after they have been laid in to help manage the weft tension.

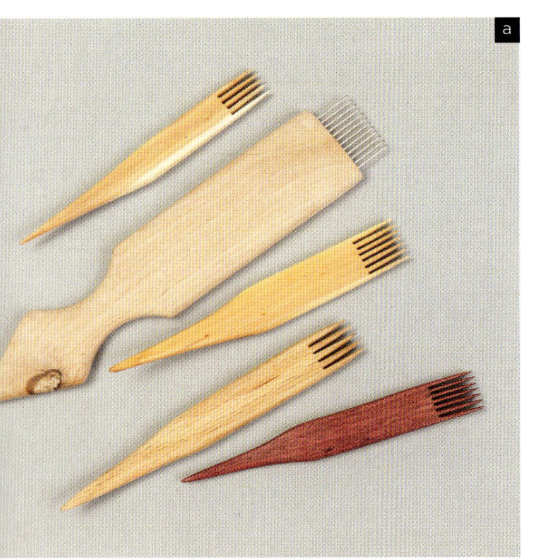

The weight of the comb helps to pack the weft tightly for a crisp design. We recommend that you choose two different sizes to try. If your hand gets tired while weaving with one, switch to the other one. If it is uncomfortable in your hand or causes parts of your hand to become chafed or sore, pad areas of the handle with foam tape, or even reshape troubled areas with sandpaper.

Please be very respectful of the comb and take care not to drop it. If weaving on hard-surfaced floors, place a throw rug under the loom to cushion the fall of the comb if it is ever dropped accidentally. Lay it down gently while you change the batten. For new weavers, trying to hold the comb while changing the batten may result in it being dropped and broken. After many weaving projects, we find that it becomes easier to handle the comb and the batten at the same time. With experience, laying the comb down while changing sheds will no longer be necessary.

The fragile teeth of the weaving comb need to be sanded with an emery board or sandpaper as chips and splinters form from regular use. This is normal. The sound of a rough or splintered part of the comb tearing fibers off of warps is an easy one to detect. When weaving, if that sound is heard, smooth the faulty section of the comb, making sure to sand it from the tip end toward the handle in the same direction the teeth come in contact with the warps. If it is dropped and any of the teeth incur more damage than normal wear, or if they break off completely, those irreparable parts can be sanded down to the nub, and the comb will still be usable.

A FINISHING COMB has fine metal teeth for use near the end of the weaving when the weaving space becomes narrow and tight. Most finishing combs b are smaller in size in every way. For weavers with hand-cramping issues, metal-toothed combs with full-sized handles are made by our toolmaker, Terry Lee. His combs work wonderfully for all weavers.

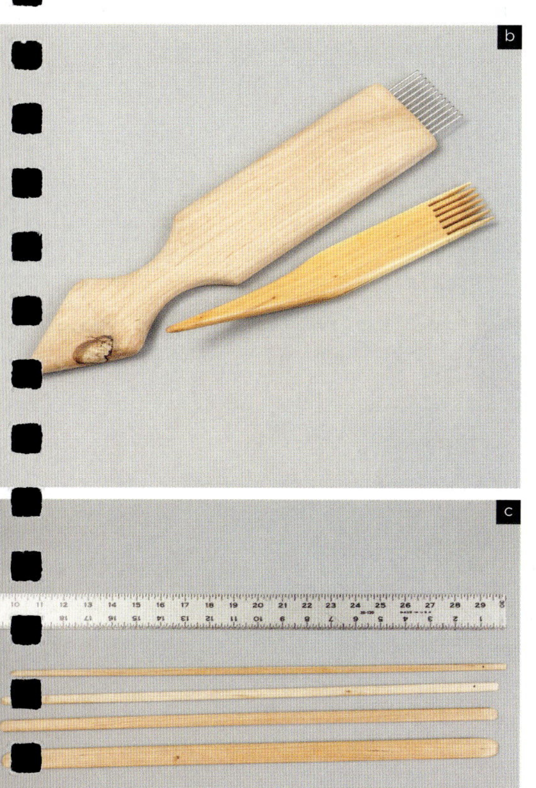

Gather BATTENS in various widths, from wide to very thin c. Start weaving with a wide batten, but once it starts to snap shut, switch to one of medium width. As the woven web of the textile grows, the weaver will graduate from using the widest batten at the start to the narrowest ones near the end of the weaving.

Not all battens are meant to be open in the warp sheds. Some of the thicker or denser ones stay inserted in one position while the shuttle or needle with the weft is taken through the open shed. As with weaving combs, if the battens develop nicks, sand them in one direction following the wood grain. If necessary, they can also be oiled with lemon oil.

Two long WIRE UMBRELLA NEEDLES with shaped blunt ends are strongly recommended for weaving the last 2″ of the textile d. This kind of needle is actually made from the metal spine of an old umbrella and is carefully crafted to work well for the finishing steps of a weaving.

(See Resources on page 127 for suppliers of this special tool.) One needle is used as a batten, and the other one is used as a shuttle for the weft yarn. Place a leader on the eye of the needle to be used as a shuttle. The umbrella needles will need to be straightened out between weaving projects.

Short umbrella needles can be used to weave design blocks in those areas where fingers can no longer fit inside the warps. Two curved needles can be used when the warps get too tight for the long umbrella needles during the finishing process. Use them in the same manner as the umbrella needles, with one as a batten and the other as a shuttle to run weft through the shed. At no time during weaving should weft yarn be pulled through the warps without the use of either an umbrella needle or a curved upholstery needle as a batten. Doing so will cause unnecessary abrasion on the warps and weft and may result in broken warps.

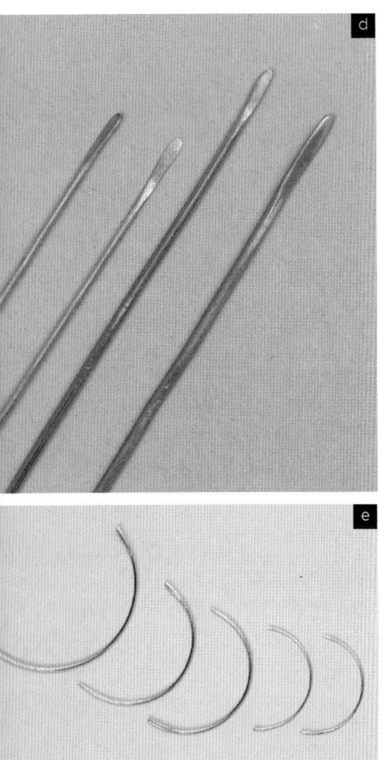

The sacking needle e, or a curved upholstery needle if you can't find a sacking needle, is a very important tool, as it helps with every process of the weaving. When there is barely any space left on the warps, the finishing process will require sewing. At that point, one sacking or curved needle is used to bring the weft between the warps. Space is created by the weaver using fingers or another sacking needle to push down the previous line of woven weft.

Wooden needles can be used as shuttles, but only after the new weaver learns how to maintain the proper tension.

Wooden hooks are used to pull weft yarns through the warps when it becomes difficult for fingers to move yarn through a shed. (See Resources on page 127 for suppliers of this special tool.)

If for any reason, the weaving tools you are using are not working for the task at hand, our first rule is to change your tools and try something else.

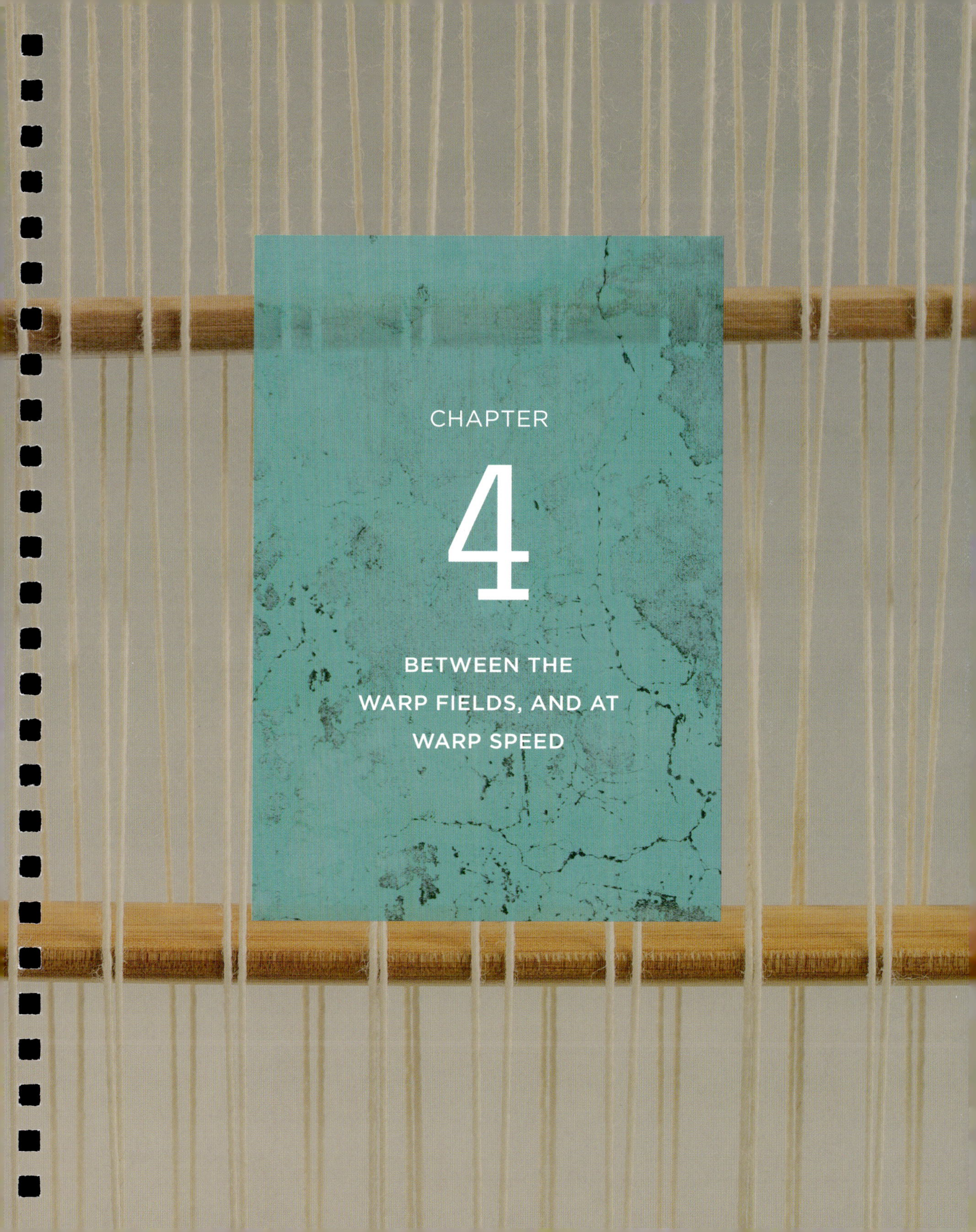

CHAPTER

4

BETWEEN THE WARP FIELDS, AND AT WARP SPEED

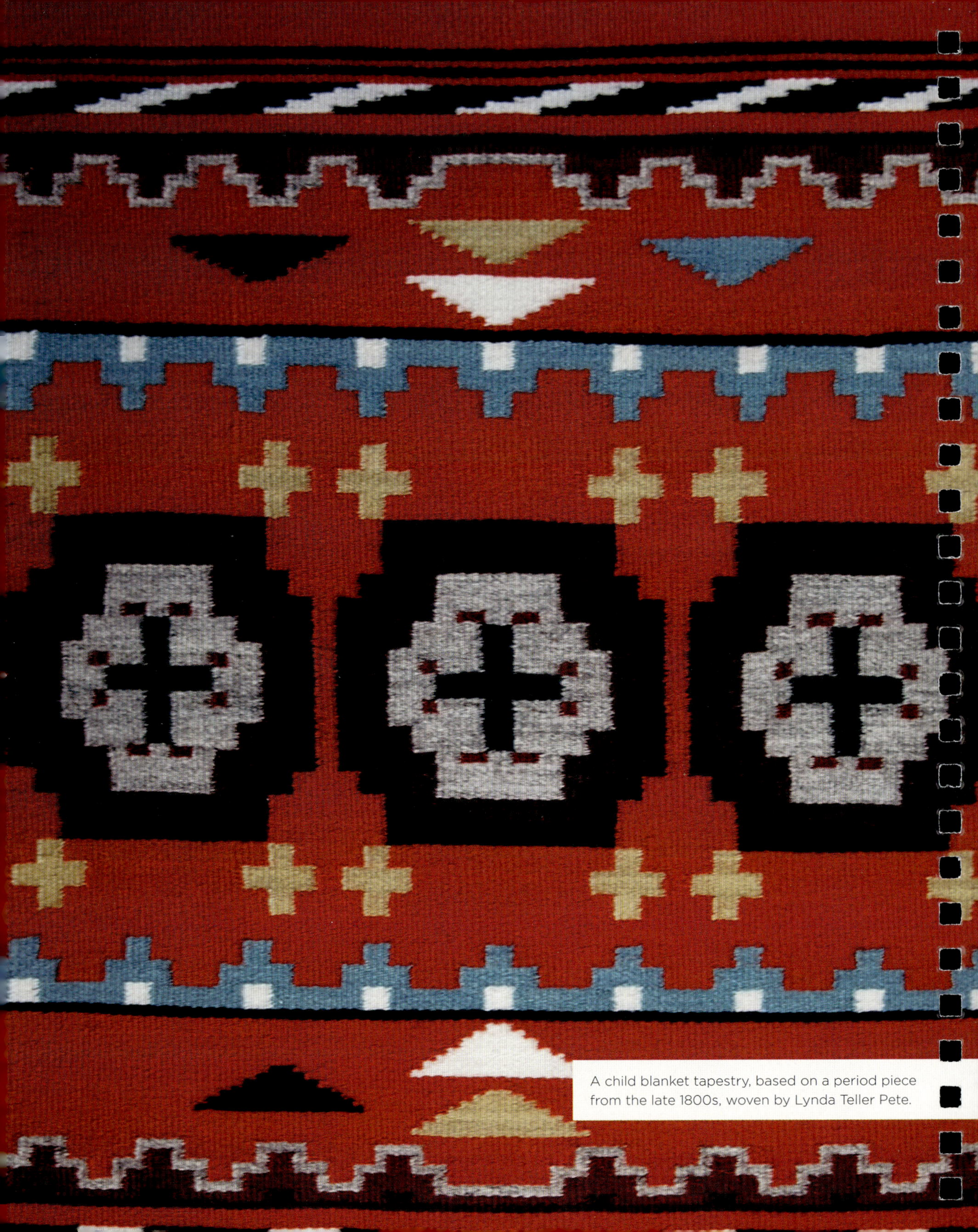

A child blanket tapestry, based on a period piece from the late 1800s, woven by Lynda Teller Pete.

STREAKS OF RAIN AND LIGHTNING

The warp on a Navajo loom represents Níłtsą́ Biką' *(the male rains) and* Níłtsą́ Bi'áád *(the female rains), the different types of moisture. When a storm is approaching, we see* K'os Diłhxił *and* Ááh Diłhxił *(male and female clouds) and* Níłtsą́ Naajin *(dark rains). When we see them in the distance, the dark streaks of rain come from the dark clouds and sky, and as the rain touches the earth, it nourishes all Earth's living beings. The streak of rain is represented by the* Nanoolzhee' *(warp). The Navajo word for warp,* Nanoolzhee', *is formed from the root word for hunting. Naalzheehí is the word for hunter and the word* naalzheeh *means to hunt. When we warp, we are actually hunting metaphorically: we are preparing to provide for our family with our weaving. The warp is held in place by* Atsiniltł'ish *(the lightning) which is represented by the rope and can apply to metal turnbuckles as well because metal conducts electricity. Male clouds are represented by the upper tension beam connected to early dawn, blue twilight, yellow evening twilight, folding darkness, sunbeam, and rainbow, which are all connected to the lower warp beam that is female.*

If you are right-handed, you will warp in the female way, inserting battens from the right. If you are left-handed, sometimes you will warp in the male way, inserting battens from the left. Each method provides an easy way to work with weaving tools. When textiles come off the loom, there is no way to tell if they were woven in the female or the male way.

BETWEEN the WARP FIELDS, and at WARP SPEED

WARP COUNTS AND WARP SPACING

The following instructions are for warping a project that is 8.5″ wide by 10.5″ high, which is the size we use in our workshops. To warp for textiles of other sizes, alter the instructions according to the chart provided after the warping instructions on page 70.

To achieve a symmetrical design, it is necessary to have an even number of warp string pairs. This count includes the pair of selvage cords. The left female selvage cord counts as one warp

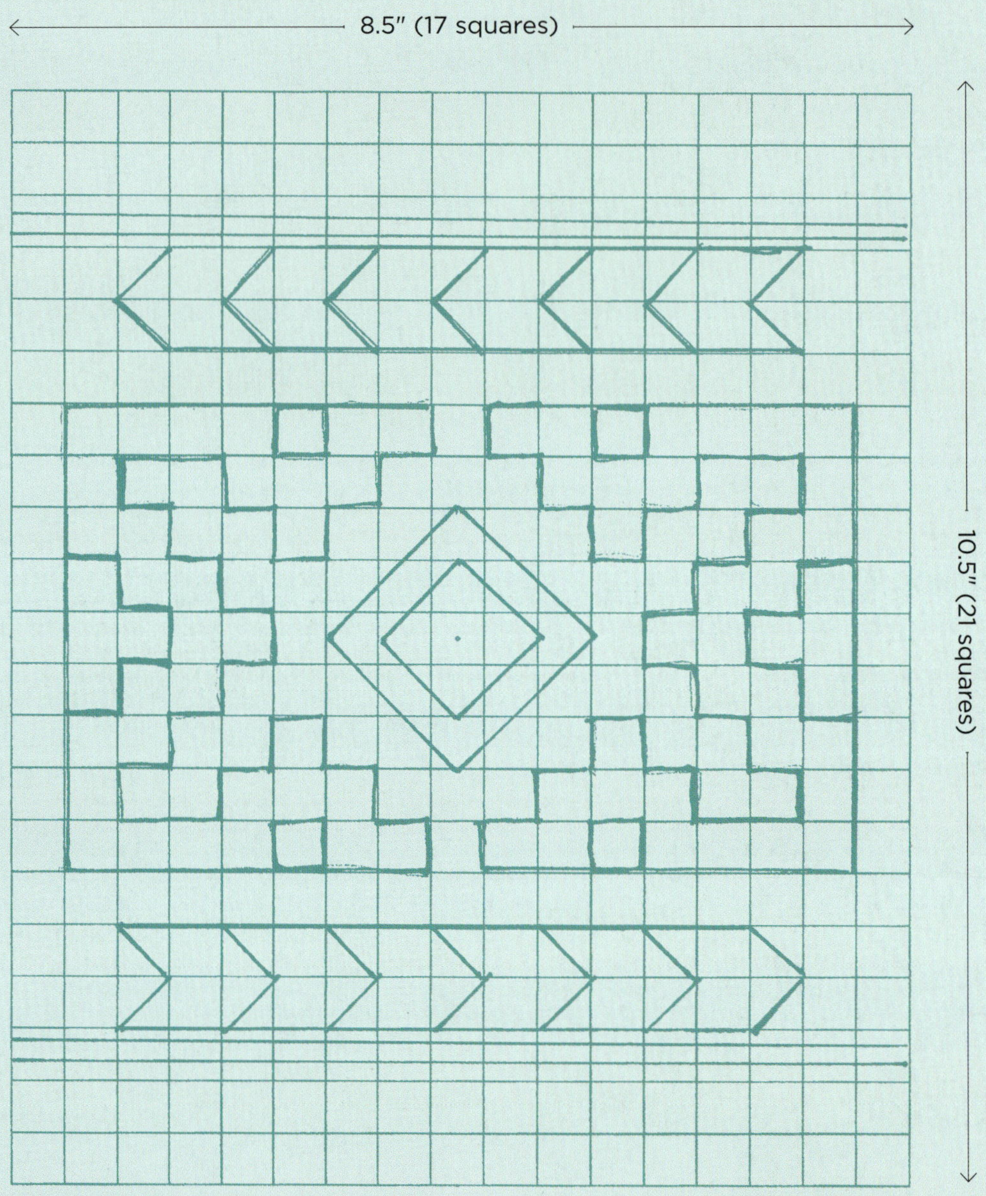

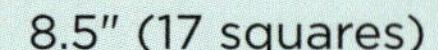

10.5″ (21 squares)

NAVAJO WEAVING GRAPH

- 8.5″ wide x 10.5″ high
- 8.5″ width x 4 warps/inch = 34 warp strings
- Selvage cords add 1 warp per side (2 total)
- Total warp count is an even number
- Each graph square = 2 warps
- 2 graph squares = 1 inch
- Mark the 2 middle warps
- Middle of rug is 10.5 squares up

when weaving in the female shed, and the right male selvage cord counts as one warp when weaving in the male shed. This is true whether you wrap or braid your selvages.

The addition of these two side selvage cords adds ½″ to the initial 8″ width of the project that has 33 warp string pairs. The selvage cords make the final count 34 pairs.

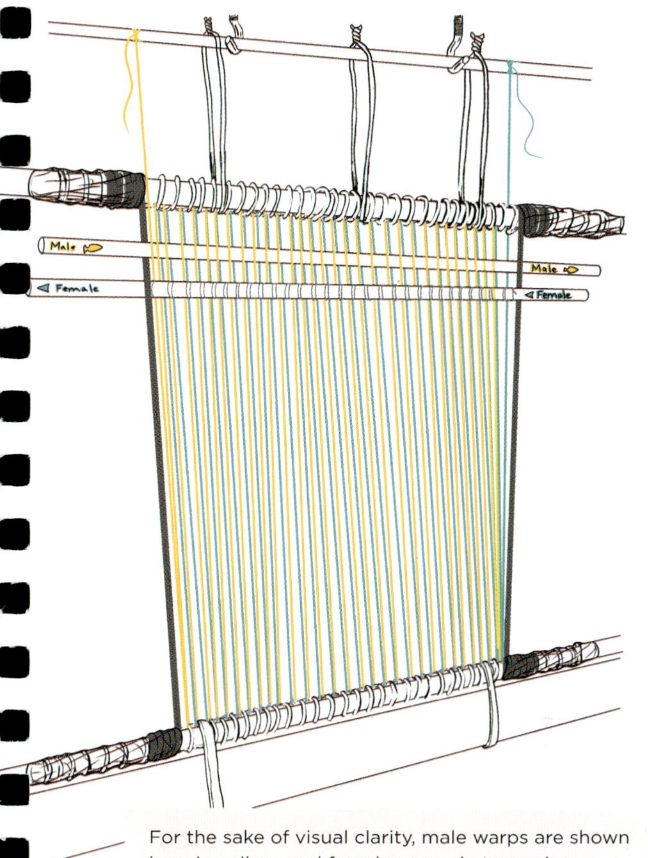

For the sake of visual clarity, male warps are shown here in yellow, and female warps in turquoise.

When the batten is inserted in the male shed, there are 33 warps plus the right selvage cord; the entire male warp count is 34. When the batten is inserted in the female shed, there are 33 warps plus the left selvage cord; the entire warp count is 34.

The warp pairs are spaced at ¼″ intervals for 8 warps per inch. They will be woven with worsted-weight single-ply yarn, which is what we recommend for beginning student weavers.

TEXTILE WIDTH

Width before addition of side selvages:
8″ (width x 4) + 1 = warp string pairs

Warp pair count without side selvages:
(8 x 4) + 1 = 33 warp string pairs

For warping, we do not need a separate warping frame. The sides of the loom have predrilled holes to accommodate three sizes of the warps that can be woven on the medium loom. We turn the loom over to the back side, and we assemble our warping kit of two marked dowels, four metal hooks, four carriage bolts, and four wing nuts.

The frame used for making the warp for a finished piece of the size we describe here has an inside measurement of 19″ wide by 27″ high; the outside measurement is 24″ wide by 30″ high.

MARKING THE WARPING POLES

The warping poles should be cut as long as the width of the warping frame or the back side of the loom, which is 24″. On both warping poles, make a bold mark with a marking pen at the midpoint and outer edges of the width of your project. The warping poles are 24″ long, and you will have bold marks at the midpoint, which is 12″ from either end, and at 6″ to the left and right of that midpoint a. Between the outside markings, lightly mark every ¼″ for the entire span of the width of your project. There should be 33 markings centered on each pole.

SECURING WARPING POLES TO THE WARPING FRAME

If you are using the back of your loom as the warping frame, simply remove the legs until you are ready to mount the warp at the front of the loom.

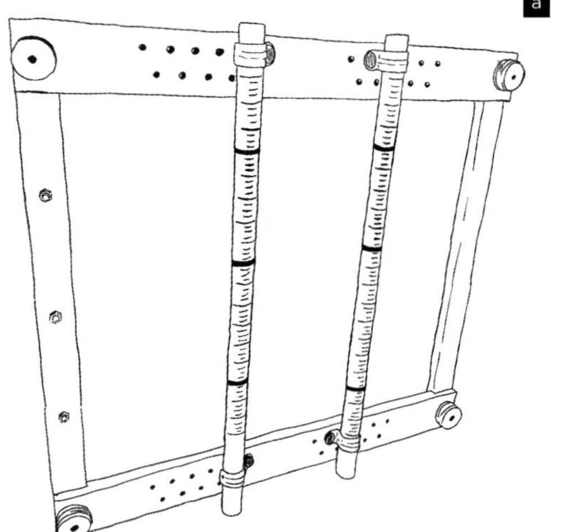

Mark the centers of both of the long sides of the 30″ long warping frame. Mark the midpoint at 15″ from either end. Then, measure and mark 4″ to the left and right of the midpoint mark.

If using a warp frame with predrilled holes at set increments, as shown in the illustration, choose a pair of holes closest to 8″ apart and secure the warping poles to the frame with the hardware that is included.

WARPING—HAVING A WARPED SENSE OF HUMOR HELPS

Position the warp frame so that the top is to your right and the bottom is to your left b. Beginning at the bold outer marking on the left-hand side farthest from your body, lay the loose end of the warp ball over the bottom (left) pole, clockwise toward the top pole. You will warp in toward yourself in a figure-eight pattern and finish at the right-hand corner that is positioned nearest to you.

Going clockwise, bring the warp ball around the bottom (left) dowel and back toward the top pole

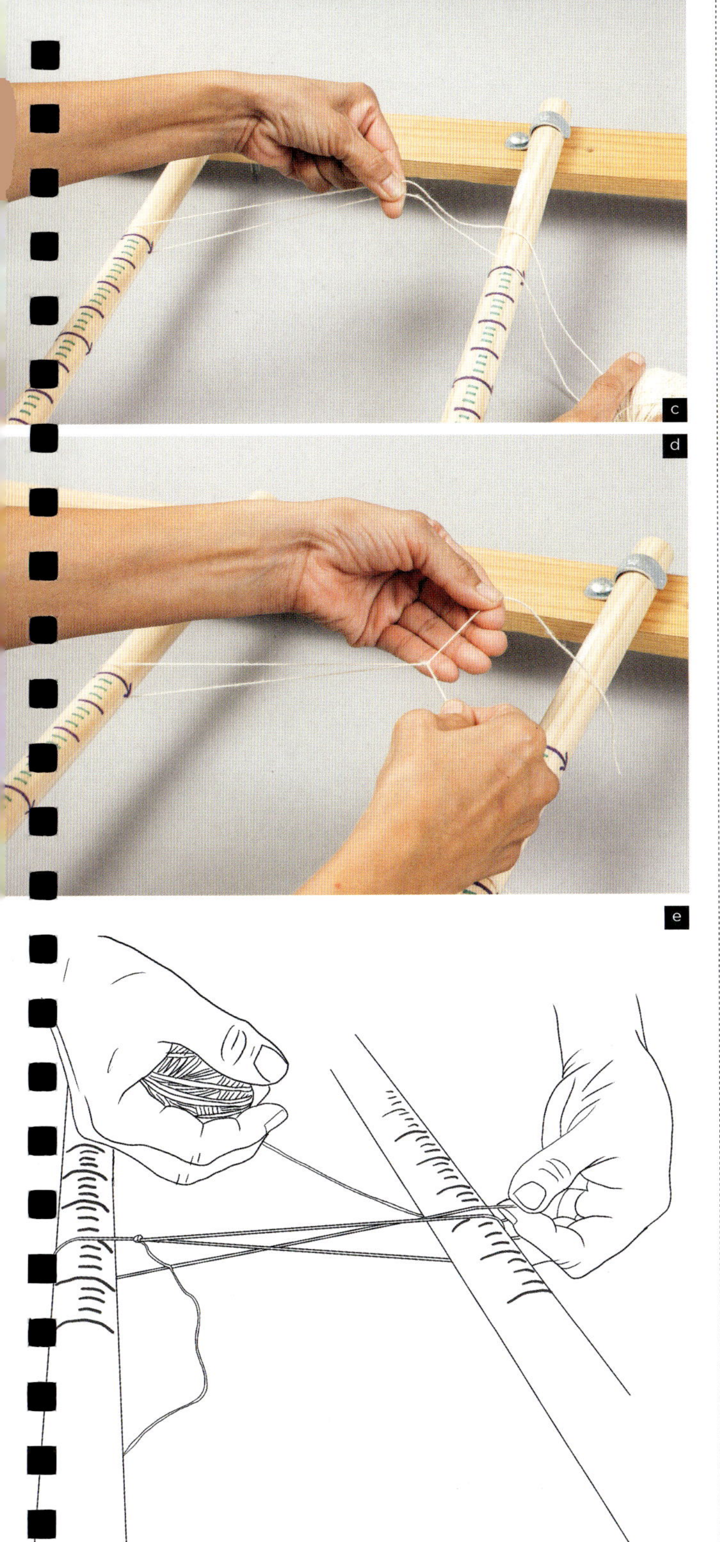

c. About ½″ before reaching the top pole, pause to tie your starting square knot. Leave a tail 5″ long. If you are unable to tie a knot that does not slip, try wrapping and taping the hanging tail end of the warp with painter's tape to the top pole while you work.

Going over the pole, wrap the warp ball around the top (right) pole, placing the first warp string on the bold outer mark. Going under the bottom pole, bring it back toward the bottom pole, placing the warp string on the bold outer mark d.

From here on, keep an even and moderate tension that is not too loose or too tight e. If it is too loose, the warps will stretch too much when they are fastened onto the loom, or they may become tangled with neighboring warps. If it is too tight, the warps could snap, or the warping poles could bend and create a lopsided warp.

Continue working toward yourself as you warp. Each time, you will pass the bottom pole going under the pole and the top one going over the pole. Continue warping in this figure-eight way until all of the markings on the top pole are covered. (See "Marking the Warping Poles.") Without dropping the warp ball or losing the even tension, reposition any warps that have moved off of the guide markings. Take the warp ball around the bottom pole one last time and bring it back toward the top one. Line it up next to the last warp on the underside of the top pole, and pinch both warps together with the index finger and thumb of one hand about ½″ before you get to the top pole. Use your other hand to tie a secure square knot.

Leaving a 12″ tail, before cutting any excess warp ends, check to see that there are 33 warps on the top (right) and 34 on the bottom (left). Also, check that the warp string figure-eight pattern has been maintained by holding the frame up horizontally and bringing it up to eye level. Then turn the frame to its side and check to see that the warps have maintained an even spacing, that they are parallel to one another, and that there are not any warps that have crossed over other warps f.

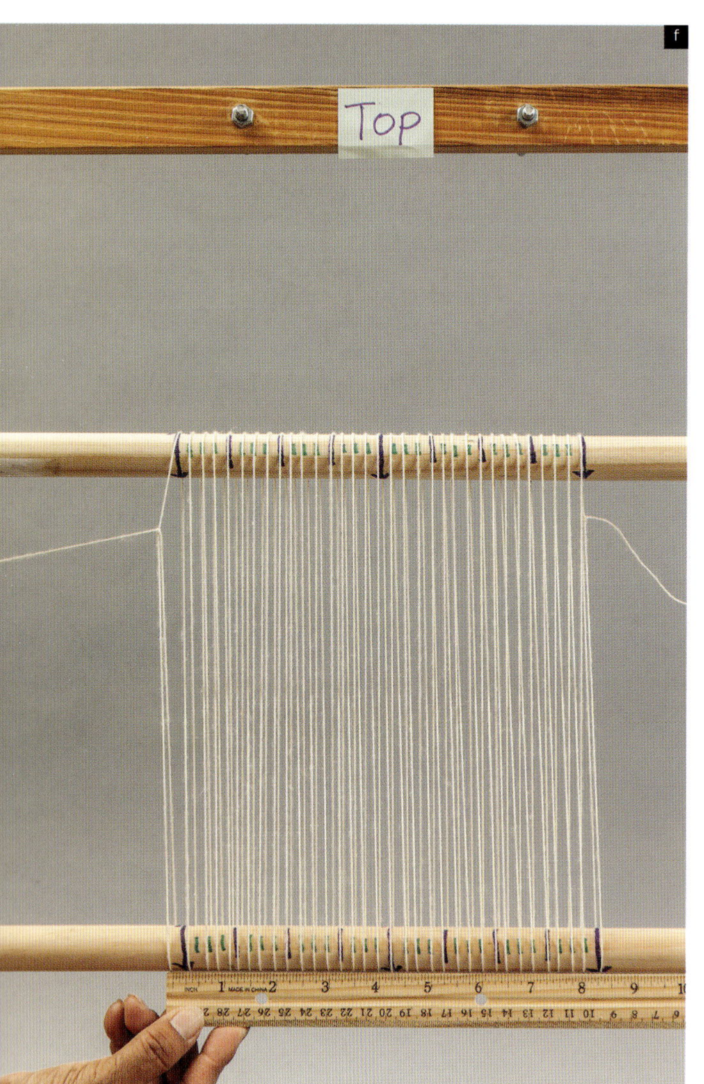

FOR THE BOTTOM POLE ONLY

The warp has been wrapped one extra time around the bottom warping pole that is opposite the side where the start and end knots were tied. If the same ¼″ spacing is used, the width across the bottom will be ¼″ wider than the top. To keep the width of the top and bottom identical, the warps across the bottom must be repositioned slightly closer than they are currently spaced. Using the markings as a guide, this step requires “eyeballing.” In other words, squeeze all of the warps on the bottom end of the warp frame into the 8″ predetermined width and do your best to keep them evenly spaced.

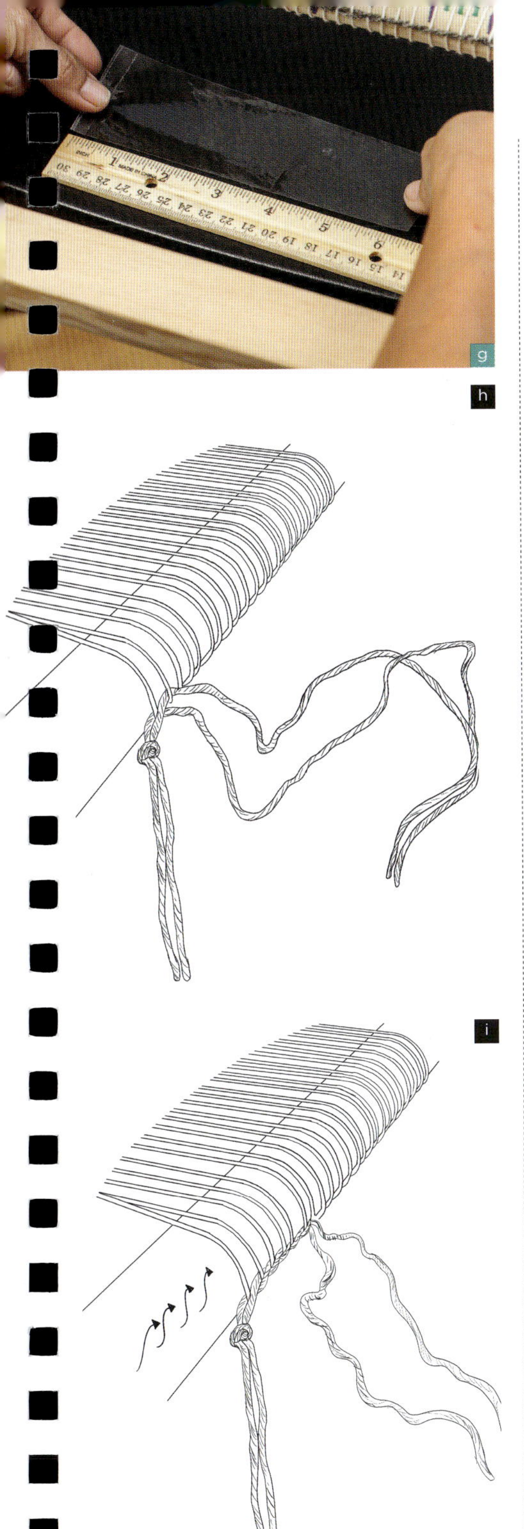

LACING THE BOTTOM (AND TOP) SELVAGE CORDS

Fold one end of a piece of packing tape onto itself for easy removal later g. Then tape the short tail of the pair of selvage cords to the warping pole, leaving a 2″ space between the knot and the tape. That space will be necessary later for sewing the warp to the top and bottom tension dowels. For right-handers, tape the cords on the left side of the bottom warping pole.

Securely taping the selvage cords is an important step. When you tug at them, they should not slip out from under the tape. If you proceed without securely taping them, the knot may slide inward, causing the warps to bunch up and ruin the even spacing you have created. Unevenly spaced warps lead to a host of weaving tension problems that are not easily solved.

To begin, separate the cords and feed one of them behind the first warp string. Drop that cord and pick up the second one. In the same manner, slide the second selvage cord underneath the second warp and over the first cord.

The next step is to lace or twine two selvage cords onto the bottom of the warp. Cut four selvage cords 10″ longer than the width of the textile. For this example, the selvage cords will need to be cut 18½″ long or rounded to 19″.

Position the warping frame so that the bottom warping pole is in front of you. Pair two of the cords side by side and tie them together with an overhand knot 4″ to 5″ from one end. Align the overhand knot on the outside edge of the leftmost warp string h. If you are left-handed and it is more comfortable for you to twine the selvages from right to left, align the overhand knot on the outside edge of the rightmost warp string i. Regardless of which

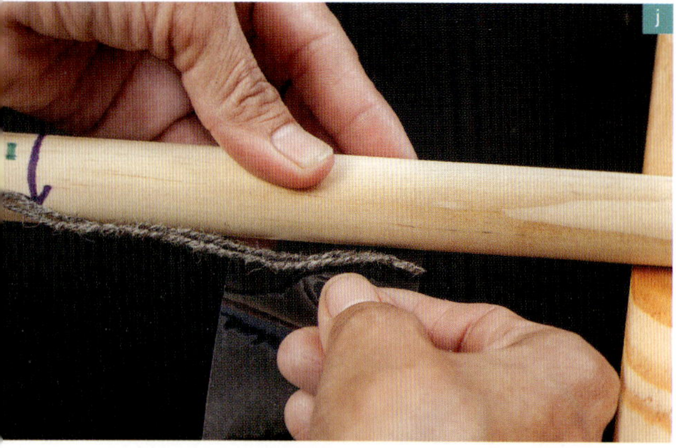

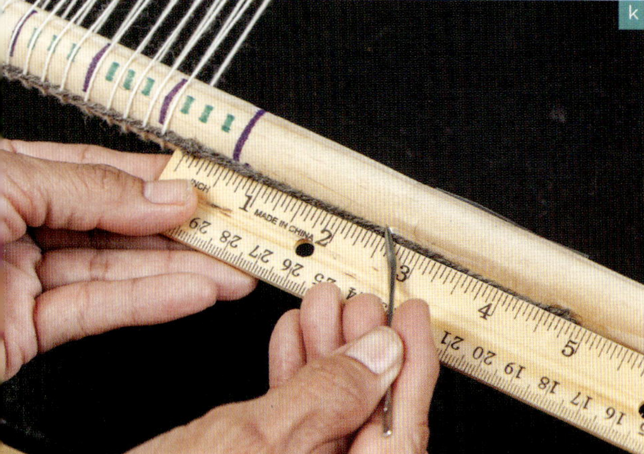

end you choose to start on, the knot should not move the warp string out of its place.

Alternate both selvage cords until all of the warps have been laced, making sure to keep the direction of twining the same all the way across. Keep a taut but not tight tension as you twine the selvage cords. When loosely twined, they sag when the warp is stretched onto the loom, making the finishing process—when it is time to sew the last ½″ with a needle—more difficult. On the other hand, top and bottom selvage cords twined too tightly between the warps will cause the corners of your finished textile to curl. Navajo warping and weaving are all about finding the right balance between loose and tight.

When finished, tie the selvage cords together with an overhand knot and align them to the outside edge of the last warp. Tape the tail end of the selvage cords to the warping pole leaving about 1½″ between the knot and the tape j k.

Before proceeding, use a needle to tug at the selvage cord at various intervals to make sure that each warp string was caught in the twining process l m. If a warp string was missed, the unlaced warp will remain "stuck" to the warping pole; it will not lift away when you pull at the selvage cord. If that happens, remove the tape and untie the knot at the end that is closest to the missed warp. Then, undo the lacing up to the point of the mistake. Retwine the selvage cords to make sure that the direction of the twining or lacing matches your previous work.

If this is not corrected, when the warps are stretched onto the loom, the unlaced warp string will fall or hang loose, and the entire warp will have to be dismantled and rewarped to fix the problem.

Repeat the process at the top of the warp.

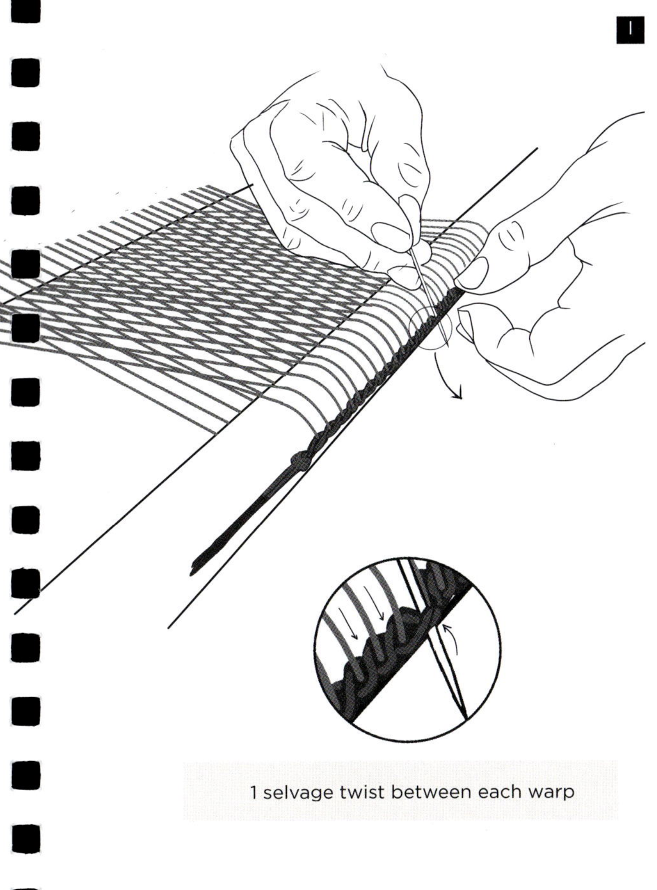

1 selvage twist between each warp

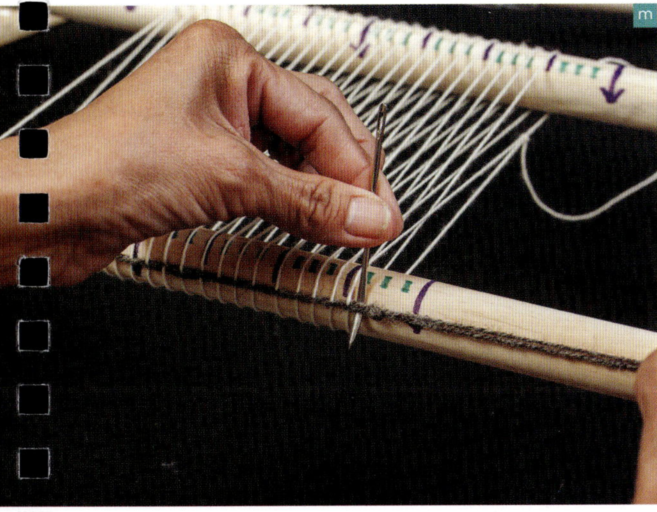

SEWING THE WARP TO THE BOTTOM TENSION DOWEL

The top and bottom dowels are 24″ in length, ½″ in diameter and marked at 12″ for the center; they will be sewn onto the warp and left in place as the textile is woven and then removed upon finishing. These dowels stretch out the warp and are called tension dowels. You will need 7 yards of household string cut in half. To measure the amount needed, wrap the string around one of the tension dowels, once for each of the (33) warp pairs plus an added 20 times for the stitches you will make at the start and the end. For this project, the string has to be long enough to wrap around the tension dowel 53 times. Ten wraps around the dowel is a 25″ length of string and so the calculation is as follows: 25″ multiplied by 5 (rounding 5.3 to 5) is 125″ divided by 36 equals 3.5 yards of cotton string for sewing one side of the tension dowel.

Position the warping frame with the bottom edge facing you. Thread the string onto a sacking needle or a curved upholstery needle. Have a small cup of water nearby to moisten the string as needed to make it easier to handle and to keep it from tangling when you work.

Center the marked tension dowel with the center of the marked warp on the warping pole. Make several secure knots

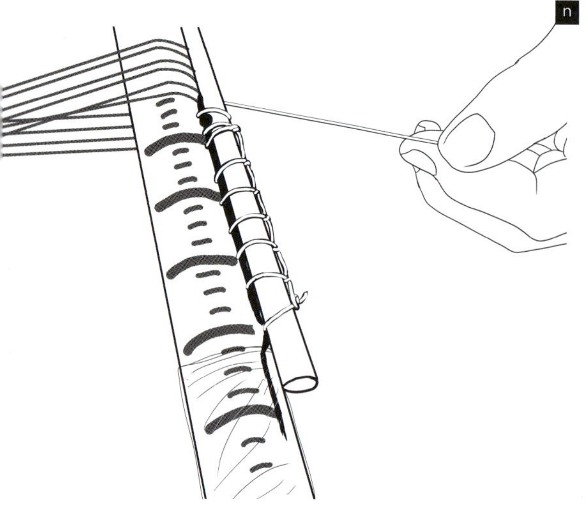

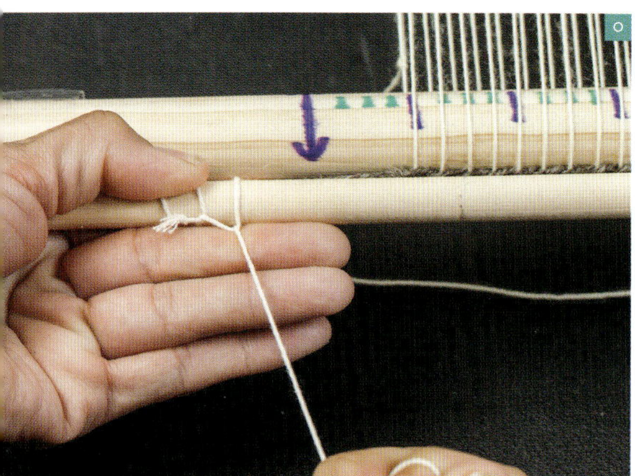

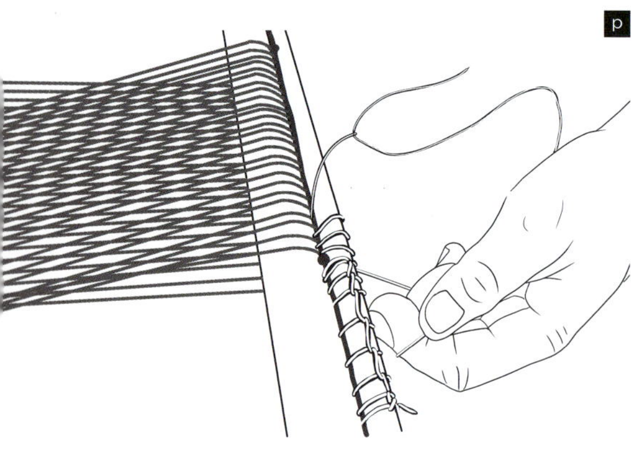

on the left side of it (for right-handers). Start sewing 1½″ to 2″ from the first warp string on the left side n and continue working toward the right side. Hold the needle with your right hand and press down on the last stitch with the thumb of your left hand to keep the stitches tight o. (If you are left-handed, start on the right side of the dowel rod and sew toward the left.)

Do the first blanket stitch to the right of the tape applied in the previous step. Keeping the needle perpendicular to the warping frame, push it down through the selvage cord and behind the warping pole. Bring it back up in front of the tension dowel through the loop just created before pulling it tight. Do that five more times. The blanket stitches should be a bit more than ¼″ apart.

After six blanket stitches, continue by making two wraps before the overhand knot without bringing the needle up through the loop p. It is important to keep your finger pressed on the wrap just made to keep the tension from loosening.

Wrap the household string once after the overhand knot but before the first warp string. Continue wrapping it between each warp pair. Maintain a tight, even tension on the string throughout by holding down the last stitch. If it is necessary to stop, make a blanket stitch, pull it tight before leaving your warp, and tape it down with painter's tape.

Throughout the sewing process, push the needle downward while aiming to keep the needle as

q

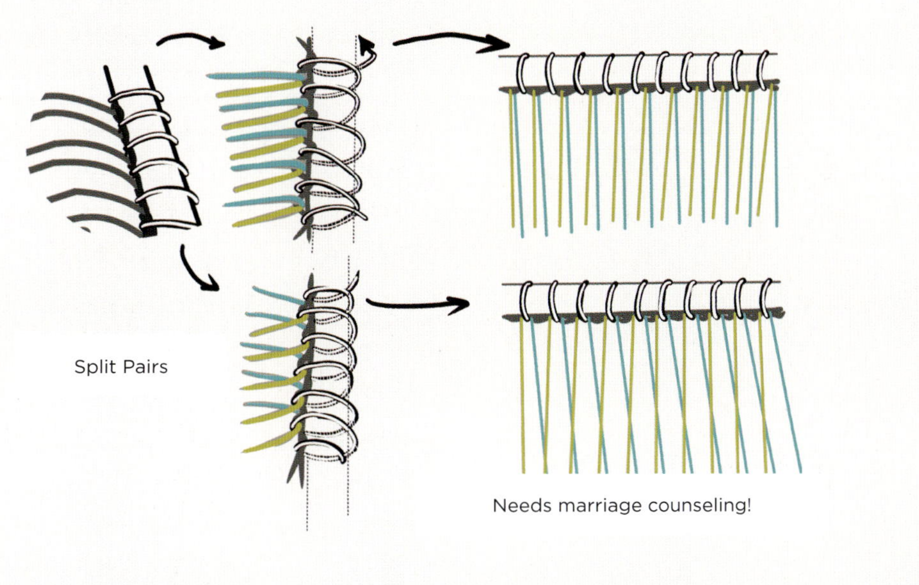

vertical as possible. Slanting the needle during sewing may result in creating a split warp pair.

A warp pair becomes split when the male and female warps get separated in the sewing process. A split warp pair on the top of the warp can cause problems in the finishing stages. If you see one that has been split, cut a separate piece of cotton string and tie the split warp pair together. We jokingly refer to this process as Marriage Counseling because the split warp pair of female and male warps need to be back together q.

After the last wrap is made between the last two pairs of warps, wrap it once before the knot, and follow that with six blanket stitches and several secure knots to reverse the process you did when you started sewing.

SEWING THE WARP TO THE TOP TENSION DOWEL

Position the warping frame so that the top edge is facing you. The process is the same as for sewing the warp to the bottom tension dowel except for the placement of the premade wire loops in three places.

Measure the string as you did for the bottom tension dowel, and thread it onto the needle. Make several secure knots at one end of the dowel. Before starting to sew, take three premade

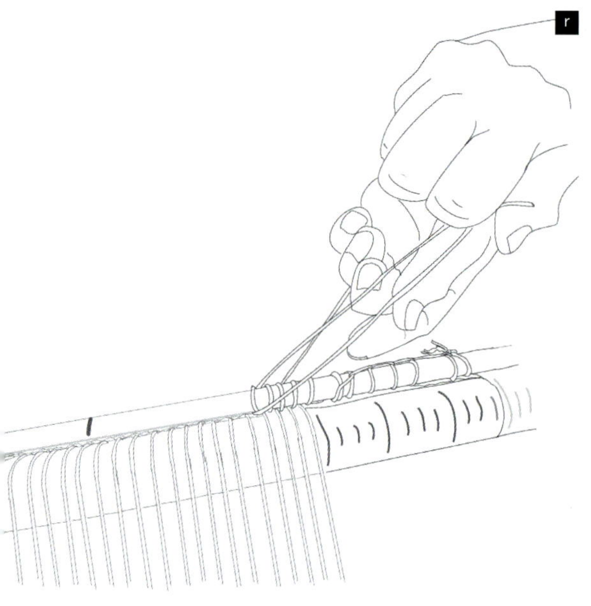

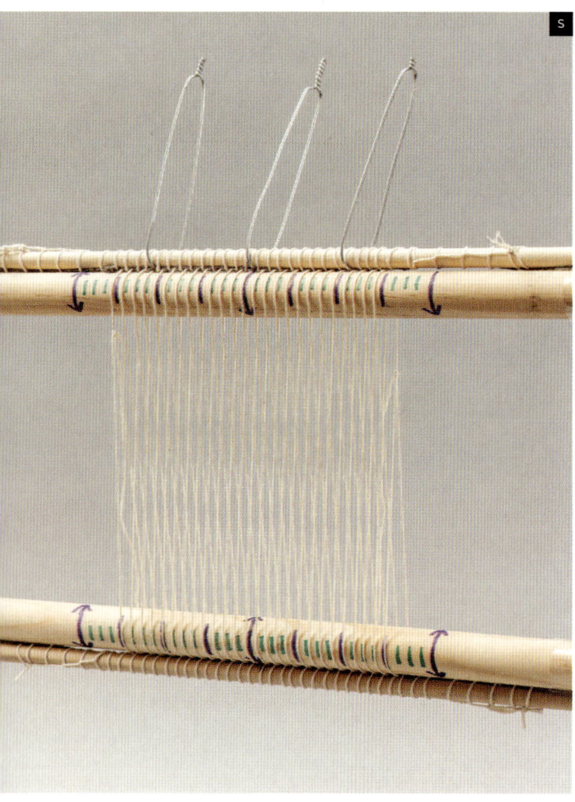

wire rings and slide them onto the top of the dowel. In the same manner as before, begin the blanket stitches followed by the wraps.

After sewing between the first four pairs of warps, slide the first wire loop on and align it to the fifth pair of warps r. Do the same with the second and third wire loops, sliding the second loop directly in the center and aligning it to the seventeenth warp pair. The final loop will line up with the twenty-ninth pair of warps which is the fifth pair counted from the right side s.

If warping a wider textile, increase the number of wire loops as necessary. After placing the two outside loops at the fifth warp counting in from both sides, use enough wire loops so that they are evenly spaced; they should be no more than 4″ apart. Wire loops should be exactly the same size although they can be small or large depending on the size of the warp compared to the size of the loom. For our project, we are using 10″ long premade wire loops.

REMOVING THE WARPING POLES

After the sewing is finished, remove the packing tape from the ends of the selvage cords on all four corners. Release the warping poles from the warping frame by loosening the hardware securing the one-hole steel clamps. Do not turn the warp frame over so that the warp ends up on its face or is allowed to slide or fall off the frame t.

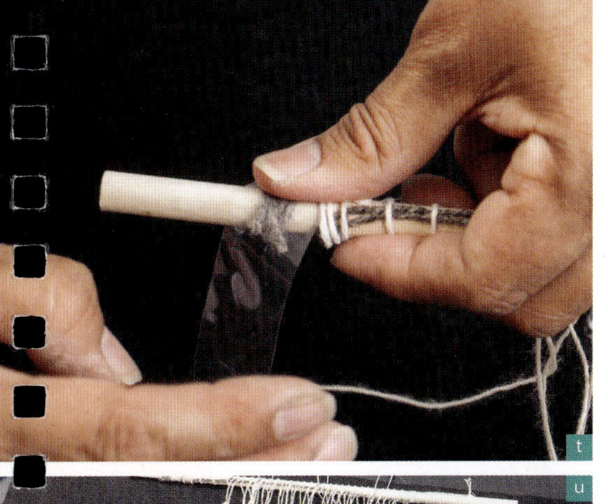

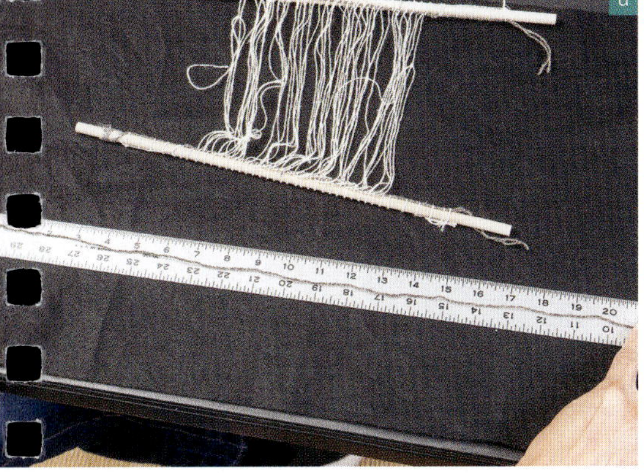

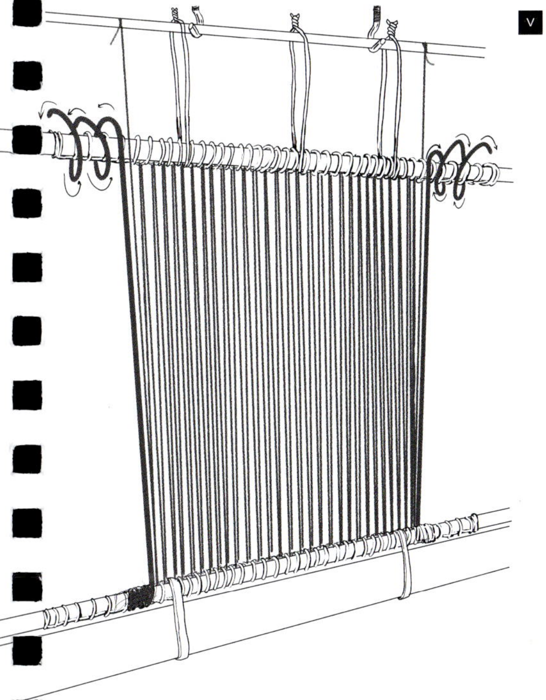

After the poles are no longer anchored to the frame, beginning with the bottom warping pole, carefully slide it out from between the warps one at a time, and set it to the side. Repeat with the top warping pole.

Straighten the selvage cords on the top and bottom tensioning dowels. Tug tautly and wrap the hanging selvage cord tails and excess household string around the tension dowels. Secure them with a long piece of tape with folded ends u. The twined top and bottom selvage cords hold the warps securely in place and help maintain even spacing. If they move, the warps move, and the weaving quality is affected. Keep the loose ends wrapped and taped up to ensure that the warps will stay put v.

SECURING THE WARP TO THE LOOM

In authentic Navajo weaving, selvage cords are used primarily to firm up the four sides of the textile. If the top and bottom selvages are laced too tightly, the ends of the textiles will curl up; if the lacing is too loose, the end warps will show through and the selvages will sag. The side selvages can be wrapped by the weft yarns, so it looks like the sides of the textile do not have edge cords; this is a beginning technique. Braiding the edges with the side selvages will look like a running stitch; this is an intermediate technique, and we begin with two cords. Advanced projects may include three cords, and we can introduce color so the selvage adds another creative dimension to the woven textile.

Before securing the warp to the loom, we need to prepare the side selvage cords. Four selvage cords are cut 10″ longer than the height of the textile. For this project, the selvage cords need to be cut to 20½″, which can be rounded to 21″.

Separate the four cords into two pairs. Measure 5″ from one end of one pair and loosely tie, but do not knot, a pair onto the bottom tension dowel on each side of the warp, ¼″ from the outer-edge double warps. This is a temporary hold.

At the top of the loom, turn each turnbuckle until both are lengthened entirely. Attach the hook side of the turnbuckles to the eyebolts in the top beam of the loom. Slip the metal rod through the first wire loop and then the eye of the first turnbuckle. Continue with the placement of the metal rod by sliding it through the center wire loop, the second turnbuckle eye, and then the last wire loop W.

Use the curved needle to lift the selvage cord away from the bottom tension dowel at the center warp and five warps in from the right and left edges. These should be the same spots where the wire loops were placed when the warp was sewn to the top tension dowel. In each of those spots, slide a plastic zip tie or a length of galvanized wire between the twined selvage cords and the bottom tension dowel.

Stretch the plastic zip ties or galvanized wires around the bottom beam of your loom. Keep the warp level and centered between the loom's side beams. Beginning at the center, lock the tapered end of the zip tie into the square end and pull and tighten the zip tie. If using wire, twist the ends of the center wire together with pliers to secure it. Do the same with the zip tie or wire on the right side followed by the left side. It doesn't matter, which side goes next, but if you're right-handed, you will generally do the right first and then the left. After checking to see that the warp is centered between the loom's two side beams, tighten all of the attachments fully. Snip the excess ends of the zip ties or galvanized wire with a wire cutter. When the warp is done, there will be 3 pre-made 10″ metal loops in place during the warping. After the warping, when the warp is being attached to the loom, the bottom wire or ties will be inserted in exactly the same places as the top metal loops. When the warp is stretched out, it is stretched out evenly from top to bottom.

Turn both turnbuckles at the same time to adjust the tension. Stop just before the final tension is achieved to attach the final side selvage cords that have already been loosely tied around the bottom tension dowel. Turning the turnbuckles one at a time can cause your warp to stretch unevenly or result in broken warps.

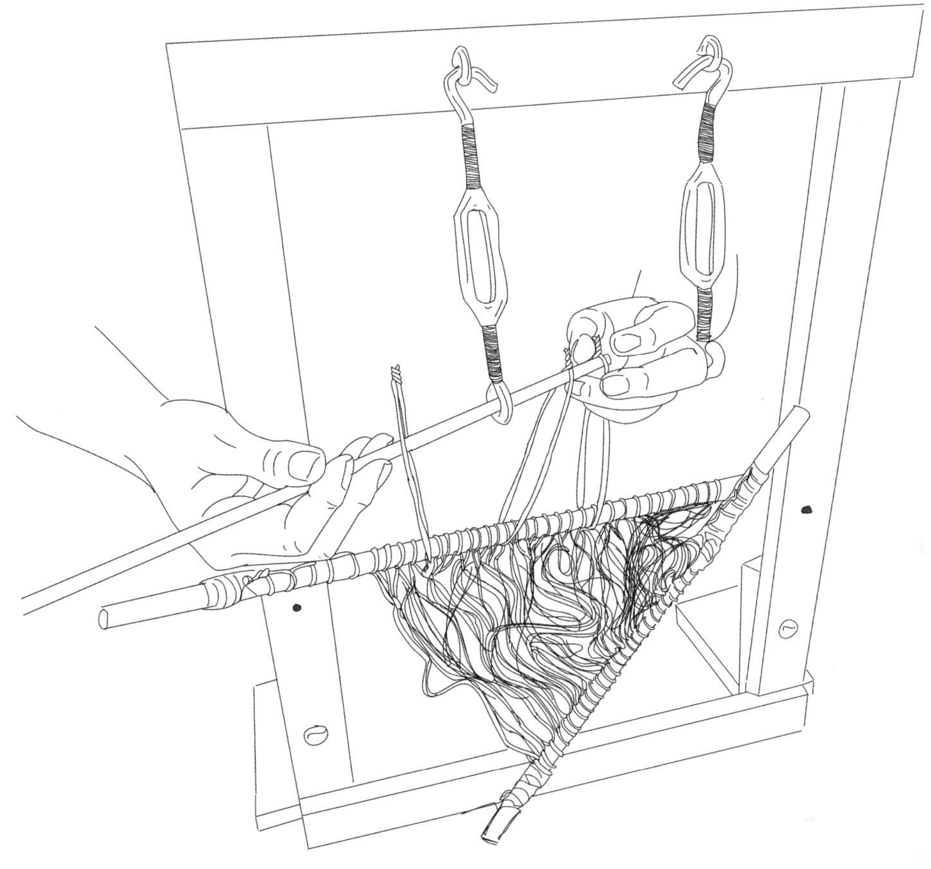

Measure both sides and the middle of the warp to ensure that they have been stretched to the same height. If one side is taller than the other, loosen or tighten one of the turnbuckles just enough so that the height of both sides of the warp are even.

Begin with the side selvage cords on the left side. Keeping the pair of selvage cords between the lower tension dowel and the bottom beam of the loom, slide them together so that they are positioned ¼″ to the left of the first double warp. Use a 5″ tail to tie the selvage cords around the lower tension dowel with a double knot that will be untied later when it is time to remove your finished textile from the loom; it is best not to tie it too tightly. Secure the wrapped selvage ends to the tension dowel with 6″ of tape with folded ends.

Repeat the process with the side selvage cords on the other side, but position that pair ¼″ to the right of the last double warp string.

After securing them around the bottom tension dowel, pull the left side selvage cords up and around the top tension dowel, and tie them with a double knot. Keep the tension on them and the warps the same and retain the same spacing of ¼″ from the outermost warp string.

Repeat the process with the side selvages on the right. Wrap excess hanging ends and the selvage cord around the top tension dowel and secure them with a long piece of tape to keep them out of the way as you weave.

Dial in the final tension by turning the bodies of both turnbuckles simultaneously one-quarter turn at a time until the warps feel taut and make a nice sound when you strum your fingers across them, signaling that they are at the right tension for weaving.

When not weaving for a few days or an extended period of time, always loosen your turnbuckles one-quarter turn. Retighten them when you are ready to resume weaving.

Measure the dimensions of the warp again to check that it is roughly 8.5″ wide by 10.5″ high. The dimensions of the warp may not exactly match the planned dimensions, but they should be close. There are seven measurements: the left side, center, and right side of the warp are measured vertically; the top and bottom of the warps are measured horizontally; and two diagonal measurements, from the top right of the warp to the bottom left and from top left to bottom right in an X formation, are made to make sure the warp is squared up.

Measure vertically on the left side, the right side, and the middle of the stretched warp. If one side is longer than the other, lengthen the turnbuckle on the shorter side a fraction of a turn at a time until the measurements at those three points are equal.

Measure horizontally at the bottom, the top, and the middle of the stretched warp. If the edges are uneven, at the tension bar of the narrower end, widen the spacing between the outer six warps until the widths at both ends are closer to matching.

Lastly, check to see that all of the warps are spaced evenly at ¼″ intervals at the top of the warp and slightly closer than ¼″ at the bottom. If there are areas where the spacing is noticeably askew, move the warps closer or farther apart as needed.

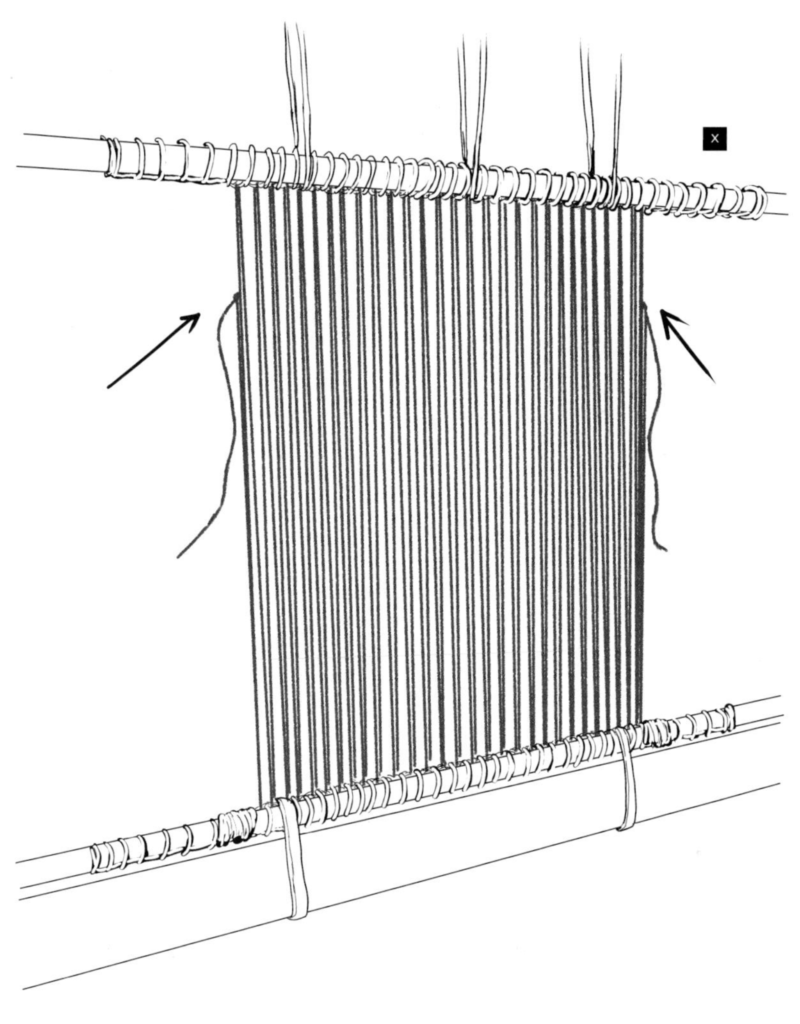

BEGINNING AND ENDING KNOTS ON THE LAST WARPS

The double warps inside the side selvage cords are the outermost ones on both sides of the warp x. They are the first and last ones that the starting and ending knots were tied onto in the warping process. They become paired as one warp string; do not separate them.

Pull the loosely hanging ends of the starting and ending warps up and secure them to the top dowel. Tie them to the top dowel or wrap the excess tail ends around it before taping them down. That will prevent the starting and ending knots from slipping down as you weave, which can cause the neighboring warps to loosen. If you do not want the knotted warps to get stuck to the female heddle warp ends, untie each knot and secure it to the metal tension bar.

The doubled warps at each end and the side selvage cords add an extra layer of strength to the sides of the textile and allow for straighter woven edges as you weave y.

When your weaving reaches the knots, it is safe to remove them. After untying them, cut the ends as close to the weft as you can. The loose ends of the warps are then tucked into and hidden in the woven web of the textile.

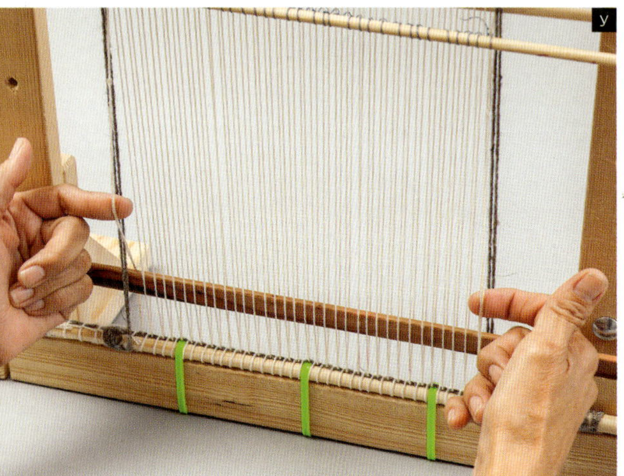

Another method is to remove both knots and tie the left and right warp ends up to the metal tension bar securely. This method will allow the female rod to slide up and down without hanging up on the knots. The double warp that is tied to the tension dowel will need to be cut 2″ to 1½″ toward the top. Students will weave up to 8.5″. With the remaining 2″on one side, and it doesn't matter which side, the double warp string that is tied up to the metal tension bar is cut off, leaving a single warp to weave on. Weave another ½″. At 9″ of woven weft, there should be 1 ½″ of bare warp space left, then the double warp string will be cut, leaving a single warp string to weave on. What are cut are the excess warp (beginning and ending warps), at no time should the warp that is attached to the inside of the rug be cut. When you untie the excess warp tied to the metal rod, it will hang down; that's what we cut. The last inch of weaving should be on single warps.

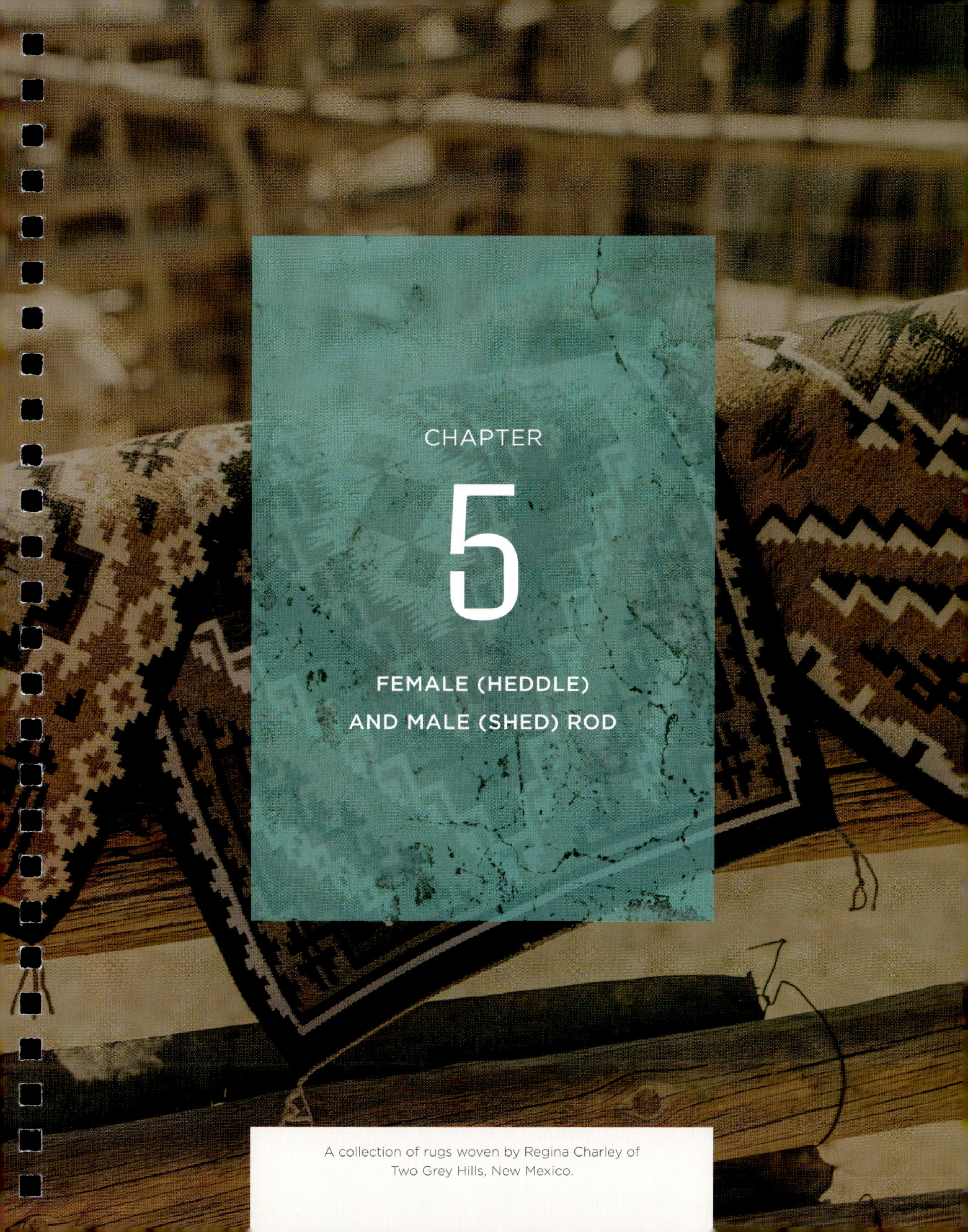

CHAPTER

5

FEMALE (HEDDLE) AND MALE (SHED) ROD

A collection of rugs woven by Regina Charley of Two Grey Hills, New Mexico.

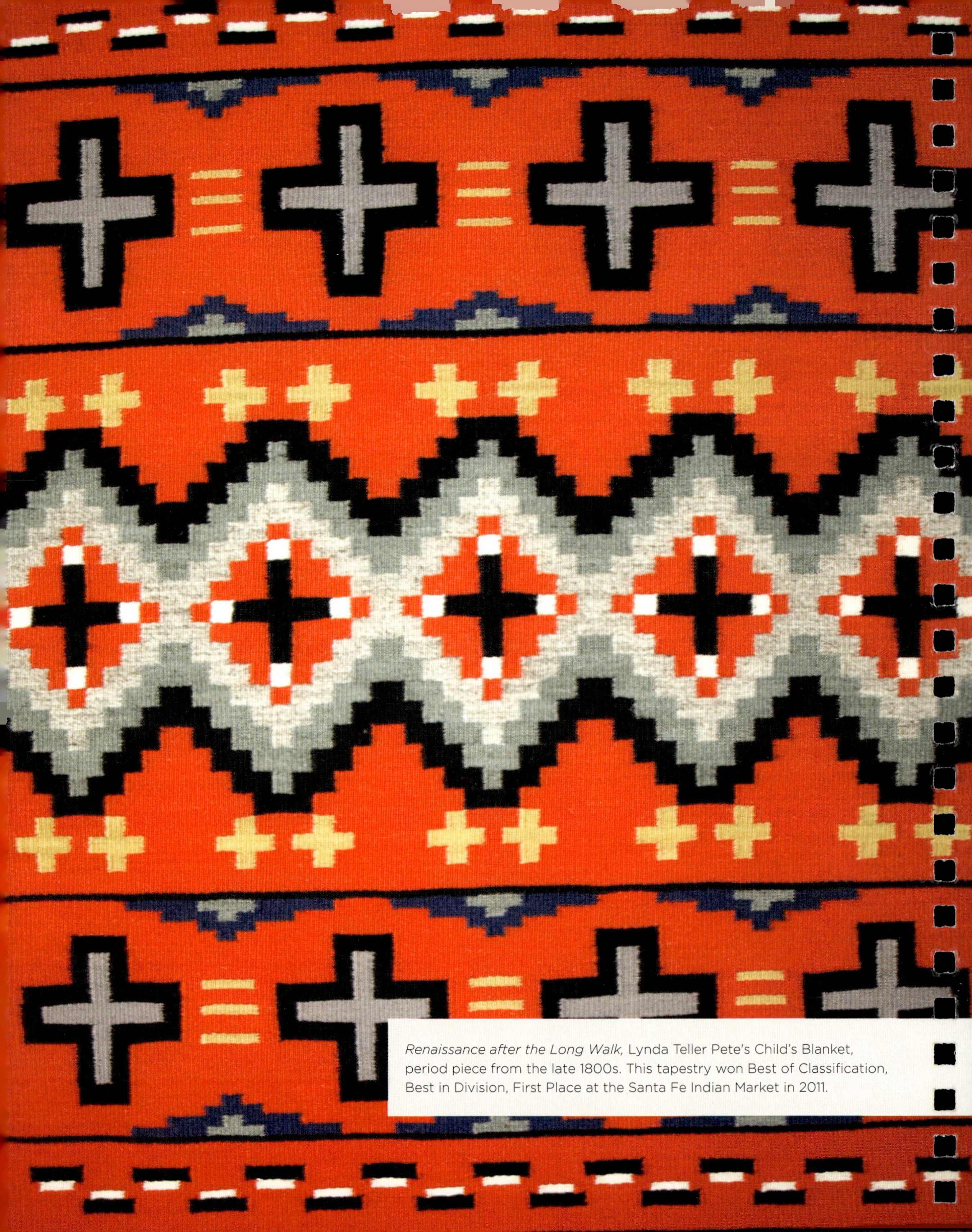

Renaissance after the Long Walk, Lynda Teller Pete's Child's Blanket, period piece from the late 1800s. This tapestry won Best of Classification, Best in Division, First Place at the Santa Fe Indian Market in 2011.

FEMALE (Heddle) and MALE (Shed) ROD

In a perfect world, the female is in charge, and the male is always right, at least in the Navajo universe. In Navajo weaving, if the weaver is right-handed, the female (heddle) is in charge of color changes and design changes; basically, she is in charge of the entire weaving until we remove her completely at about 1″ from the top. In our sample project, the male shed rod should not move at all. It should just be on top and look pretty until we lose the male completely at about 1½″ from the top. The male shed can be moved up and down in a larger project, and if you are in a female row, the male has to be pushed back up to the top; otherwise, he prevents the female heddle from doing her job. The female heddle works best on her own and has to be far from the male to open widely. The male works best when the female heddle is very close—the male does not work well by himself. When the batten is inserted in a female row, the weft yarn is woven to the left. When the batten is inserted in a male row, the weft yarn is woven to the right. Thus, the male is always "right."

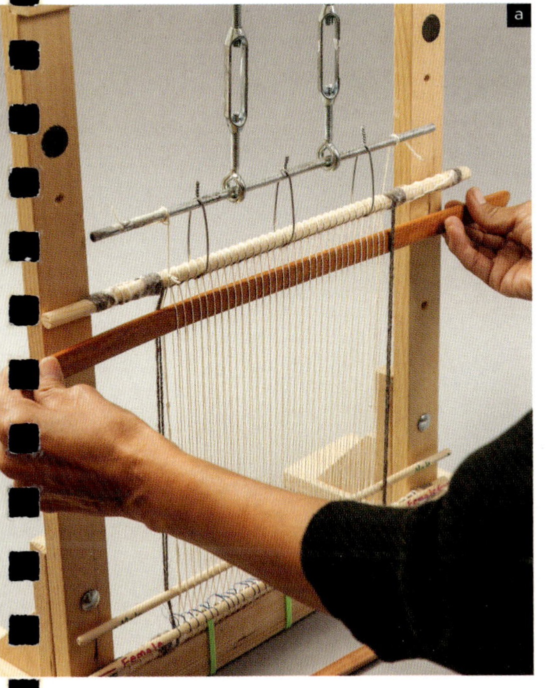
a

PLACEMENT OF THE RODS

To find the male warps, use a batten to pick out the front warps on the top of the loom. They are the male warp ends a. Leave the batten in place b.

With another batten, pick out the front warps on the bottom of the loom that are the female warp ends c d. Take the last left warp off the batten for the double warp for the male set of warps. Take the last right warp and place it on the batten to create the double warp pair for the female set of warps.

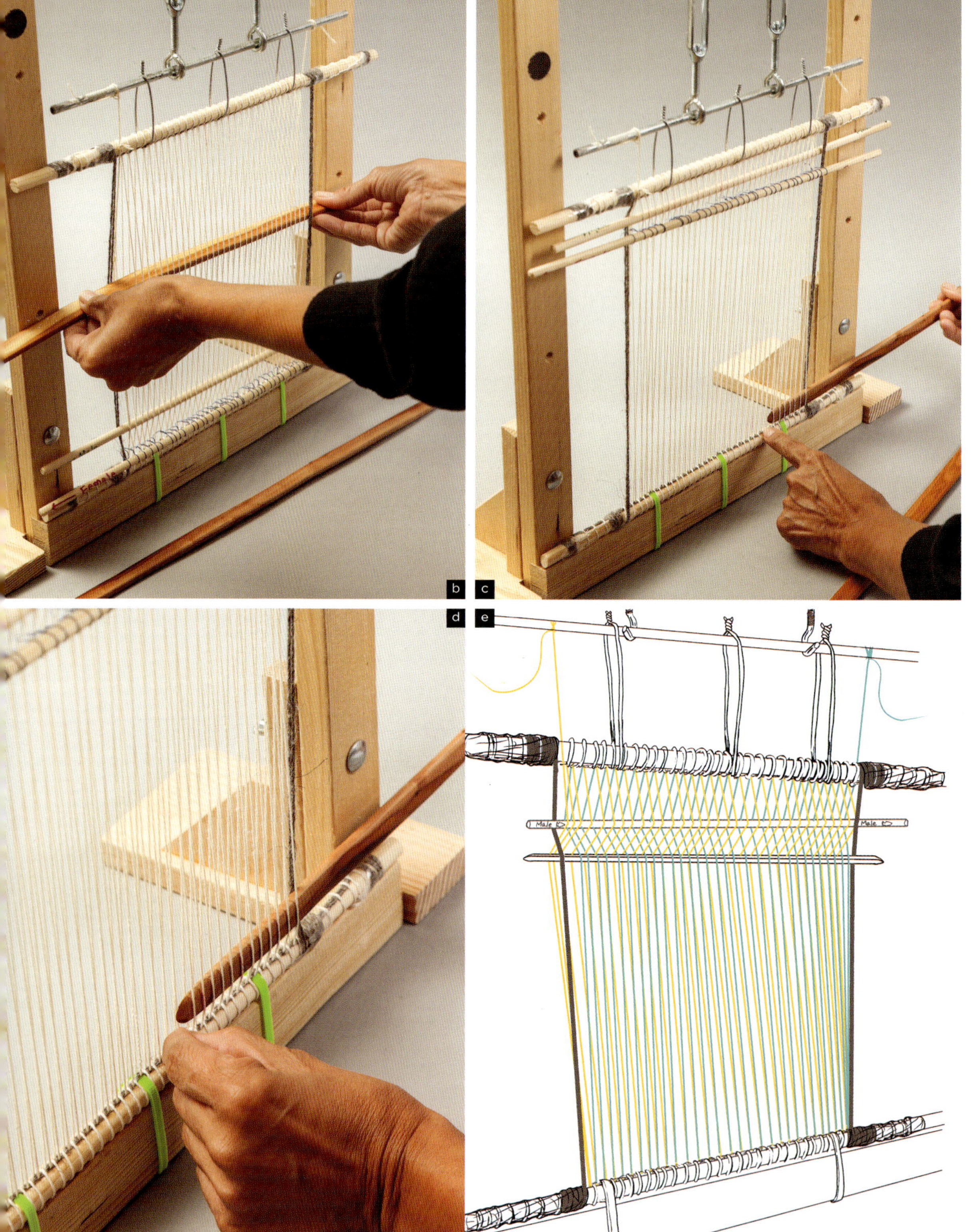
b
c
d
e
Male
Male

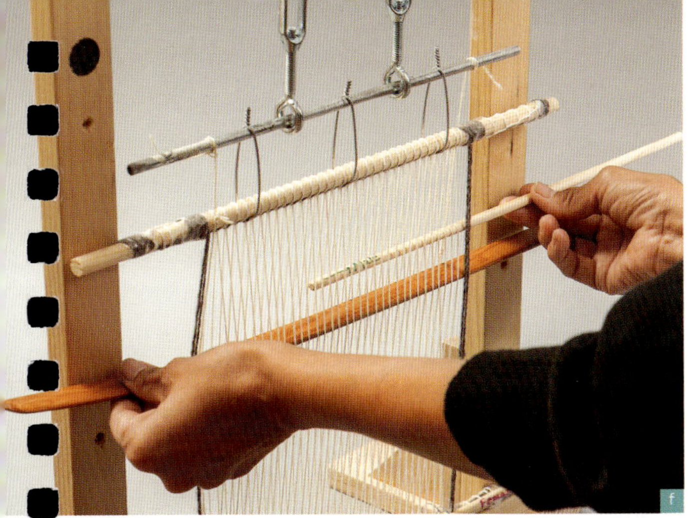

f

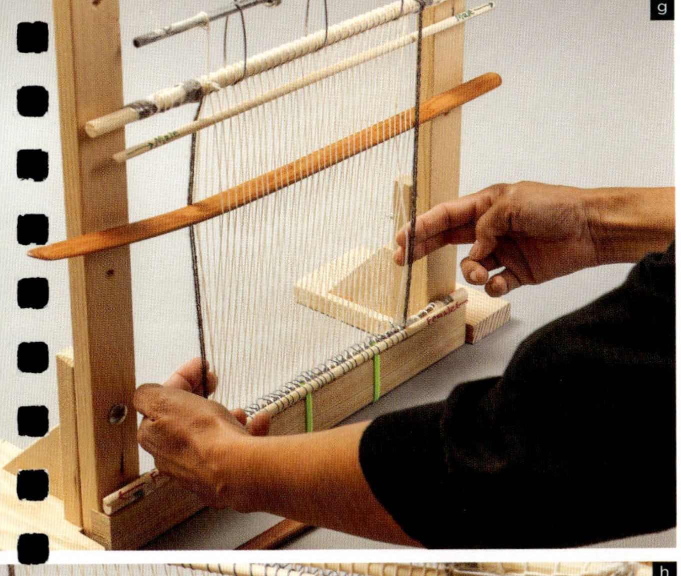

g

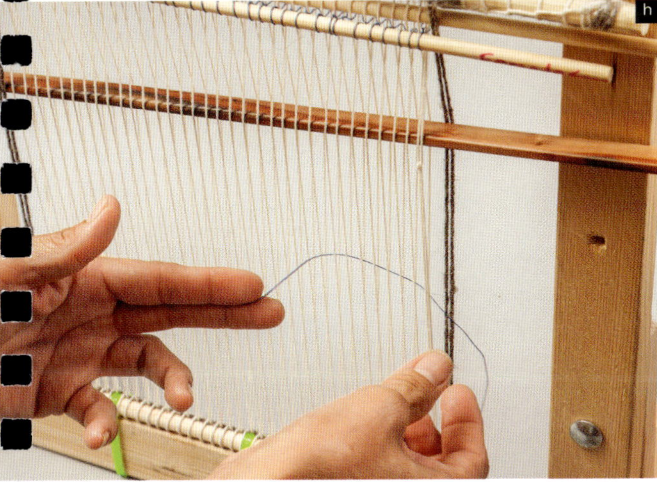

h

Also leave that batten in place. Bring the two battens together to see the crisscross of the warps **e**. If there are any areas where the crisscross pattern is disrupted, remove one or both battens up to the problem areas, and try again to find and separate the male and female warps.

To place the male shed rod, return to the batten at the top. Turn it horizontally to open the shed and place the shed rod through the opening between the warps **f**. Then, leaving it in place, pull the top batten out. Mark that rod "male," and draw an arrow on it pointing to the right **g**.

The female heddle rod floating in front of the warp is secured to the female warps with loops of nylon thread. Placement of the female heddle rod is a more involved process than for the male shed rod. To begin, return to the lower batten. Turn it horizontally to open the shed and thread a long piece of nylon string through the opening between the warps **h**. (*Note:* Thread made of synthetic material such as rayon or nylon is best for this step as it is less abrasive on the wool warp yarns than materials made of natural fibers such as cotton or wool.) For right-handers, thread the heddle from the right side of the warps.

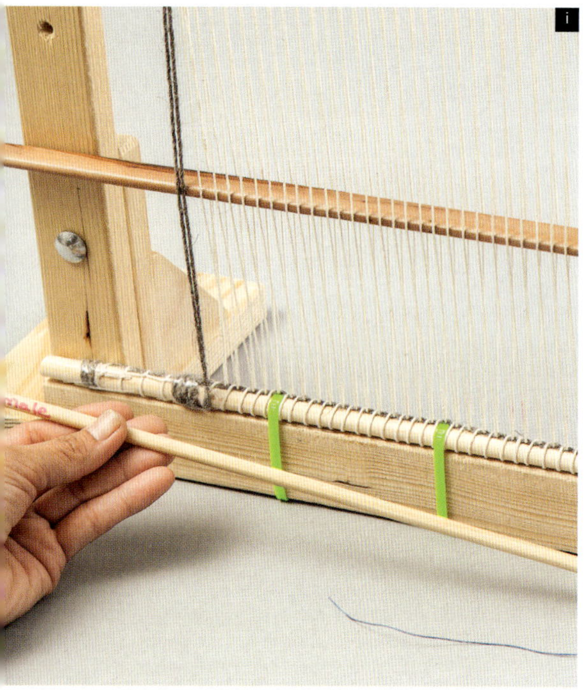

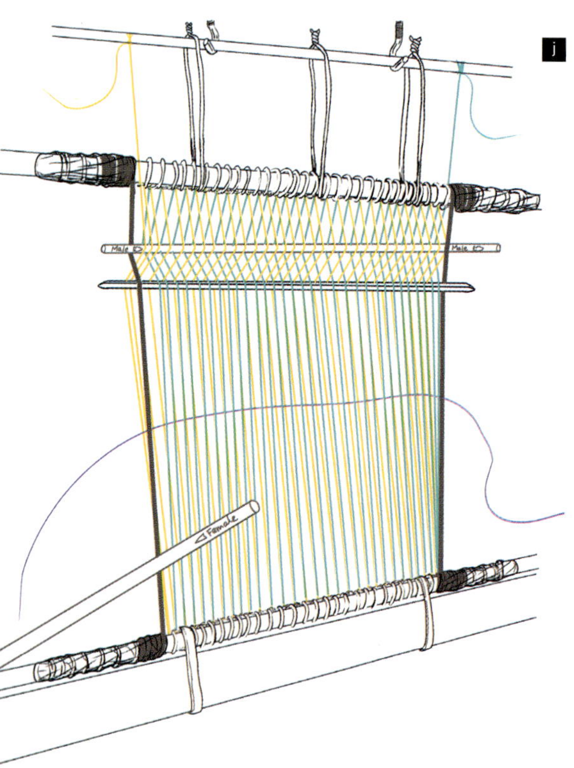

Once the nylon thread has been pulled through the shed, make a loop on the left end of the string and slide the rod through the loop. To prevent the loop from undoing itself, create another knot next to it on the tail end of the string i j k.

FINGER LOOPING

Starting between the selvage on the left-hand side and the first female warp string, pull the nylon thread with your right index finger. Twist it twice in a clockwise direction, and slip the loop created onto the heddle rod. Attach it between the first and second female warp ends. We will refer to this process as finger looping. (For the left-handed process, thread the nylon thread from the right side, and then secure the loop and twist it twice counterclockwise with your left index finger.)

Throughout this process, keep the dowel spaced about ¾″ away from the warp l. If it is too close or the loop is too tight, it will interfere with the male shed rod's ability to bring the male warps forward. Tug on the unlooped portion of the nylon thread if needed so that the female rod stays the correct distance away from the warps. Try to keep the loops equal in size.

Continue twisting and looping each female warp to the female heddle rod. After the last warp, loop the nylon string around the female heddle rod one last time and double knot it to

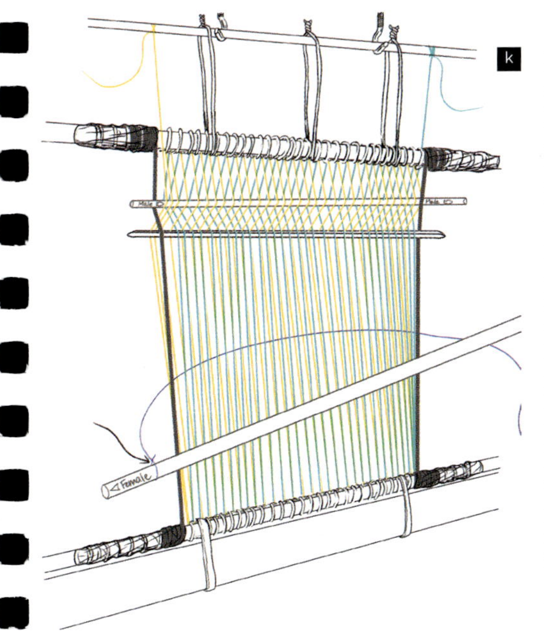

the last loop made. Tie another knot next to the one on the tail end of the string. Cut off any excess nylon string taking care not to cut it too close. Mark that rod "female," and draw an arrow on it pointing to the left m.

FEMALE AND MALE WARPS: THE LAST CHECK

When the batten is inserted in the female shed, all of the warps attached to the female heddle rod will be in front of the batten n. That will include the side selvage cord on the left and the double warp on the right.

When the batten is inserted in the male shed, all of the warps plus the side selvage cord on the right and the double warp string on the left will be in front of it o.

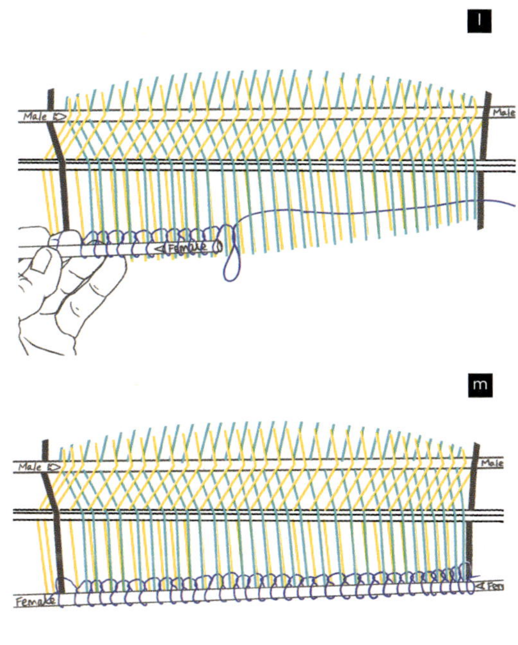

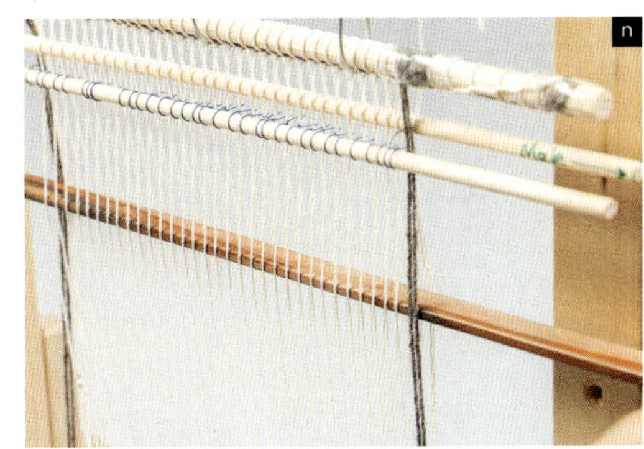

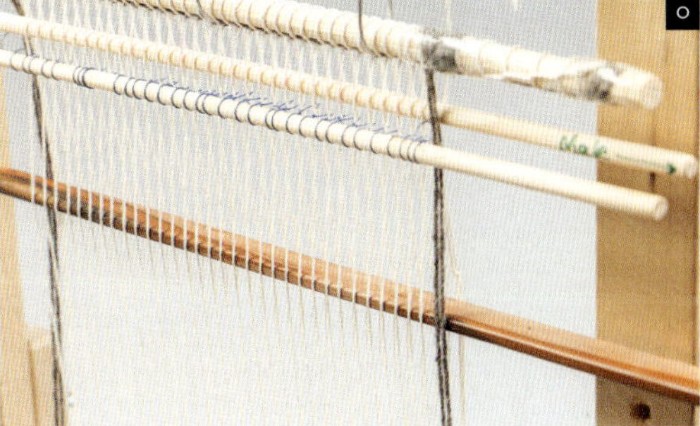

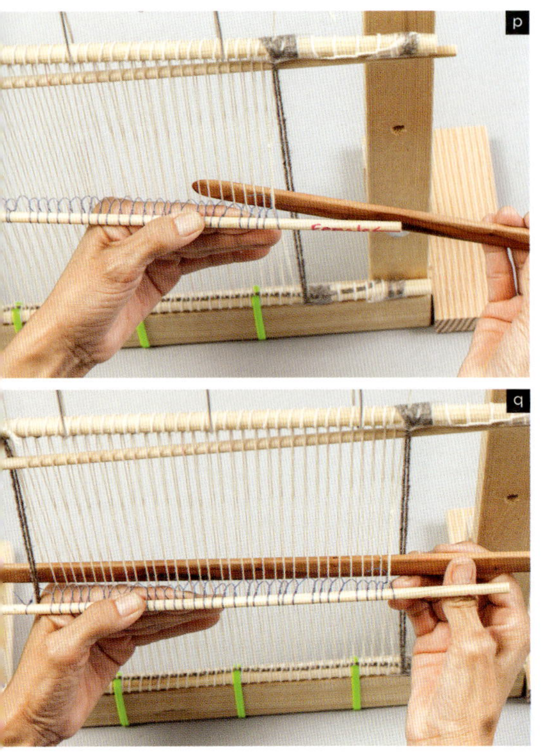

USING THE FEMALE (HEDDLE) AND THE MALE (SHED) RODS

A turnaround consists of a row woven on the female warps with the weft traveling from right to left followed by a row woven on the male warps with the weft traveling from the left side back to the right.

For the warps to be fully covered, the weft has to complete that entire back-and-forth path. The shed is changed each time the weft makes it all the way to the left or the right side. After bringing the yarn back and forth a few times, if the same warps remain uncovered, it means you are weaving in the same shed. Undo that section of your weaving and reweave it, paying closer attention to the direction of the arrows and labels marked on the heddle rod and shed rod.

The male warps are in front of the male shed rod, which is their normal resting position. Nothing else has to be done to bring them forward. The male shed rod is left in place at the top of the loom for the duration of the weaving process.

The female heddle rod is looped to the female warps, which are the ones behind the male rod. Slide the female heddle rod down and away from the male shed rod and pull it toward you to bring the female warps forward. If they are not easy to pull forward, let the female heddle rod go, and slide it farther down and away from the male shed rod.

Once the female warps are pulled away from the male warps p q, slide the batten through the opening created between the warps to hold the female warps in position r. Sliding the female heddle rod down and away from the male shed rod and pulling it forward away from the loom should be a gentle motion. Do not yank or tug it with a lot of force.

Right-handers pull the female heddle rod with the left hand, and left-handers pull it with the right hand s. While holding the heddle rod between your index finger and thumb, use the rest of your hand to press the warps back simultaneously. When you have woven just beyond the halfway point, the female dowel gets harder to pull. At this point, you will divide your pulling into three or more sections to determine where to pull the female heddle rod. That will allow you to pull the warps to be woven on forward with the least amount of strain.

After the female warps have been separated from the male warps, all weavers will use the dominant hand to slide the batten into place behind the female warps.

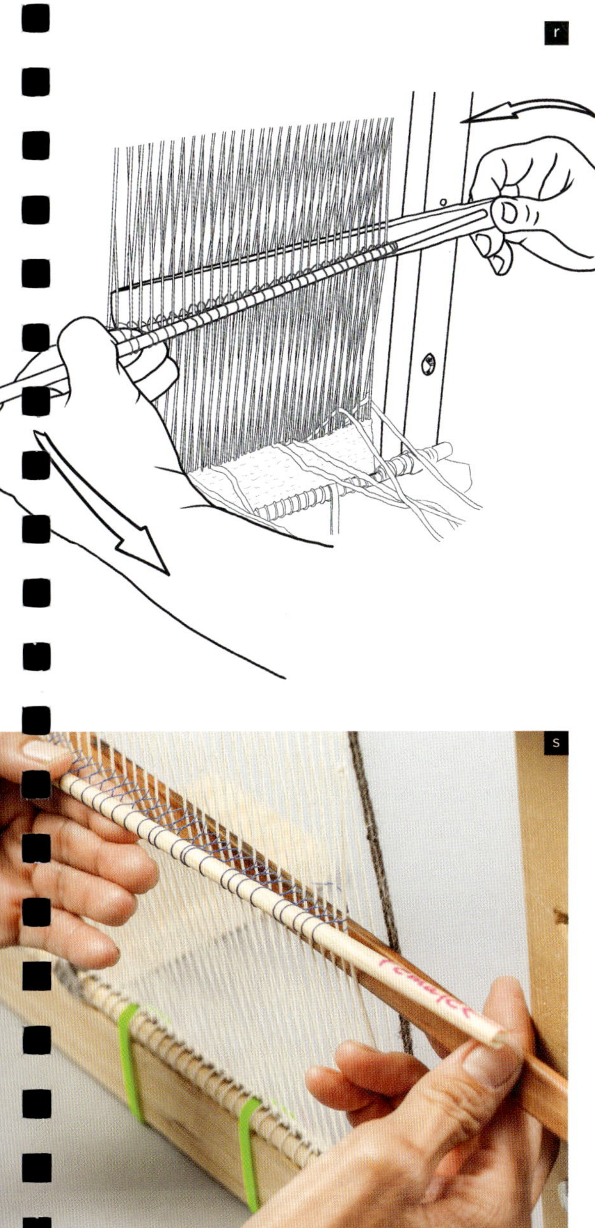

At times, the loops on the right or left side of the female heddle rod will become uneven in looseness or tightness. The tightness of the loops around the heddle becomes irregular if the female heddle rod is pulled with more force on one side than on the other. If that occurs, begin at the end with the larger loops, and use the sacking needle to tighten each loop in order, one at a time, so that the female heddle rod returns to its original position of one finger's width away from the face of the warp and the loops are even all the way across.

Unlike the female heddle rod, the male shed rod works best if the female heddle rod is nearby. Once the female heddle rod slides up and is positioned under the shed rod, you may insert the batten beneath the female heddle rod.

At no time should the male and female rods slide up and down together. That action is very abrasive to the warps and will result in weakening and ultimately breaking one or more warps.

While weaving, if the female heddle rod falls into your weaving space, use one or two hair clips to clip the rods together and prevent them from falling.

ADDITIONAL SUPPLIES TO HAVE ON HAND FOR WARPING

There may be times when warping does not go according to plan. If the stretched warp is too short, add S-hooks to the turnbuckles to lengthen. If the stretched warp is too long, use shorter turnbuckles. Turnbuckles come in various sizes and lengths; check that each set has the same "L" or "R" on the hook side. A rope can be used for tensioning instead of turnbuckles.

CALCULATIONS FOR WARPING OTHER SIZES

10.5" W x 12.5" H	12.5" W x 16.5" H	16.5" W x 20.5" H
41 warps + selvage = 42 warps	49 warps + selvage = 50 warps	65 warps + selvage = 66 warps
31 yds warp, 5 yds selvage	48 yds warp, 5.5 yds selvage	77 yds warp, 6.5 yds selvage
8.5 yds string, cut in half	10 yds string, cut in half	12.5 yds string, cut in half
Three 8" metal loops	Three 6" metal loops	Four 4" metal loops
Two ¼" turnbuckles	Two 7/32" turnbuckles	Three 3/16" turnbuckles

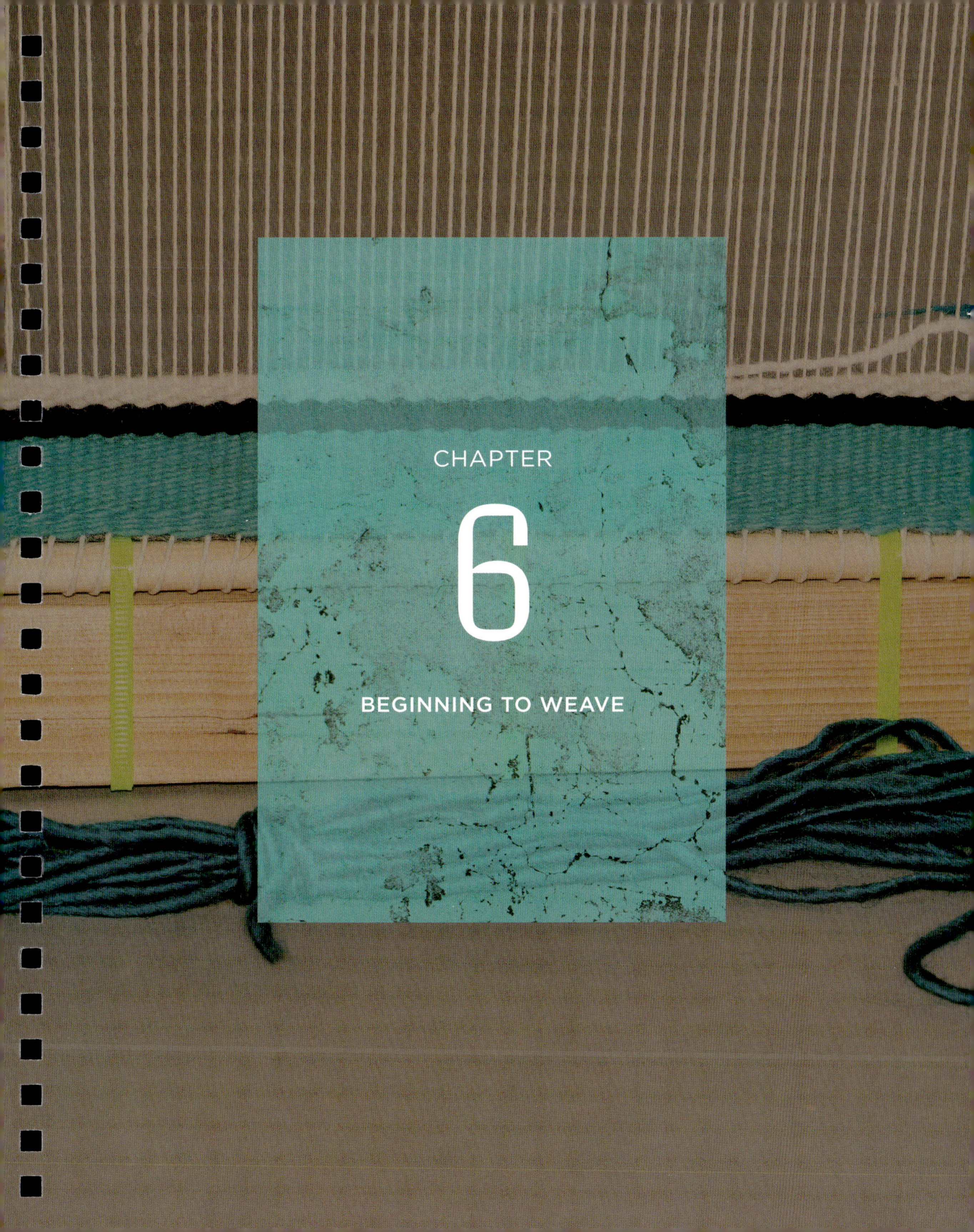

CHAPTER

6

BEGINNING TO WEAVE

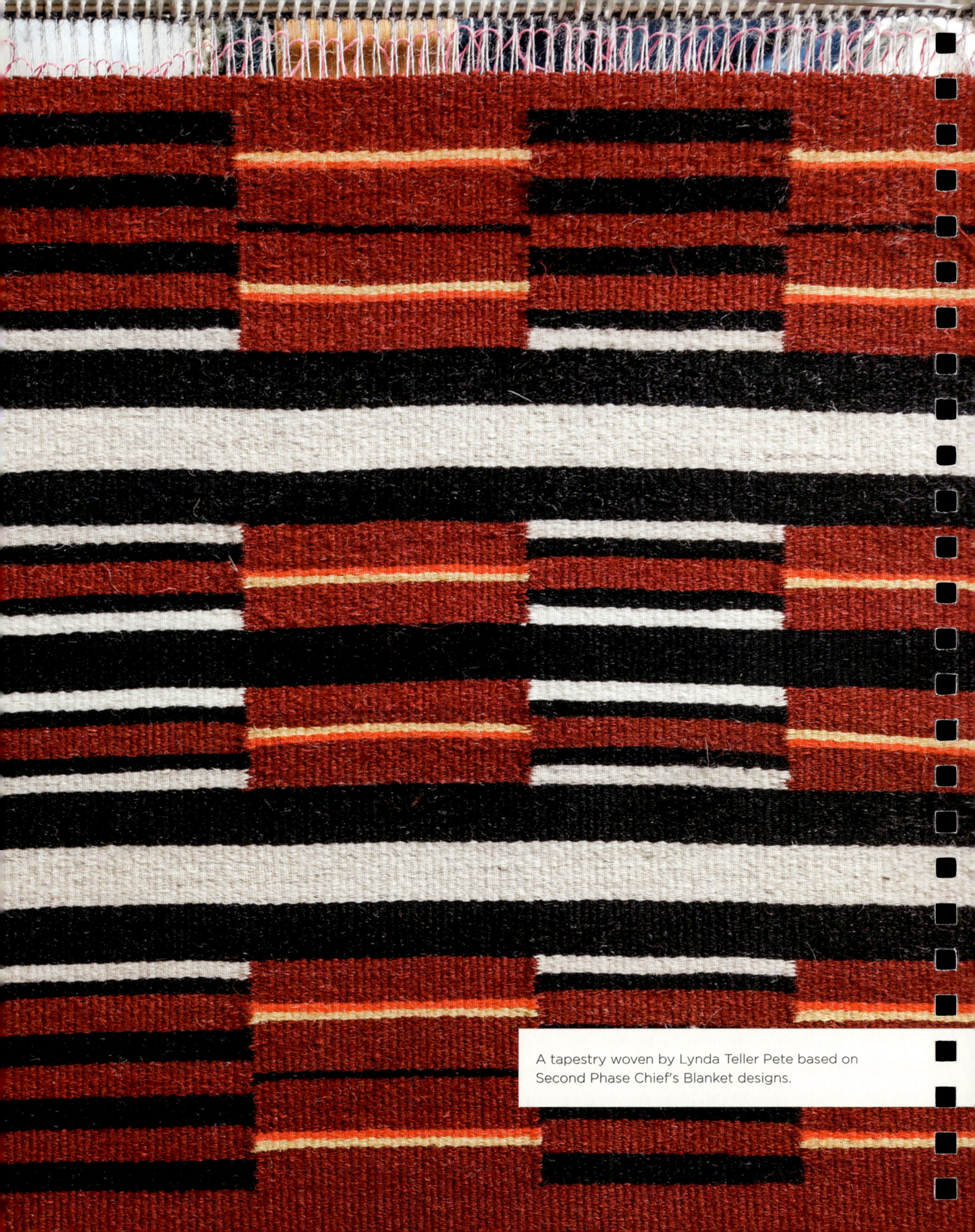

A tapestry woven by Lynda Teller Pete based on Second Phase Chief's Blanket designs.

WEAVING LIFE, WEAVING BALANCE

We begin with a foundation of weaving pairs of male and female warps together, a technique we call "two by twos." We equate weaving the two by twos to a child taking her first steps. The balance of the design, the color combinations, and the patterning to achieve symmetry or asymmetry are symbolic of the teenage years. The finishing of the textile, which involves letting go of the male shed and then the female heddle, is equated to children leaving and moving on with their adult lives. Every action requires forethought, and we are aware that these actions also represent a balance of female and male energies; they parallel female and male fertility, childbirth, the rearing of children, and the final takedown of a textile. Cutting the selvage cords is equated to the cutting of the umbilical cord of a newborn.

BEGINNING to WEAVE

THE TWO BY TWOS

Weaving the two by twos is accomplished by going over and under pairs of warp ends, a male and a female pair, instead of going over and under one warp at a time. Weaving two by twos is done at both the start and the end of a textile.

We weave the first and last four turnarounds of our project (that is, weaving across right to left and back, left to right) with two by twos so that we can bury the warp ends on both ends of the rug. If you skip the two by twos and go straight into weaving on single warps using the male shed rod and the female heddle rod, you will have specks of warp showing at the top and bottom of the textile.

Your outstretched arms are your wingspan. Break off a length of yarn that is five wingspans long. Break the yarn to create a tapered end instead of cutting it with scissors. Organize the length of yarn into a long butterfly or loose skein by wrapping it around your hand, and then wrap the bundle with the last few inches of yarn. You will pull weft from the starting end of

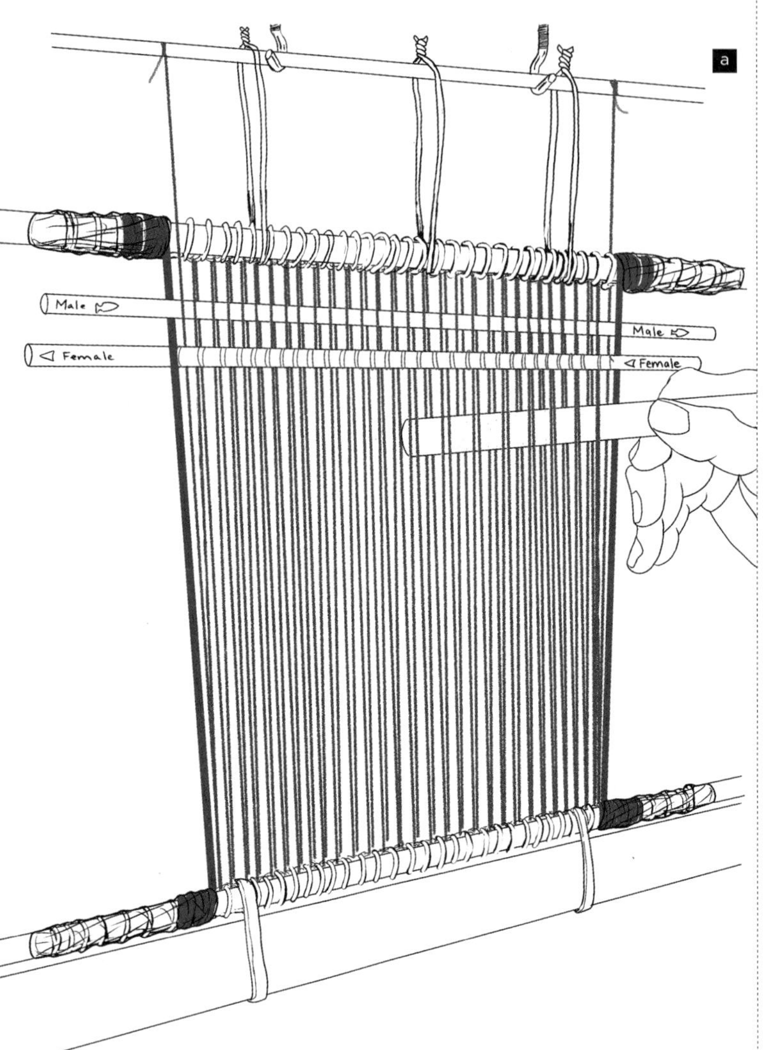

your bundle to release more yarn. Beginning weavers, please do not whine about using a shuttle. That treat is coming later, but first you need to bond with the yarn.

Do not worry about measuring the exact amount of yarn needed for this section. It will end when it ends, and we will address how to add more yarn to continue weaving in a later section.

To begin weaving the two by twos, push the male shed rod and the female heddle rod to the top of the loom so they are out of the way, as they will not be used for this part of the process a. Hold the batten in your left hand in its vertical position (we will call it the closed position because the shed is closed when the batten is not turned on edge) and starting from the left side, slide it behind the selvage cords and then across the front of the first pair of warps. (Illustration a shows the process for a left-handed person, who would hold the batten in the right hand and skip over the right-hand selvage cords.) Keep going in this manner, alternating going in front of and behind each pair of warps with the batten until you've reached the last pair on the right side. The right-hand side selvage will be behind the batten.

With the batten in the closed position, push it up to give you some room, and anchor the frayed end of the weft into the warp on the right side. Using your fingers, pick up the right-hand selvage cord and the first three warp pairs behind the batten. Holding the shed open with

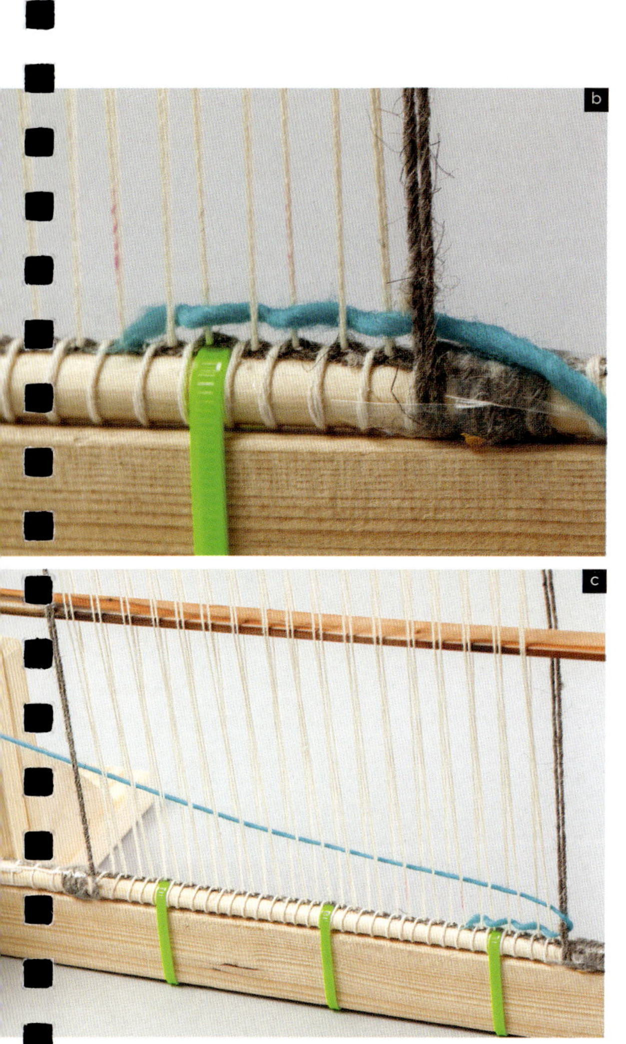

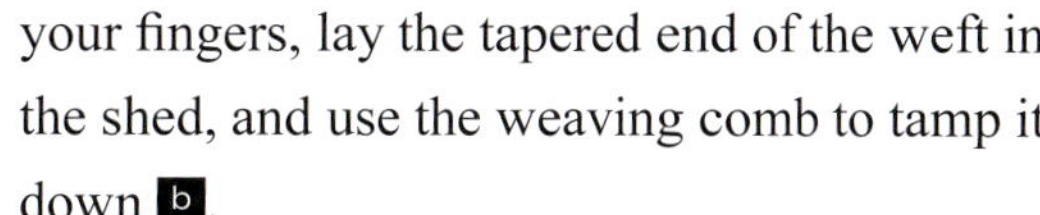

your fingers, lay the tapered end of the weft in the shed, and use the weaving comb to tamp it down b.

Next, turn the batten to open the shed and, in one large arc, insert the long end of the weft through the shed from the right side to the left side. Leave the excess yarn hanging out of the left side of the warp c.

Using your index finger or the tail end of the weaving comb, begin at the right side and push the yarn down at two points to form three smaller arcs of about the same size d. These "bubbles" will keep the weft from pulling in at the sides when you tamp it down. Beat the weft down with the comb, from the right side to the left (in the direction the yarn was laid into the shed) e.

You have just woven half of a turnaround. The weft will now be hanging out on the left side of the loom. The start of the weft for this row should lie in front of the right selvage cord, and the end of it should lie behind the left side selvage cord. Turn the batten to the closed position, push it to the top of the warp, and leave it there as you weave the first four turnarounds of two by twos.

Beginning on the right side of the warp, slide a second batten behind the selvage cords and then across the front of the first pair of warps. Then alternate going in front of and then behind two warps with the batten until you reach the last pair on the left side f. Repeat the process of laying the weft in and forming three

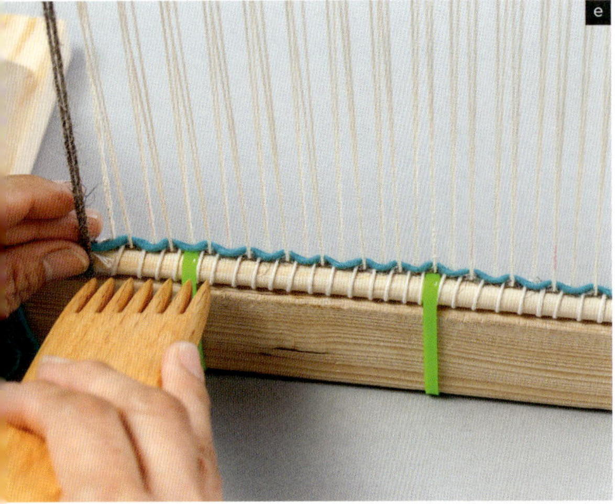

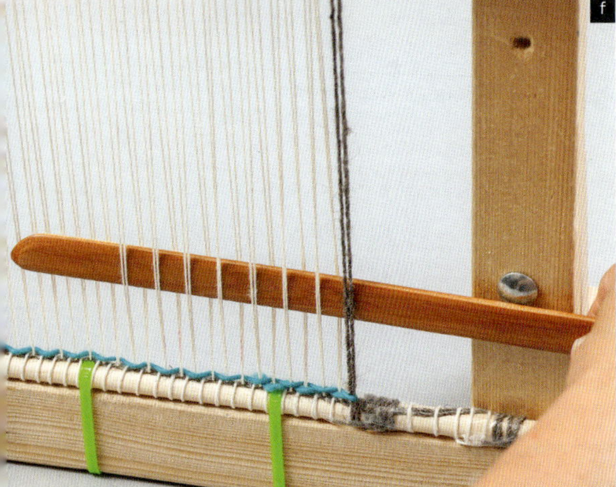

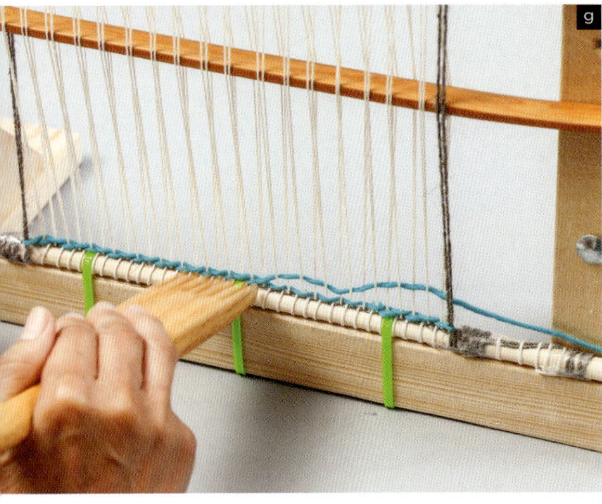

arcs with the weft across the width of the warp, and tamp it down moving from left to right. That is one complete turnaround.

To begin the second turnaround, remove the batten just used. Bring down the first batten that was left in the warp and pushed to the top g. Open it, that is, turn it so it is horizontal, and lay the weft in the shed from right to left. Make a large arc and divide it into three sections with the tapered end of the comb to create tension bubbles h. Beat the weft so it lies flat, moving from right to left. Close the batten and push it back to the top of the warp to rest again.

With the other batten, pick up all the opposite warp pairs, starting with the selvage cord on the right-hand side. Take the weft from the left side to the right, form the tension bubbles, and beat the weft so that it lies flat to finish the second turnaround.

Repeat the process until you've completed four turnarounds i. If you are weaving a larger rug or using finer wool than worsted-weight, do six or more turnarounds. If weaving your larger textile with bulky weight wool, stay with the initial number of four turnarounds.

To count the number of turnarounds you have woven, first make sure that you have completed a full turnaround by checking to see that the weft end hanging from the right side of the warp is behind the right-hand selvage cord. Then count the number of loops woven around the left-hand selvage cords. Or select one warp or warp pair and count the number of wefts that have been stacked onto it.

We will return to weaving four turnarounds of two by twos at the end of our project when the weaving is ⅛″ from the top of the warp. The finishing turnarounds will be woven with a sacking needle. Even though they will be difficult to weave, do not skip the final two by two turnarounds. Like the hem of a garment, they provide added stability to the top and bottom edges of the textile while keeping the warp ends completely hidden.

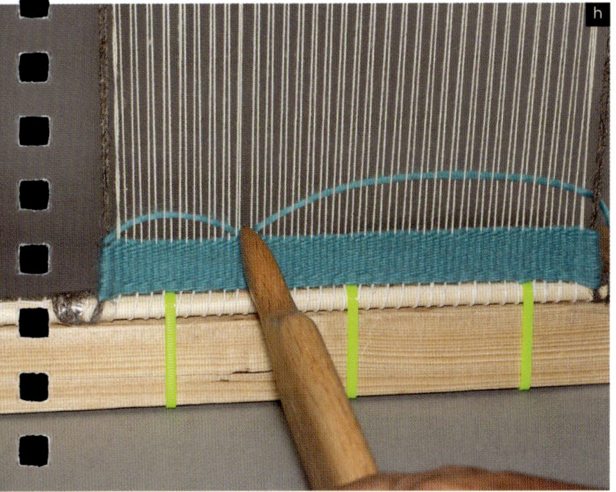

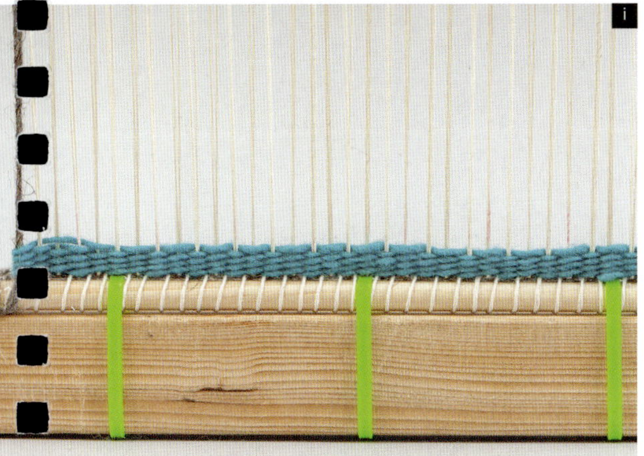

We are now ready to weave on single warps using the male shed rod and the female heddle rod.

Single-Warp Weaving Using the Male Shed Rod and Female Heddle Rod

Remove both battens that were used to weave the first four turnarounds. The weft yarn will be hanging out on the right-hand side of the warp.

Now pay attention here. On both sides of the warp, there is a double warp inside both the right and left selvage cords. Do not separate it into single warps, as the two warps work as one and will be woven on together as one. This will give your edges strength and stability. While in the female shed, the double warp on the right-hand side and the side selvage cords on the left-hand side will be treated as female warps. In the male shed, the double warp on the left-hand side and the selvage cords on the right-hand side will be treated as male warp ends.

To begin weaving the female row, bring the female heddle rod down and away from the male shed rod. With your left hand, hold the shed rod with your index finger and thumb, and pull the female heddle rod toward you while simultaneously pressing against the warps with the back of your hand to keep the male warps from lifting **j**. Insert the batten into the shed from the right-hand side of the warp before traveling to the left **k**. You may have to reposition your left

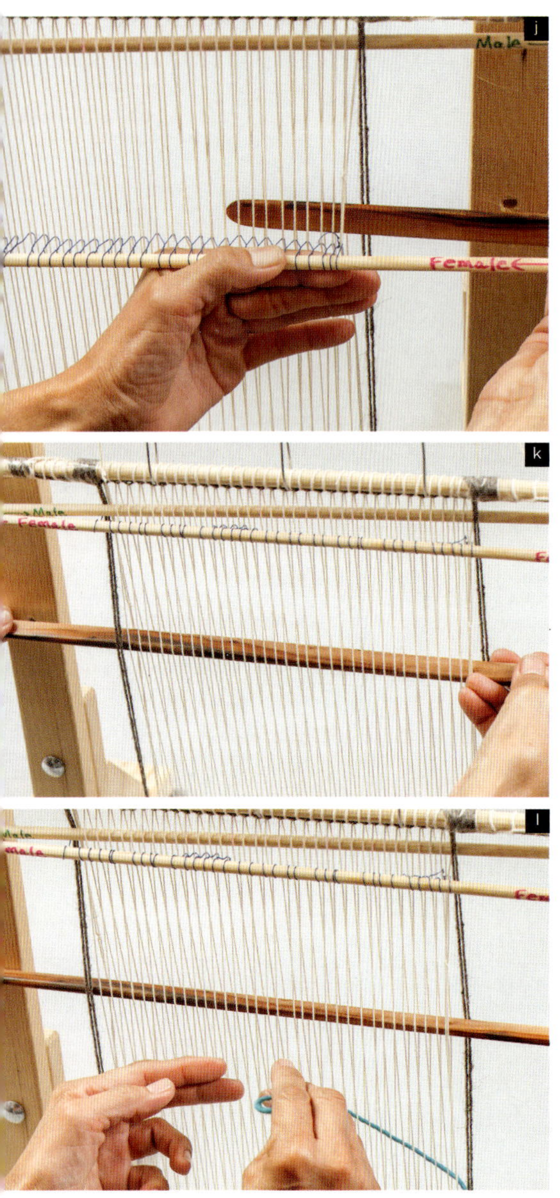

hand to pull the female heddle in one or two more places while inserting the batten in sections across the entire width of the weaving. Lift the female heddle away from the batten and bring it to the top of the warp until it is aligned just under the male shed rod. Rotate the batten so that it is horizontal in the open shed position.

TENSION ARC BUBBLES

Lay the wool in the open shed going toward the left in one large arc l. Just as you did while weaving the turnarounds, divide the arc into three tension bubbles, starting from the right side and working to the left. Measure the height of the middle arc: ¼″ is too tight, ½″ is perfect, ¾″ is good, 1″ is too loose. Beat the weft down with your comb, moving from right to left. After completing this half of a turnaround, remove the batten.

With the male shed rod and the female heddle rod aligned next to one another at the top of the warp, the male warps are naturally separated from and resting in front of the female warps. Beginning on the right-hand side, insert the batten under the male and female rods. Bring it down and away from them and rotate it so that it is in the open shed position.

Lay the yarn into the open shed, starting on the left and traveling to the right side of the textile. Place the weft in an arc and divide it into three tension bubbles. Measure the middle arc vertically: ½″ to ¾″ arc is good tension. Tamp down the weft, moving from left to right. You have now completed one full turnaround. To weave a band or design block that is ½″ high, you will need to weave approximately eight turnarounds if you are using worsted-weight wool. When you've woven the eight turnarounds, you'll find that they are a little higher than ½″, but the weft yarns will pack down as the weaving progresses.

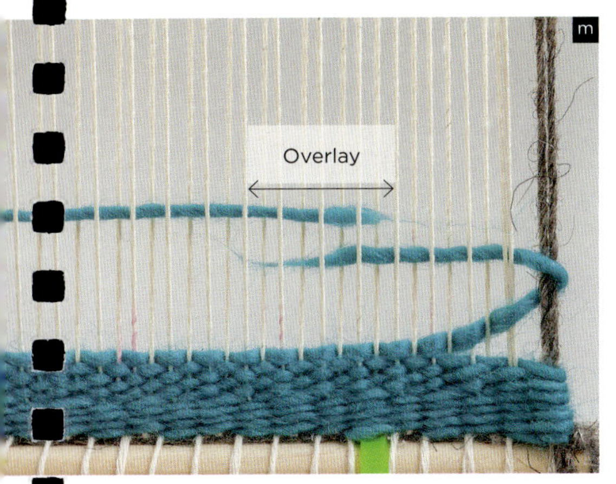

Take measurements frequently. Measure the width of your project every ½″ as you weave to ensure that the variation in width is never greater than ¼″. Measure the middle of the three arc bubbles vertically until you get to know the right height by eye.

Feel free to mark your dowels or stick notes on your loom if you find yourself needing reminders to help you figure out which shed to weave in. Label the male shed rod that remains between the sets of warps "male" and add an arrow pointing to the right. Label the bottom heddle rod that is looped onto the warps "female" and add an arrow pointing to the left. The direction of the arrows on the dowels indicates the way the weft will travel when it is in that shed. For example, if after the completion of a row, the weft is hanging out on the right side of the weaving, it needs to travel to the left, so it has to be woven next in the female shed. If the weft is hanging out on the left side of the project, it needs to travel to the right, so it needs to be woven in the male shed next.

We advise you not to change colors or introduce a design element in the first 2″ or so of the textile. If your design is symmetrical, the top and bottom will mirror one another, so starting your piece with a 2″ band of solid color will make the finishing process much easier.

By now, you have woven most of the initial five wingspans you started out with. Lay the remaining weft into the shed and tamp it down with the weaving comb. Break off another few wingspans of the same color of weft. If five wingspans were too much, take less this time. Lay in one of the tapered ends of the new weft and overlay it with the tapered end of the weft just finished with no more than ½″ overlap of the adjoining yarns m. Continue weaving as if you were weaving with a continuous unbroken strand of weft.

WOVEN WEFT PACK-DOWN—IS IT ME, OR IS MY RUG SINKING?

The weight, width, and length of your comb can affect the pack-down of the weft. We recommend that you use a heavier comb that fits comfortably in your hand at the beginning of your weaving project, a medium-weight comb toward the middle, and a small, lightweight finishing comb at the end of the project. Toward the end of the weaving, when very little space is left, the finishing comb will be pushed down rather than beating down the weft. Hold the comb with your thumb, index, and middle fingers resting on top of the handle and your

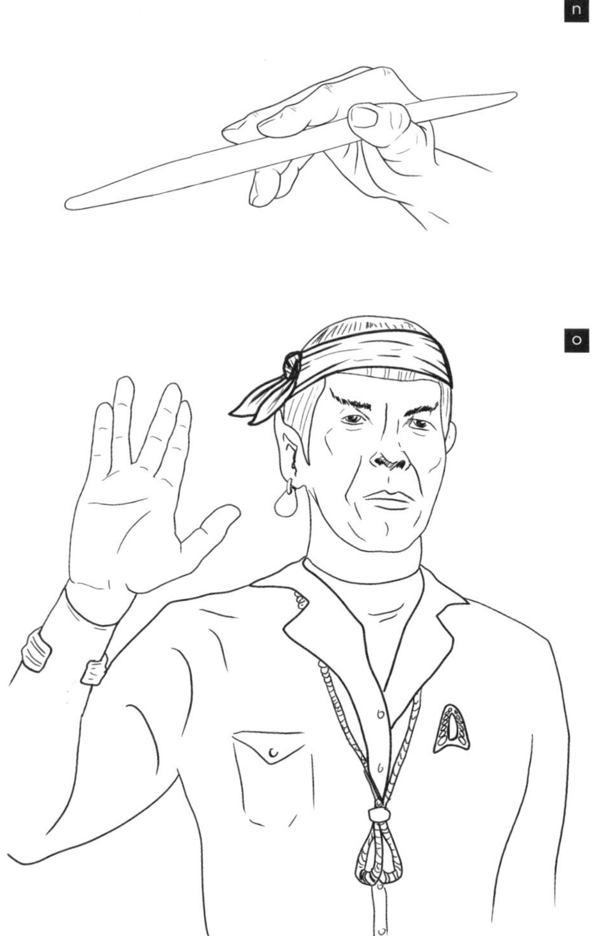

ring and pinkie fingers positioned underneath n. That should give you a balanced hold. *Star Trek* fans, let Hastiin Spock show you how to separate your fingers o.

The pack-down of the weft will vary depending on how firmly or softly you use your weaving comb to tamp down the weft. If you have a light touch, the weft will not pack down as much, and you may even see some warps through the weft. If you have a heavy touch, the pack-down may be more than ½″ of weft. Having a hard touch can lead to your hand and wrist hurting after a day of weaving. Finding a medium touch will allow for a more consistent pack-down of the weft and prevent injury or soreness to your hand and wrist from overzealous pounding.

All yarn is not the same. It will pack down differently depending on whether it is heavily or lightly dyed, blended or carded wool, and single- or multiple-ply. For example, black worsted-weight yarn of the kind we are using here packs down less than white or blended yarn of the same weight. As you weave and beat black yarn, 2¼″ may pack down to closer to 2″. Compare that to white worsted-weight yarn or blended yarn, both of which may pack down from 2″ to approximately 1⅞″. Over time, that small difference will become more and more noticeable if the two types of yarn are stacked next to one another as you create patterns. Fill-ins will be required to bring the height of the white or blended wefts up to match the black.

Other factors affecting the pack-down of your weft are the height of the tension arc bubbles and where you are in the progress of weaving your textile. If the weft yarn has been pulled through the warps too tightly or if your tension arc bubbles were not high enough, you may notice that the warps in some area have pulled together. In sections where the warp spacing has become narrower, the woven weft will "hill up." If the warps have moved closer together in one section, it is likely that they have become farther apart in other areas where the woven weft will sink more. You will have to do short rows or zigzags to fill in the low areas and then work to manage your tension better as you continue to weave.

Lastly, the bottom portion of the weaving will pack down more than the top. Keeping similar design elements equal in height requires keeping careful track of the number of turnarounds woven in each one. That is true until you get to the top portion of the project. Since the weft at the top of the weaving will not pack down as much as at the bottom, you may omit a few turnarounds from a design block at the end, and it will still match the height of the matching block in the bottom half.

As you approach the halfway point of your design, if it seems to have packed down more than you intended, be flexible and willing to improvise the center of your design to create a new "middle."

CHOOSING WEFT YARNS—BUT I WANT MY RUG WOVEN WITH AUTHENTIC NAVAJO COLORS! CALM DOWN, THIS IS YOUR FIRST PROJECT.

We recommend single-ply worsted-weight yarn for beginning students p. Bulky-weight yarn is used for weaving saddle blankets and floor rugs. Sportweight is thinner and can be used by experienced or advanced students. Laceweight is extremely thin and is used for fine-weave tapestries. The first rule of Navajo weaving if you are using mill-spun yarns, is not to mix yarn sizes or brands; stay with one brand, one weight, and always single-ply.

If you're a beginning weaver, choose a dark color of heavily dyed yarn for a base color (but preferably not black, which is hard to see without direct lighting, especially at the finishing stage). To keep things simple, combine a dark yarn with one light and one medium. As you weave more and learn about designs and balance, more colors can be combined for interesting stripes or bold design blocks. We don't recommend using blended, white, or cream-colored yarns as a base color until you've done several weaving projects. Take a black-and-white photo of your yarns. If you cannot see a difference, the values of the colors are too similar.

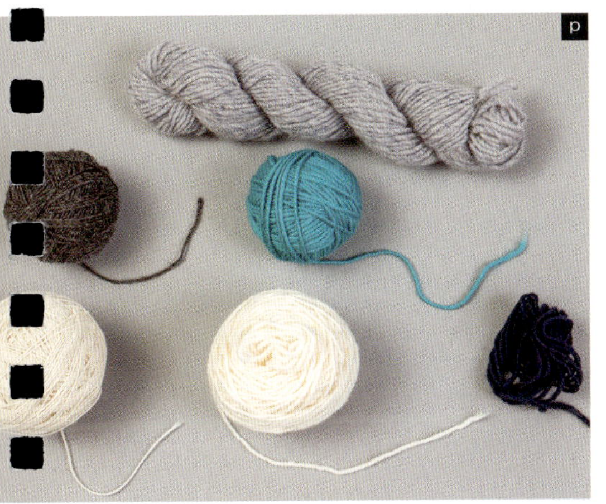
p

Table 1 is a guide for determining the amount of wool you will need for your weaving project. Once you've chosen your yarns, if it is in skeins, roll it into balls.

TABLE 1

Project Dimensions	Area (square inches)	Amount of Worsted-Weight Yarn (ounces)
8.5″ tall x 6.5″ wide	55.25	4
9″ tall x 7.5″ wide	67.5	5
10.5″ tall x 8.5″ wide	89.25	6
12.5″ tall x 10.5″ wide	131.25	8 to 9
16.5″ tall x 12.5″ wide	206.25	14 to 16

HOW MANY TURNAROUNDS OF WEFT SHALL I WEAVE?

The guidelines in Table 2 apply mainly to darker-dyed worsted-weight yarn manufactured by the Brown Sheep Company, which is readily available in the Navajo Nation and yarn shops around the country. Remember that light-colored or blended wool is less dense, so it will pack down more and will therefore require more turnarounds to achieve the same woven height as dark yarn. Thicker yarns require fewer turnarounds and thinner yarns require more turnarounds to achieve the same woven height.

TABLE 2

Height	¼″	½″	1″
Turnarounds	4	8	16

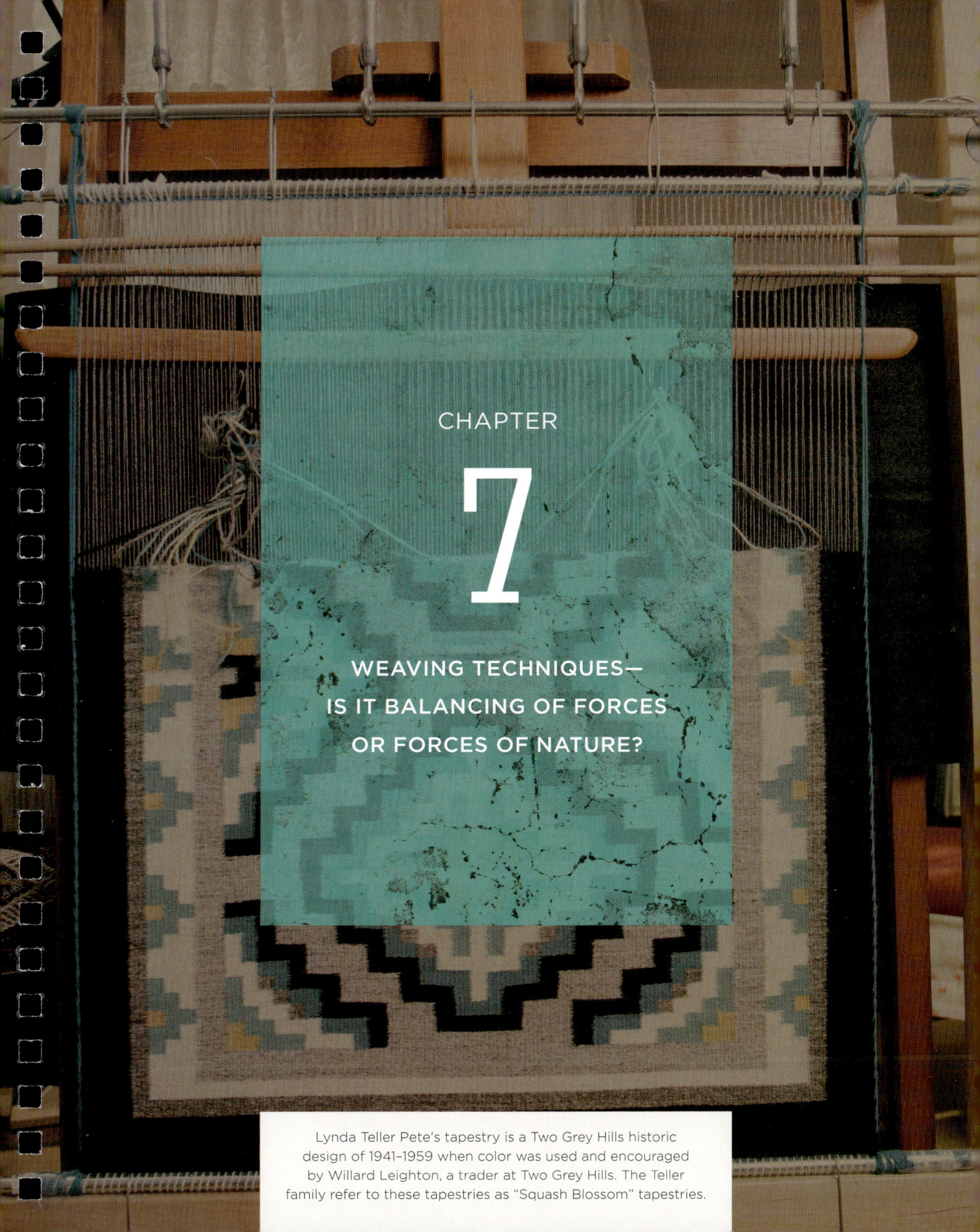

CHAPTER

7

WEAVING TECHNIQUES—IS IT BALANCING OF FORCES OR FORCES OF NATURE?

Lynda Teller Pete's tapestry is a Two Grey Hills historic design of 1941–1959 when color was used and encouraged by Willard Leighton, a trader at Two Grey Hills. The Teller family refer to these tapestries as "Squash Blossom" tapestries.

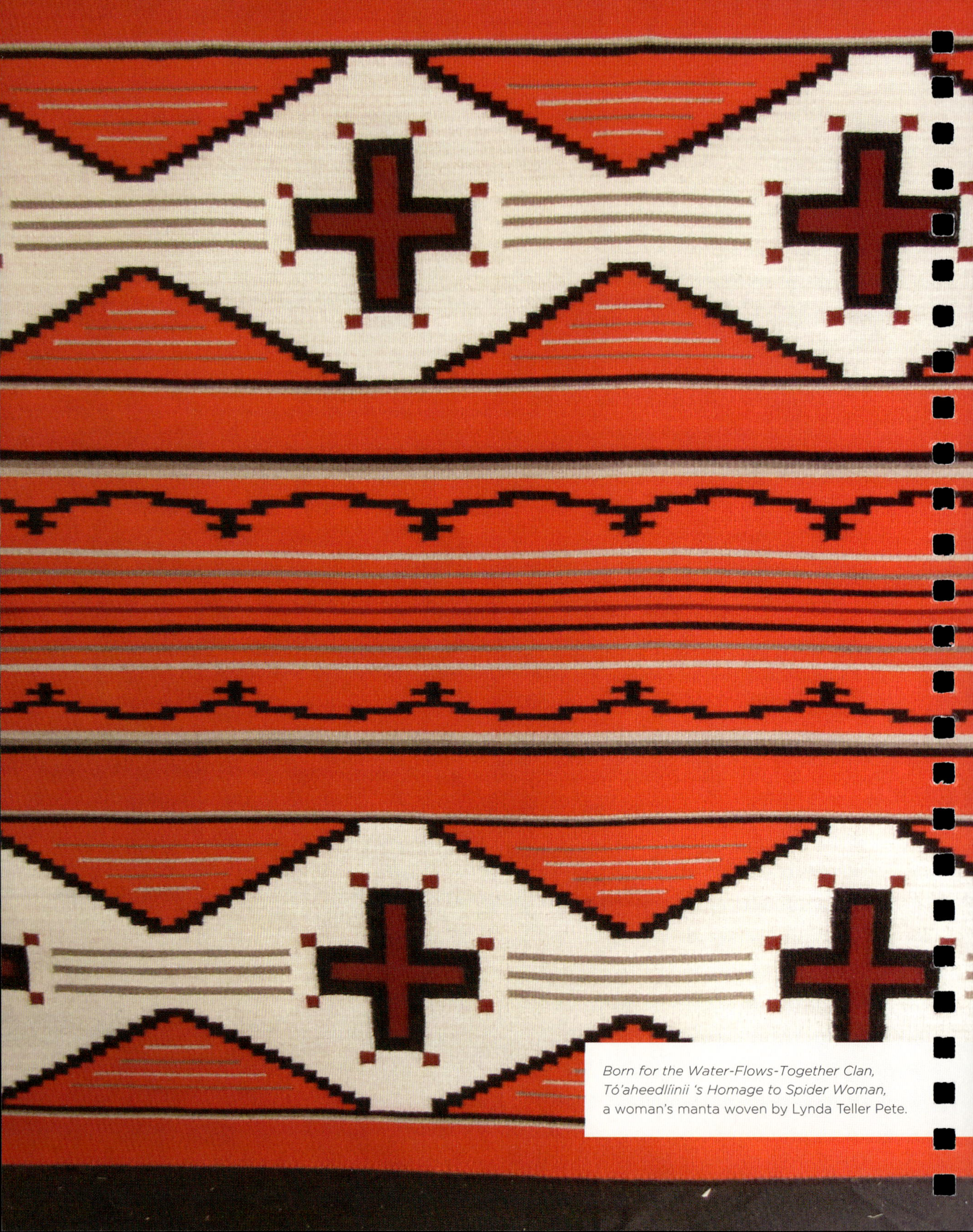

Born for the Water-Flows-Together Clan, Tó'aheedlíinii 's Homage to Spider Woman, a woman's manta woven by Lynda Teller Pete.

WEAVING TECHNIQUES — Is it balancing of forces or forces of nature?

MAINTAINING A BALANCED WEFT TENSION

The most reliable technique for getting a "just right" tension as you lay in the weft is to work in sections. Lay the weft into the shed opening about a third of the way in. Do not pull; let the weft lie naturally and form a ½″ arc. After tamping down the first section of weft with the weaving comb, lay the next section of weft into the shed about two-thirds of the way in. After tamping it down, weave in the last section of weft for that row for the remaining width of the project.

If you lay the weft in all the way across, create half-moon arcs to form three tension bubbles, with the first arc placed in the direction the weft is traveling. For example, if the weft is laid in from right to left, the arcs are made from right to left. Measure just the middle arc vertically. Good heights for the tension bubbles are ⅜″, ½″, and up to ¾″. Bubbles as small as ⅛″ or ¼″ will result in an hourglass edge. A 1″ bubble is too loose and will cause the bottom part of the textile to buckle.

Always beat the weft down in the direction the weft is traveling. Never begin from the direction of the excess hanging weft. Holding the end of the weft gently as you tamp the arcs down will prevent it from being too loose, but do not pull it. If it is too loose after it has been tamped down, it will bubble out from in between the warps. Lift the weft again and form a slightly shorter arc. Then tamp it down again with the weaving comb. It will take a little bit of work to find the middle ground, but with time and practice, it will come naturally.

After completing each inch of weaving, measure the width across the top row of your weaving. Check to see that the row currently being woven is the same width or close to the same width as the very beginning of the textile. It is normal for the measurement of the width to vary slightly, but if the current row's width is ¼″ narrower than the bottom of the textile, you need to do what you can to loosen the weft tension before the hourglass shape becomes unmanageable. It is much easier to troubleshoot tension differences when they are caught early rather than later.

The first thing to try in a narrower section is to pull the textile from the middle outward. You are depending on the middle arc bubble to stretch out. After that, as you lay the weft in the shed, pull and hold the side of the textile that is gravitating inward as you beat it down with the comb. Never pull on the warps to stretch out the width because they may break.

If the hourglass shape returns or is still noticeable after you try both of these suggestions, thread some household string onto a sacking needle, and push the needle through the woven web about an inch from either the right or left selvage. Tie it securely around the side beam of the loom frame to help straighten the side edges of the textile. Repeat the process on the other side if needed. As you weave up, continue to make ties at 1″ intervals. If multiple stretcher ties are placed on just one warp, it will weaken the affected warp string, so make sure to stagger the points at which the ties are inserted by choosing different distances from the edge of the textile.

YOU CAN'T FIGHT GRAVITY

As you progress, there will be areas in your weaving that sink or dip lower than the surrounding areas that will need to be filled in. It happens most often on the sides of your weaving, and there really is no way to prevent it from occurring. However, when dips form in other areas of the textile, it could be the result of subtle differences in yarn types that affect the pack-down. (See "Choosing Weft Yarns," page 81.) Also, a skein of yarn may have variations along its length, causing some sections to be of different thicknesses. That is mostly true with handspun wool, but it can also happen with machine-spun yarn.

Variations in the warp spacing can also cause "hills" and "valleys" in the weaving. The weft will sink more readily in areas where warp threads are spaced farther apart. In areas where the warp spacing is closer, the weft may pile up or "hill." Warp spacing that starts out uniform can become altered over the course of your weaving if you don't maintain balanced weft tension. You can work the warp ends at the top dowel back into place by gently pushing them together or apart until they are evenly spaced at ¼″ intervals.

Weaving a fill-in to level the design can be thought of as weaving a "short row" a. As you weave the fill-in, use the male and female rods and the batten to move between the warp sheds as you do when you are weaving normally. Instead of weaving across the full width of the project, you only need to weave back and forth in the dip or low area. When doing fill-in, do

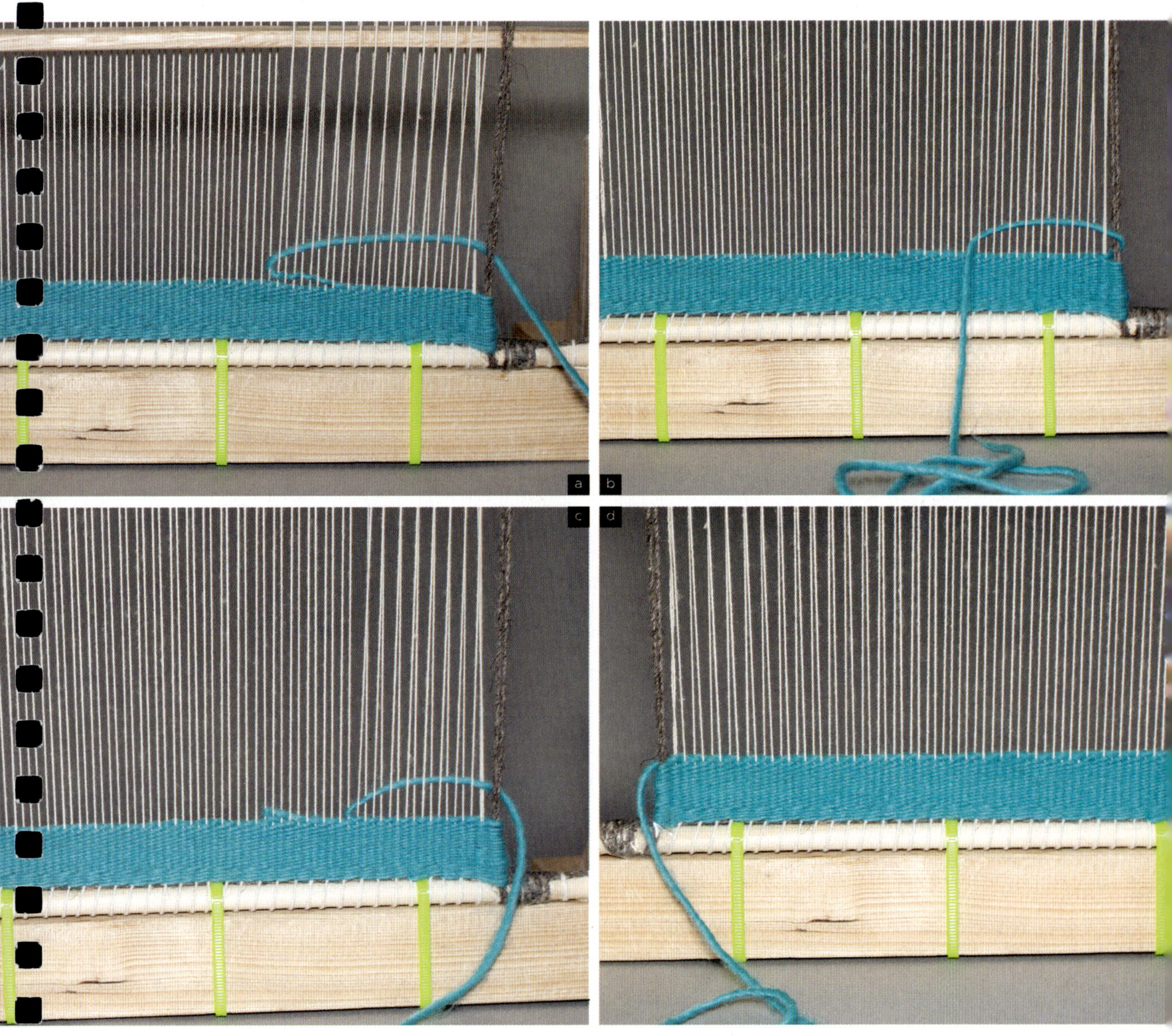

not end your short rows in the same spot b. Do no more than one or two short rows or fill-ins before returning to do a full turnaround c. It helps to gently tug the textile at both edges after every turnaround to help the wefts settle in. The important rule of fill-ins is to keep to the male and female direction of weaving, with male to the right and female to the left d.

GOOD NIGHT COMB, GOOD NIGHT BATTEN, GOOD NIGHT LOOM (WINDING DOWN AT THE END OF YOUR WEAVING SESSION)

Turn the batten to the closed (flat) position after every weaving session or when you step away from your loom to take a break. Do not leave the shed open when you are not weaving.

At the end of a weaving session, it is a good idea to clip the female and male dowels together with hair clips or tie them together with string. That is especially important if you are moving your loom or traveling with it. If the loom is tilted or turned sideways, the female heddle and male shed rod are at risk of falling out, and the process of sewing the female heddle back into place is time-consuming.

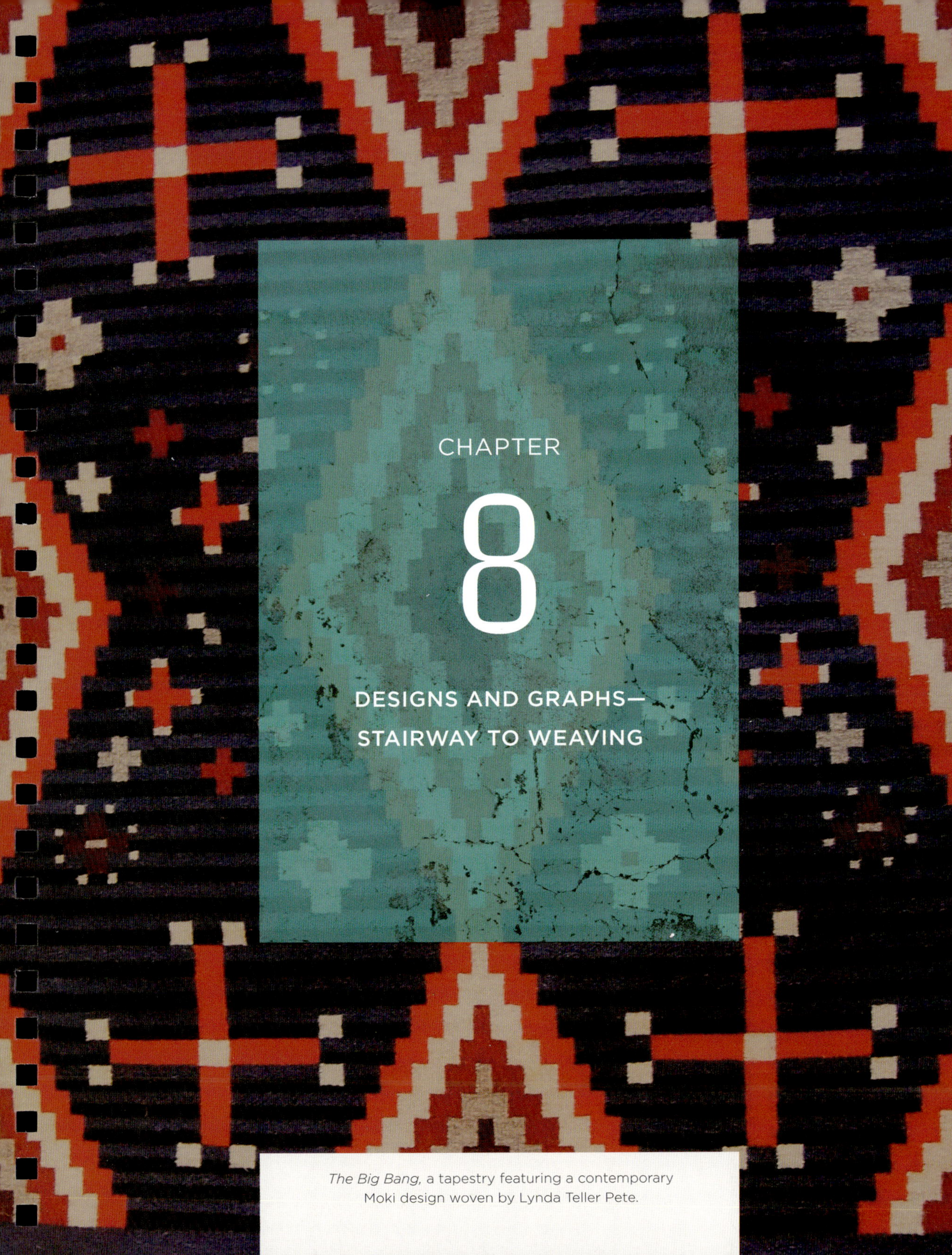

CHAPTER 8

DESIGNS AND GRAPHS—STAIRWAY TO WEAVING

The Big Bang, a tapestry featuring a contemporary Moki design woven by Lynda Teller Pete.

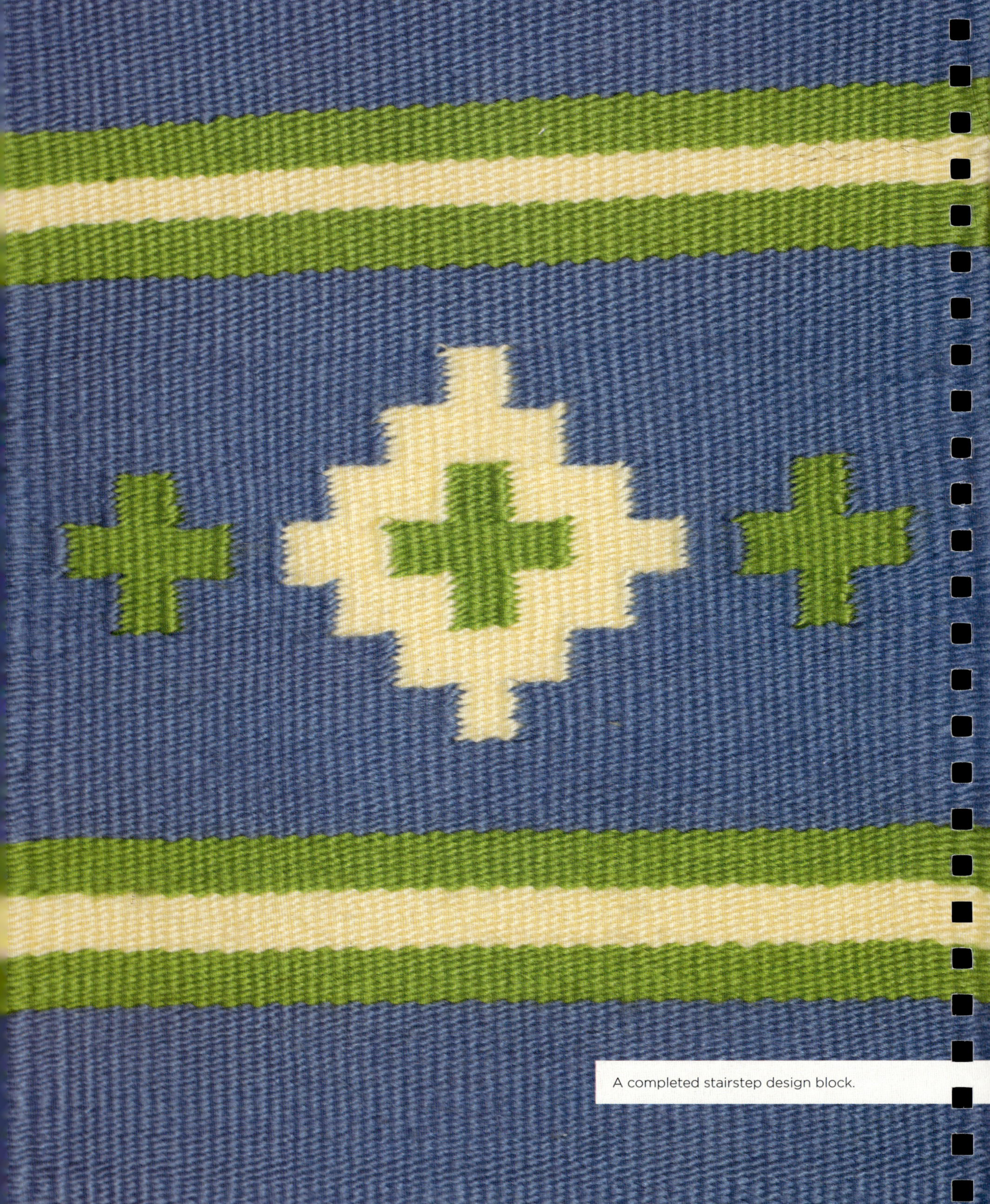
A completed stairstep design block.

DESIGNS and GRAPHS — Stairway to Weaving

When using graph paper to plan your design, assign each square on the graph paper to represent a ½″ by ½″ area in the weaving. Our warp measures 8.5″ by 10.5″, which should cover an area of 17 squares across and 21 squares high on the graph paper. To plan a symmetrical design, count inward vertically and horizontally to find the center lines and divide the graph paper into four quadrants. For beginning weavers, place the most intricate elements of your design in the central 3 ½″ horizontal band of your project. By the time you reach the central band and begin weaving your design blocks, you will have given yourself adequate practice with solid-color bands or stripes.

On the loom, horizontal distance is measured by counting the warps. Two warp pairs (one male and one female) equal ½″; four warps pairs equal 1″, and so forth. For a warp 8.5″ wide, you have a total of 34 warp pairs. (Remember, the side selvages are included in that count and will be treated just like any other warp.) It means that whether you are weaving in the female shed or the male shed, there are 34 warps in each set. On your graph paper, each square in a row represents two male or two female warps, depending on which shed you are weaving in.

The width is established since our warps are set, and it does not change. However, the height of the weaving distance is measured by the building up of wefts, and many factors contribute to how the weft stacks. For that reason, the vertical distance can only be approximated by the number of turnarounds. Brown Sheep Company worsted-weight wool packs down at an estimated 8 turnarounds per ½″ or 16 turnarounds per inch.

Your rug or textile is at the mercy of its environment. The warps may stretch and shrink, causing your project dimensions to be longer or shorter than planned for. During high-humidity days, a rug may stretch, and during a long run of low-humidity days, it may shrink. The stretching or shrinking may be as little as ¹⁄₁₆″ or ⅛″, or it may be as much as ¼″. However minute or large the stretching or shrinking of the warp turns out to be, it will affect the symmetry of your design. For that reason, remember to be flexible with your design. You may even want to draw out three versions of it on graph paper in case the first one has to be altered.

A NOTE ON COPYING OTHER WEAVERS' DESIGNS

Barbara and I have woven many tapestries, and some of our designs have been published. Each of our woven designs, whether published or unpublished, is protected under the guidelines of the Indian Arts and Crafts Act of 1990. To copy a Diné weaver's design(s) is illegal.

Our students sometimes ask if they can copy our designs, and as flattered as we are, we would prefer for students to come up with their own designs. It is up to Navajo and non-Navajo weavers to attach meaning to the elements in their designs, so each of our textiles is not a universal design; each one is a personal creation with personal meaning attached. You'll find more discussion on appropriation on page 108.

BE-WEAVE IT OR NOT: MOVE ON TO COLOR CHANGES AND DESIGNS

When you are ready to begin your first design block, complete a turnaround to the male side with the excess weft yarn hanging on the right side of the weaving. Then, keep the batten in the male shed open as you lay the weft into place. This is called the "prep row." The remaining unwoven weft should be hanging out on the right side of the warp. Without tugging at it, snip the weft with scissors close to the woven part of the rug. Now, unweave the weft 6 to 8 warps. Use scissors to shave off or taper about an inch of the ending weft. Lay the frayed end back into the male shed. Proceed to either "Weaving a Stripe or Band of Solid Color" or "Weaving Sections of Design with Two or More Colors."

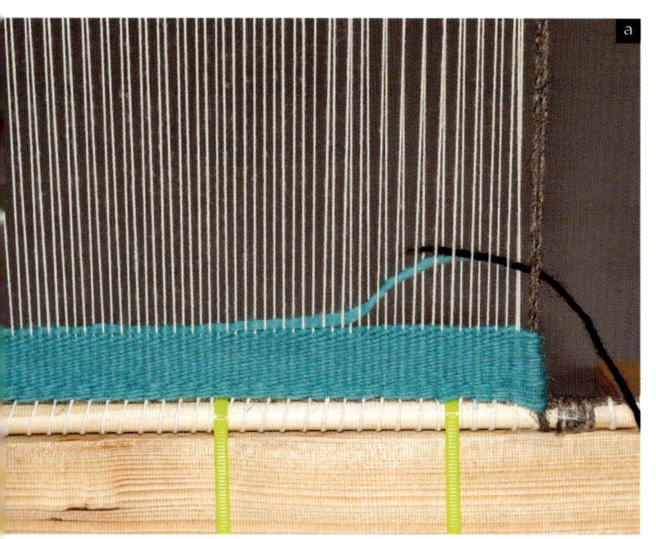

WEAVING A STRIPE OR BAND OF SOLID COLOR

Take the new color of weft and lay the frayed starting end over the tapered end of the weft that was just finished on the left side of the male row a. Switch the warps to the female shed, and weave with the new color as before.

For each striped color change, stagger the overlay of frayed ends of old and new color wefts so that they do not always begin and end on the same warps, which could possibly create a hump in that spot.

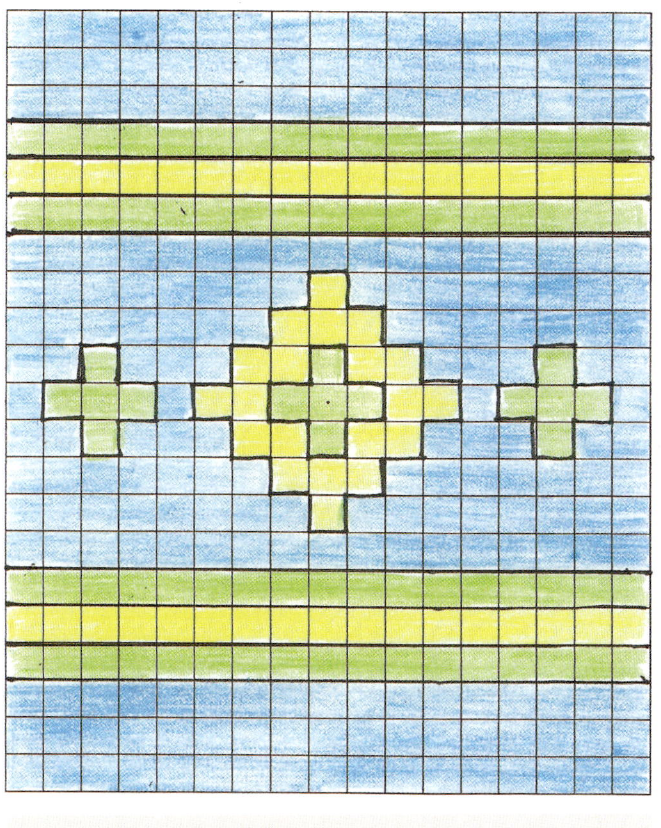

Graph of the design, not to scale.

Change to the female shed, and weave with the new color. This is the first "true row" of the first turnaround of this band of color. Weave until your stripe is as high as you want it to be. End it by weaving the weft back to the right edge in the male shed to fully complete the turnaround, and then cut and taper the end of the weft.

WEAVING SECTIONS OF DESIGN WITH TWO OR MORE COLORS

Using the graphed design, there are seven design rows, three separate colors—blue, yellow, and green—and three design elements. The first row of the design and each section of the design will span across 34 warp pairs. Tear off a length of weft for each section of the design block. Since the area of each section of the design block is smaller than the solid-color bands you were weaving before, you will need less weft for each one. For example, if a section of the design block spans only ½″ or 2 warps, 12″ or less of weft is plenty. If the section of the design block is 3″ wide or 12 warps, you may want to start with one wingspan of weft.

Do not worry about trying to gauge the exact amount of weft you will need to finish the design block. Focus instead on keeping the length of weft you are weaving manageable. At any time during the weaving, you can extend a weft that has run out by overlaying the tapered end of a new weft of the same color over the tapered end of the old weft. Having too long of a weft yarn creates major issues like getting the weft tangled, unspinning it, or preventing it from passing smoothly between the sheds.

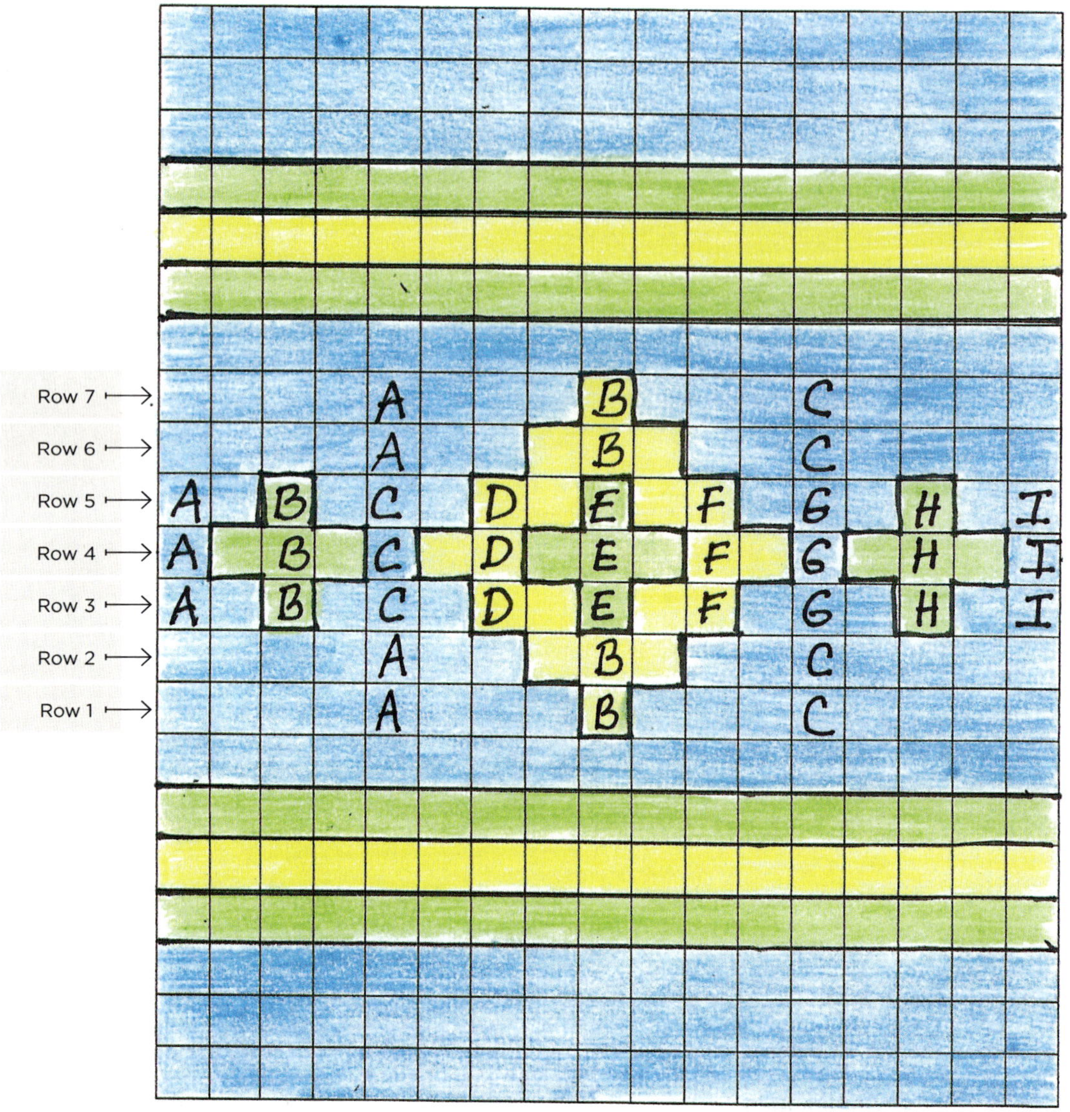

Row 7 A B C
Row 6 A B C
Row 5 A B C D E F G H I
Row 4 A B C D E F G H I
Row 3 A B C D E F G H I
Row 2 A B C
Row 1 A B C

With the batten in the male shed and starting from the left-hand side, begin your prep row by laying in the wefts behind their assigned warps with the long ends hanging from the right side of the design blocks. Remember to include the male selvage cord on the right-hand side in your warp count.

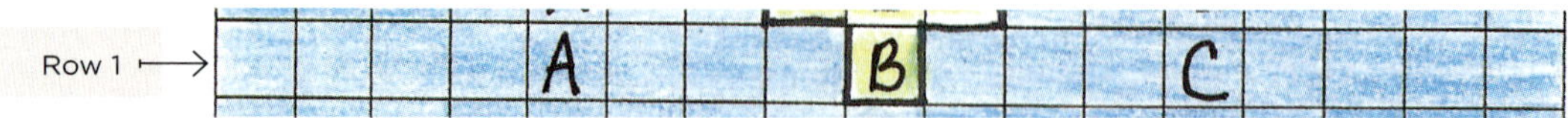

DESIGN ROW 1

1. Weft C on the right is in its starting position, so it does not need to be moved. Weft B has a new starting position 2 warps to the right **b**. Since that is the direction that weft travels while it is in the male shed, we can move Weft B 2 warps to the right now. Weft A has a new starting position of 2 warps to the left. We have a couple options for how to move Weft A. We can "unweave" 2 warps in the male shed, or we can switch the shed and move Weft A 2 warps to the left in the female shed **c**.

2. Weft B has 2 warps and Weft A has 16 warps; both are new design blocks and are laid in the male prep row. Following this sequence, weave 8 turnarounds, which should measure ½″ high when packed down **d** **e** **f** **g** **h** **i**. Notice how the wefts interlock as you weave across. When you have double-checked to see that all of the wefts are in their correct positions, pull each weft slowly toward the right side until only the tapered ends are anchored behind the male warps.

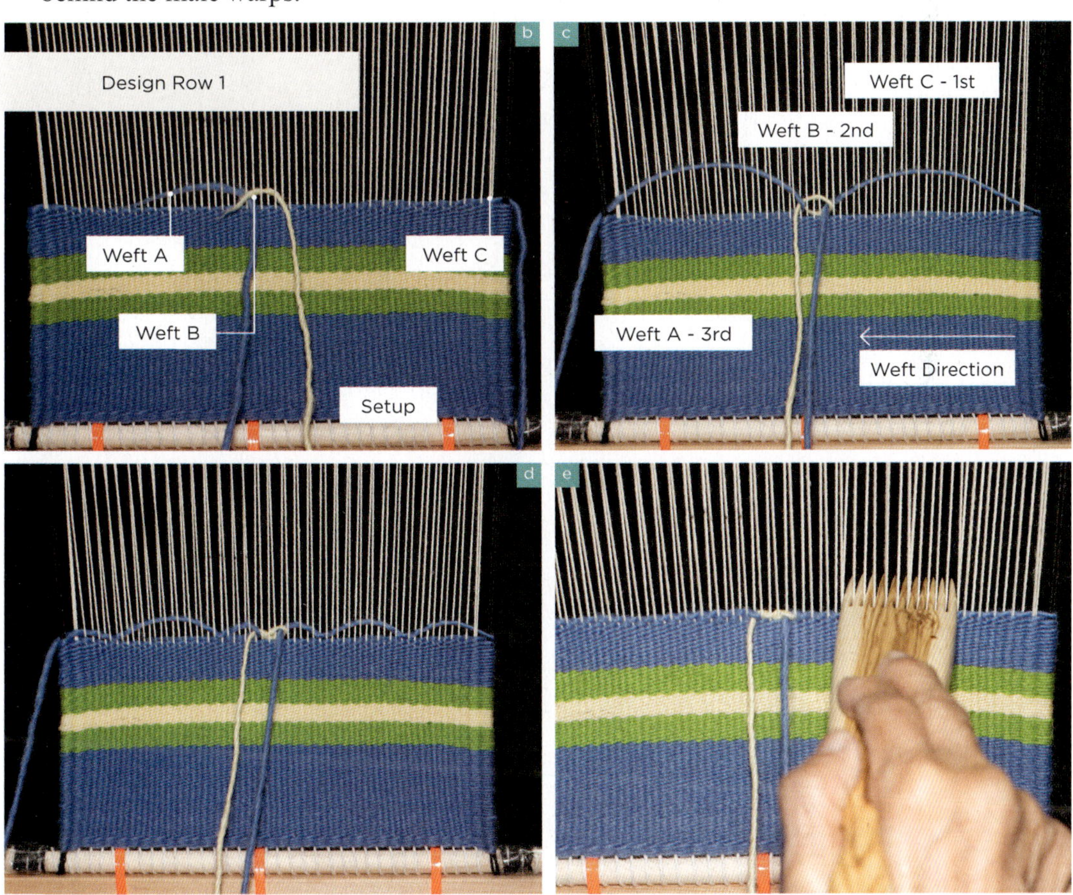

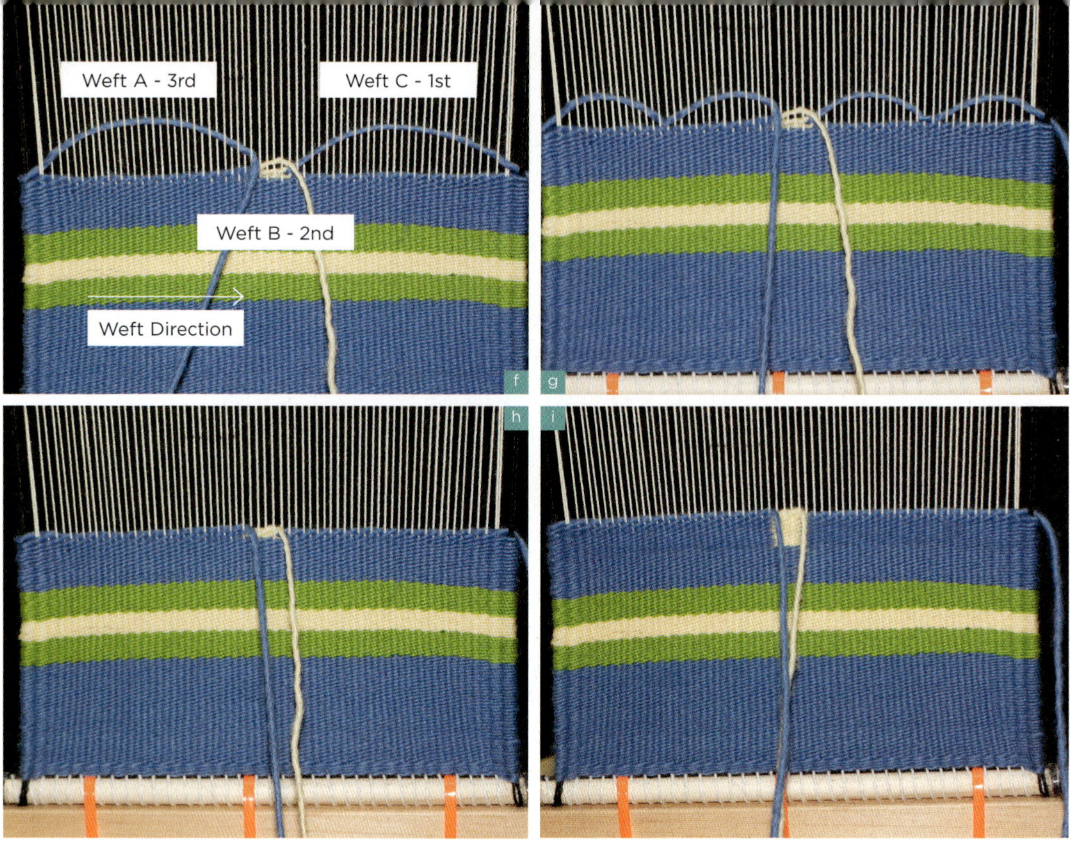

Increasing and Decreasing Design Width

In our example, the central design element is a step diamond. After finishing the first row of the design, we are ready to expand the step diamond outward in both directions, which means that the background color on both sides of it will decrease in width. Position the batten in the male shed to weave all of the wefts to their starting positions. Remember to begin weaving the male row with the weft on the far right. Make your way to the neighboring wefts until you reach the weft on the far left. Only after all of the wefts are resting where they started at the beginning of this design block section is your turnaround complete f g h i.

Continue weaving this section until the design section reaches the intended height. Approximately 8 turnarounds are needed for ½ inch in height. After completing the last turnaround of this section of your design, you are ready to prep for the next section. We do not have any other elements in this section of the design, so the weft count remains for A, B, and C. For the next section of the graphed design, we need to move the existing wefts to their new starting positions. Most of that will be done in the male shed, so we will remain in the male shed while doing as much preparation for our "true row" here as we can.

DESIGN ROW 2

Now that everything is prepped for Row 2 of the design block, we can begin weaving the "true row" with weft C with the batten inserted in the female shed. Weft C will begin at the right-side selvage cord and stop 2 warps early, where it will meet Weft B a. Interlock Wefts C and B, and weave Weft B its new assigned number of warps; Weft B begins 2 warps early and will end 2 warps past its previous end warp. Interlock Wefts B and A, and weave with Weft A to the left-side selvage cord to complete the female row. As it meets the next weft, let the hanging end of

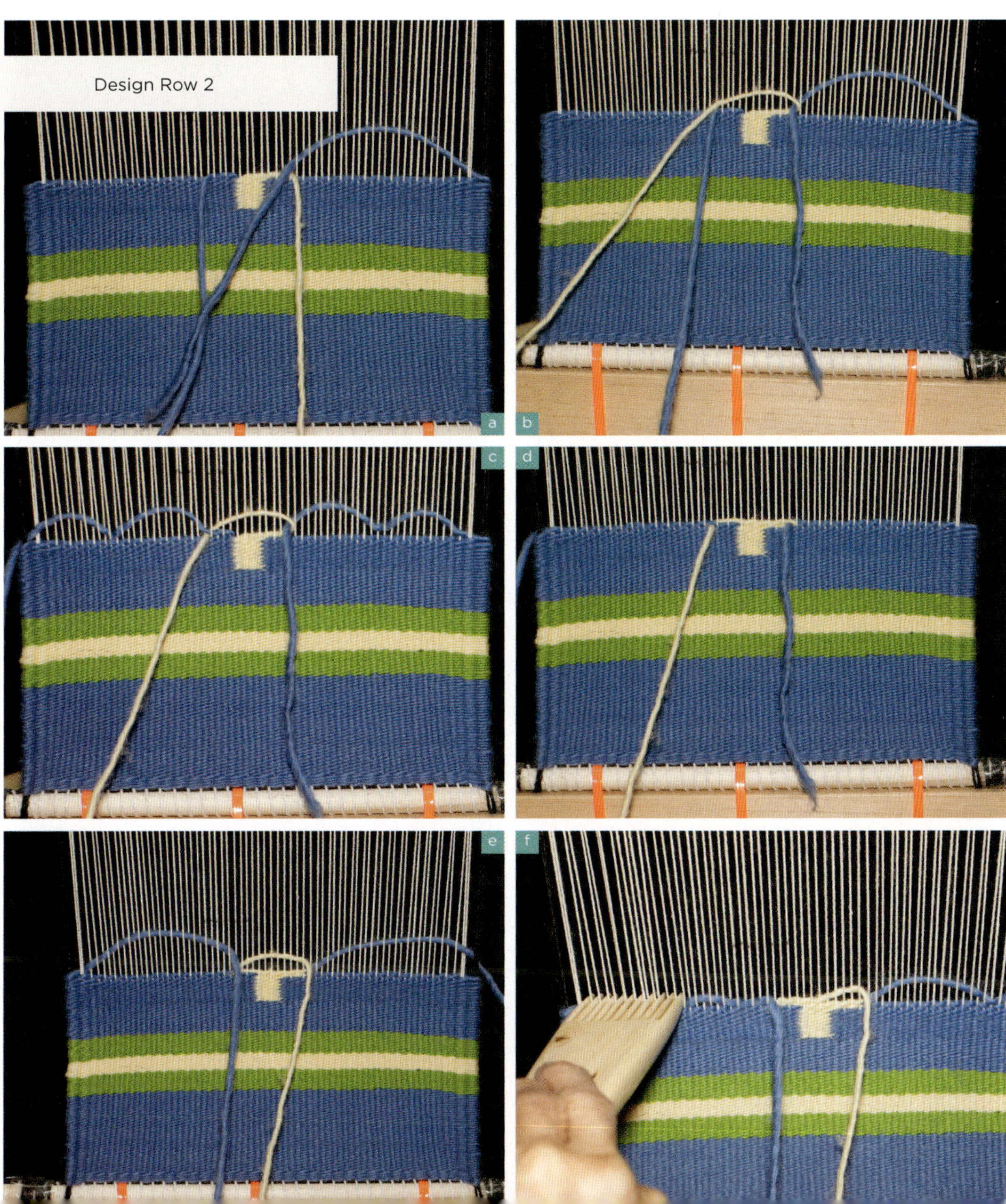

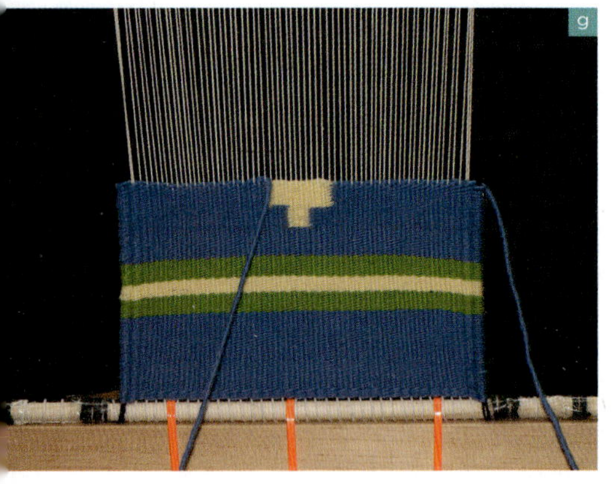

Weft B cross over the hanging end of the neighboring Weft A b.

Wefts A, B, C are the same as for Row 1, except that Weft B advances by 2 warps to the right over Weft C during the male prep row and advances 2 warps to the left over Weft A during the female prep row. For this sample, 3 wefts are in our design row, but the same steps will work for designs with any number of wefts or color changes in a row. Just remember to start weaving the row with the weft on the right-hand side and work your way across the female shed to the neighboring weft, interlocking the 2 wefts as you go until you get to the other edge c d.

1. Crease the weft between your index finger and your thumb at interlock joins to help the joins look tidy. This is half of a turnaround.
2. Once all of the wefts are on the left side of their design block sections, you have completed the female row. Insert the batten from the right to change over to the male shed.
3. Again, start weaving with the weft that is farthest to the right. Weave Weft A back to its starting position at the right edge of the warp where it will rest behind the right-side selvage cord. Next, weave Weft B through its assigned number of warps, and do the same with Weft C. The first turnaround is now complete, and all of the wefts are resting where they started at the beginning of this design block section e f.
4. Warp counts are as follows: Weft A spans 14 warps, Weft B now spans 6 warps, Weft C spans 14 warps. Weave a total of 8 turnarounds g.

DESIGN ROW 3

Position the batten in the male shed to weave all of the wefts to their starting positions a. Weave Weft C, then Weft B, and finally Weft A to the right. Remember to begin weaving the male row with the weft on the far right. Make your way to the neighboring wefts until you reach the weft on the far left. Your turnaround is complete only after all of the wefts are resting where they started at the beginning of this design block section b.

Continue weaving this section for 8 turnarounds until the design section is about ½″ high. After completing the last turnaround of this section of your design, you are ready to prep for Row 3 c d.

As we prep for Row 3 of the design block, we will be adding new wefts and moving current wefts to new starting positions. In Rows 3, 4, and 5, we will refer to the wefts (including the newly added ones) with the letters A through I. In Rows 6 and 7, the design rows will mirror Rows 1 and 2. Get ready.

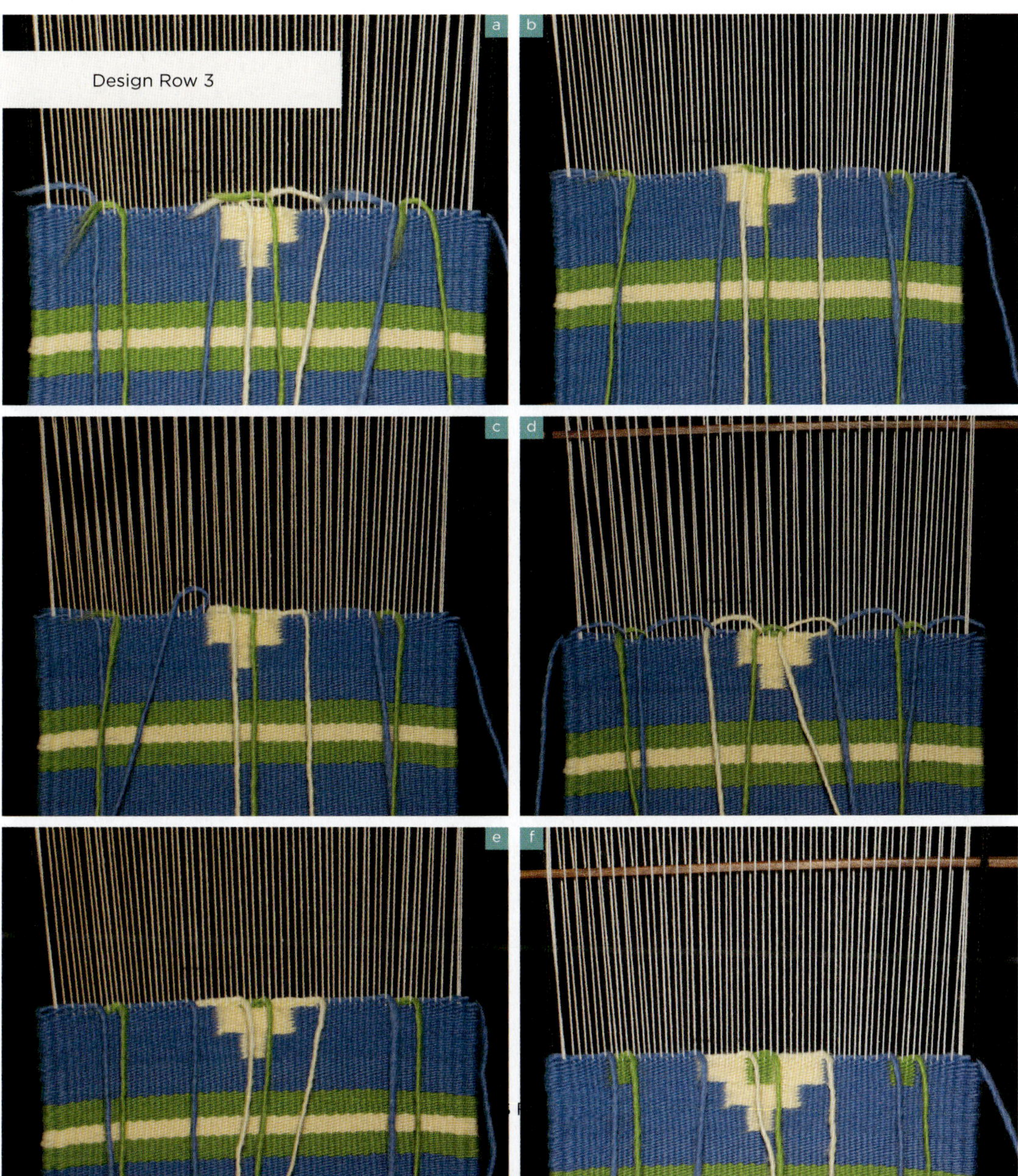

Design Row 3

1. Our chart adds three new design blocks with new wefts in Row 3 in the male prep row. Weft A now spans 4 warps, Weft B spans 2 warps, Weft C spans 6 warps, Weft D spans 4 warps, Weft E spans 2 warps, Weft F spans 4 warps, Weft G spans 6 warps, Weft H spans 2 warps, and Weft I spans 4 warps.
2. Wefts A, B, D, E, G, and H are new additions in the male prep row. Weft F is increased by 2 warps to the right in the male prep row. Weft C will be moved to the left by 2 warps in the female prep row e.
3. Weave 8 turnarounds of this sequence to complete Row 3 of the pattern f.

DESIGN ROW 4

1. This is the middle of the design. It is important that the middle measures 5¼″ high, keeping in mind that there will be ¼″ of yarn packing down. If you have more or less than that amount, you will have to be flexible with this design block, adding or deleting a row as needed.
2. Row 4 does not have new design additions, just some advancements and reductions done first in the male prep row and then in the female prep row.
3. In the male prep row, Weft B is moved to the right by 2 additional warps over Weft C. Wefts E, F, and H are also moved to the right by 2 warps a b.
4. In the female prep row, Weft A is reduced and moved to the left by 2 warps, along with Wefts C, D, G, and H moving to the left by 2 warps c d e.
5. Warp counts are as follows: Weft A spans 2 warps, Weft B spans 6 warps, Weft C spans 2 warps, Weft D spans 4 warps, Weft E spans 6 warps, Weft F spans 4 warps, Weft G spans 2 warps, Weft H spans 6 warps, and Weft I spans 2 warps.

Weaving continues in the female shed, and Row 4 will be woven with 8 turnarounds f g h.

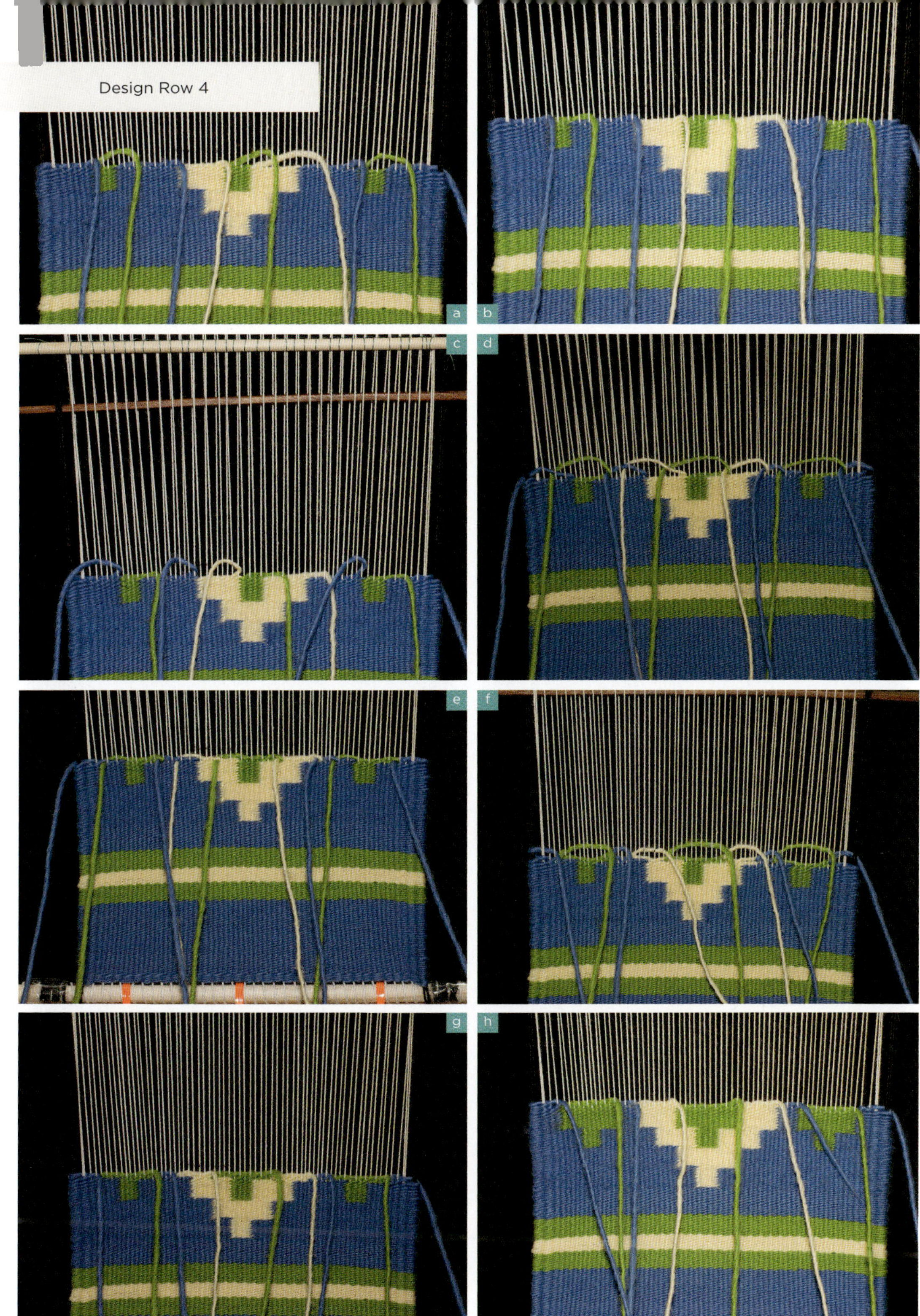
Design Row 4
a
b
c
d
e
f
g
h

Design Row 5

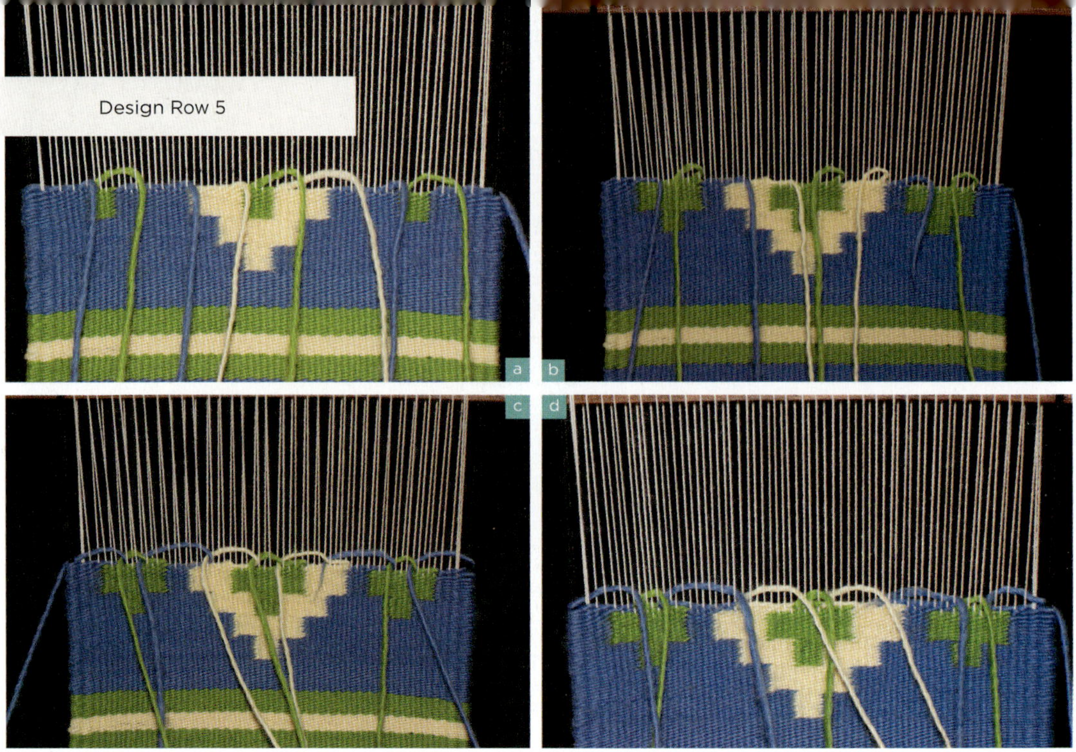

DESIGN ROW 5

1. Wefts A, C, D, and G need to be moved to new starting positions 2 warps to the right. That can be done in the male prep row. Continue weaving this section of the design the same way you have been until it is the desired height. Before moving to the next part of your design, make sure to complete the current turnaround. All hanging ends of the wefts should be on the right-hand side of their sections. For now, keep your batten in the male position, and revisit your graphed or sketched design plan to see what comes next.
2. In the female prep row, Wefts B, E, F, and H will be moved 2 warps to the left before the true row begins a. Warp counts for Row 5 are as follows: Weft A spans 4 warps, Weft B spans 2 warps, Weft C spans 6 warps, Weft D spans 4 warps, Weft E spans 2 warps, Weft F spans 4 warps, Weft G spans 6 warps, Weft H spans 2 warps, and Weft I spans 4 warps b c.

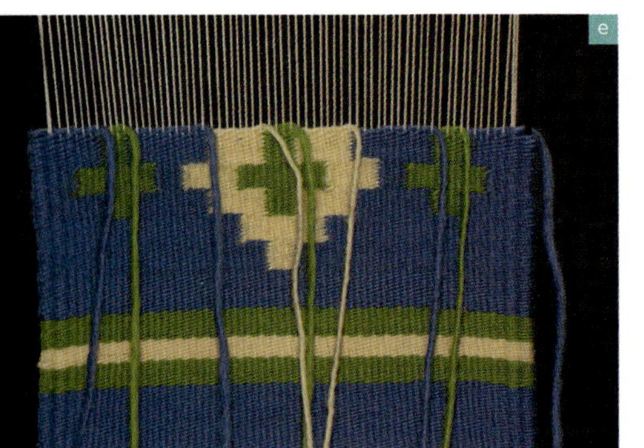

Weave 8 turnarounds to complete Row 5 d e.

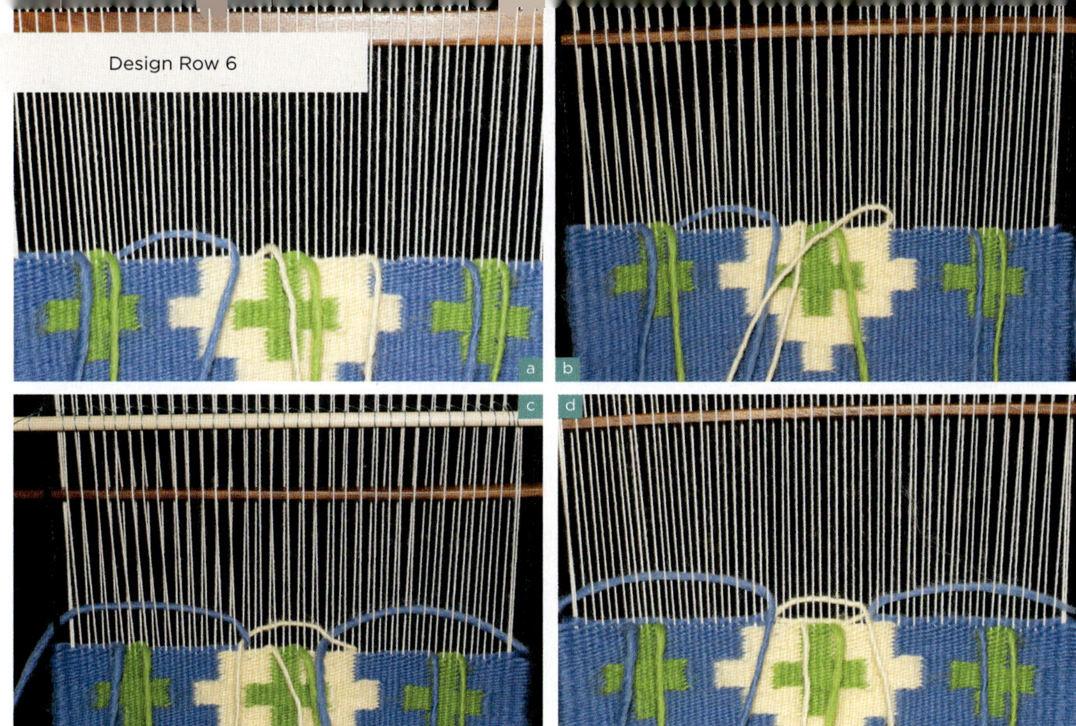

DESIGN ROW 6

1. In Row 6, we eliminate Wefts D, E, F, G, H, and I, and the row will mirror Row 2. You can snip the leftover weft yarns in each block to about an inch a; do not snip them completely off or the comb pounding the textile will work out the woven weft and create a hole. The leftover weft yarns will be clipped close when the textile is finished.

2. In the male prep row, move Weft C 2 warps to the right, over Weft B. Wefts A, C, D, E, G, and H will be eliminated.

3. In the female prep row, move Weft B to the right 2 warps b. Weaving will continue in the female shed; Weft C is woven to the left first by 14 warps, over Wefts H and G which ended in Row 5, and interlocked with Weft B which now spans 6 warps c. Weft B will interlock with Weft A to complete the first female row.

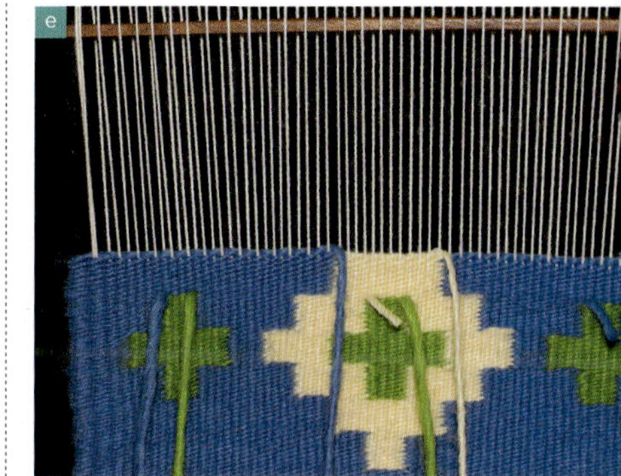

4. In the male shed row, Weft C is woven to the right by 14 warps, Weft B is woven to the right by 6 warps and Weft A is woven to the right by 14 warps d.
5. After 8 turnarounds, Wefts A, B, and C will hang on the right side of each design block in the male shed row e.

DESIGN ROW 7

1. In the male prep row, take Weft A to the right by 2 warps over Weft B a.
2. In the female prep row, take Weft B and move it 2 warps to the left. Take Weft C and weave it to the left by 16 warps so it is adjacent to Weft B, and interlock. Weft B spans 2 warps and will interlock with Weft A, and it will span 16 warps to the left to complete the female row b. In the male shed row, take wefts to the right c.

Design Row 7 is woven with 8 turnarounds.

Seven design rows are now completed, with each row having 8 turnarounds, more or less. When packed down, the entire section should measure 3½″ high d.

Return to plain weave g h i j.

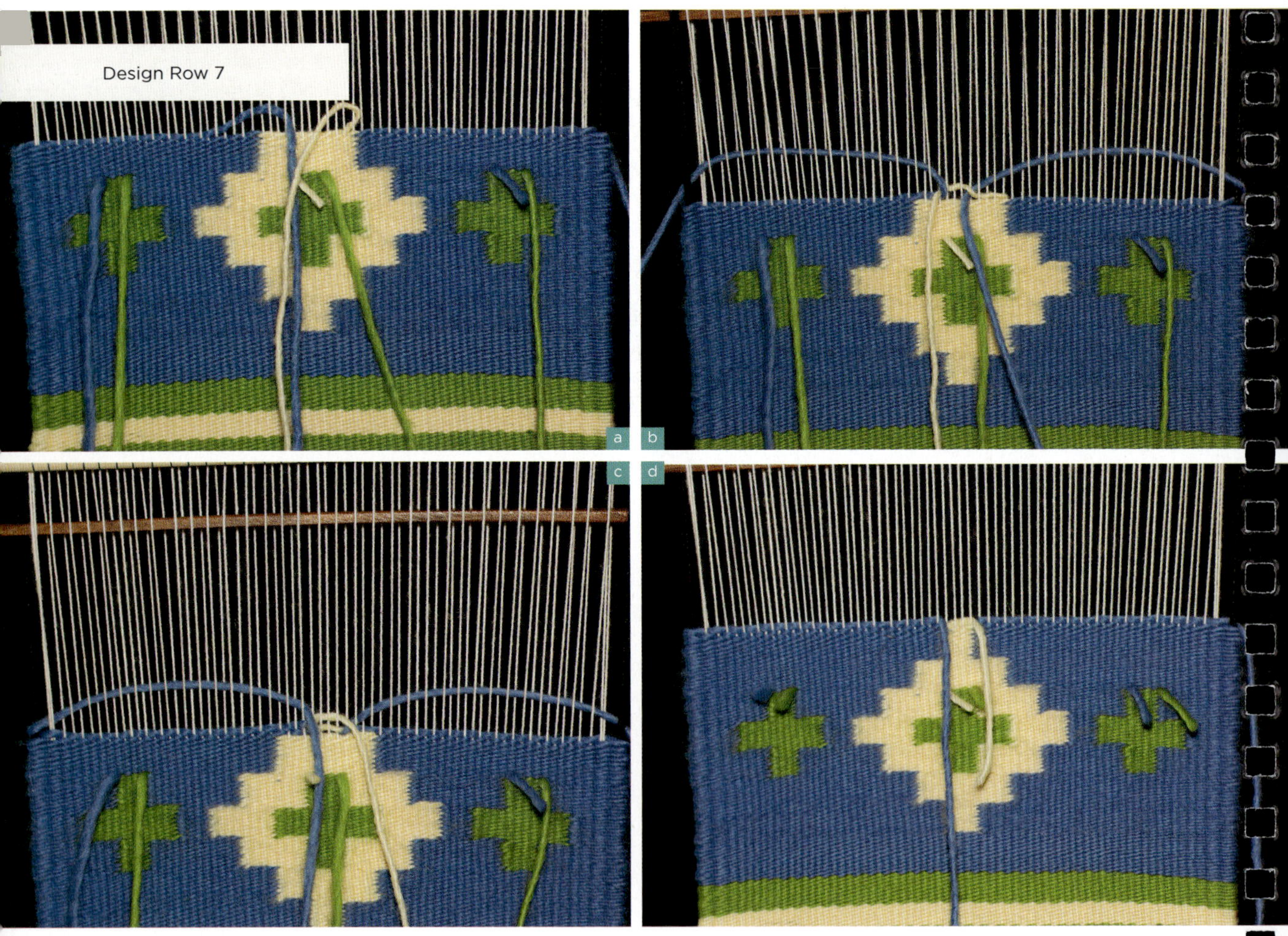

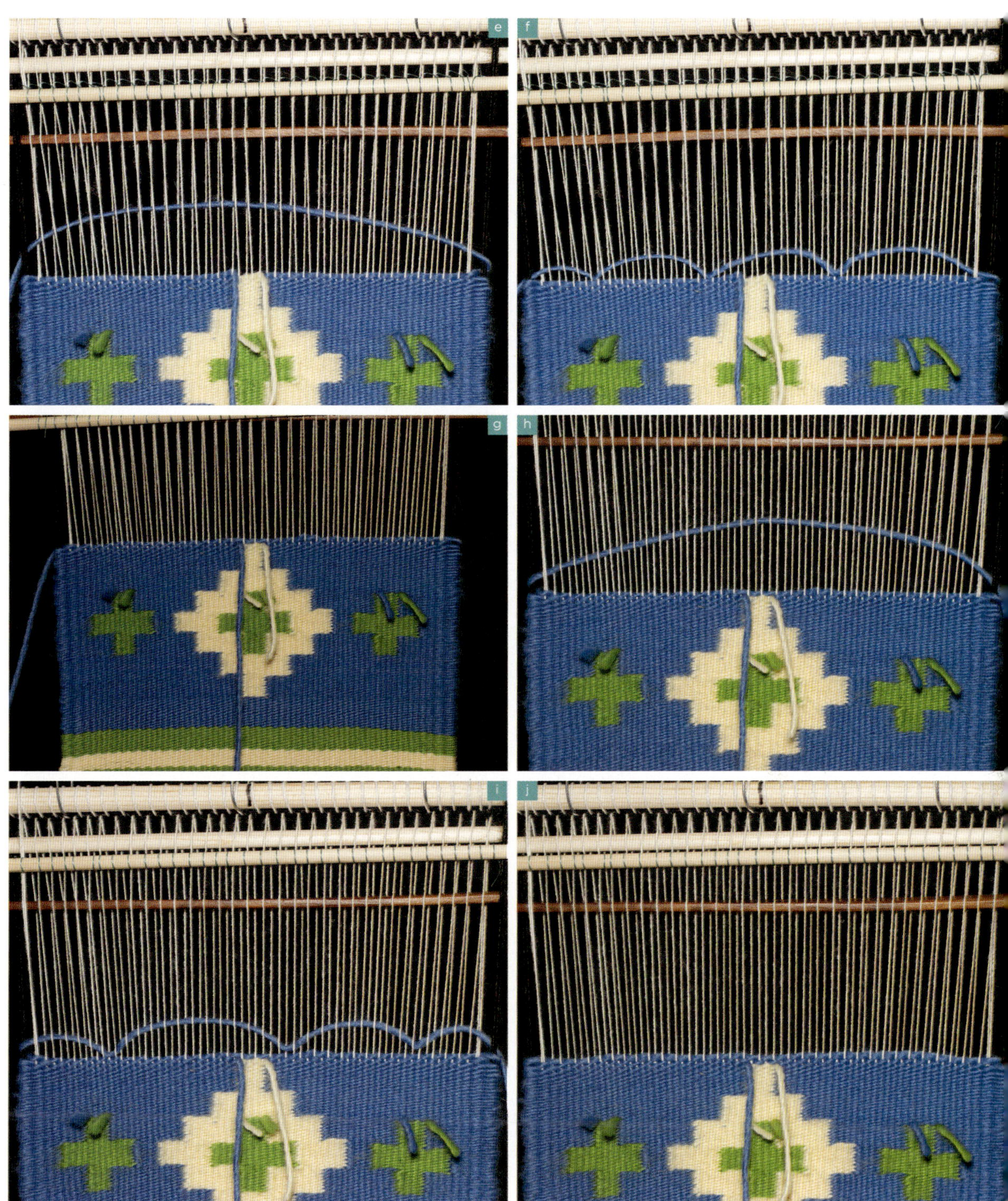
e
f
g
h
i
j

INCLUDING ADDITIONAL DESIGN ELEMENTS

The main thing we want to illustrate in this section is that the complexity of the weaving process can increase pretty quickly with the addition of design elements. In this sample design plan, we have added three crosses. Two crosses are disconnected from the primary design element, and one is inserted within the step diamond. Each time a design element is added, its insertion requires "breaking up" the current design and adding more wefts into the row. In this case, the addition of three small crosses has caused the number of wefts to increase from 3 to 9.

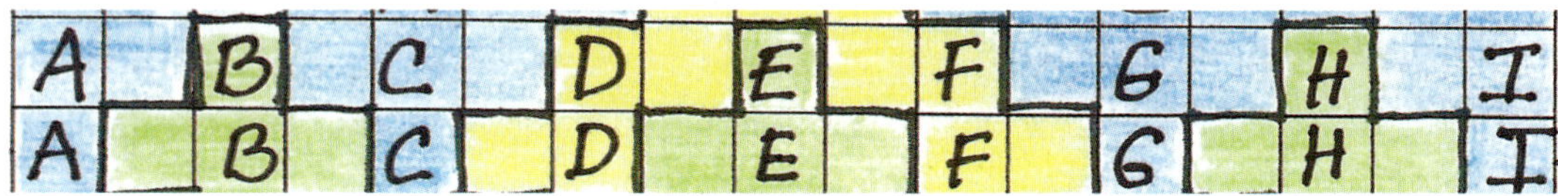

DECREASING THE NUMBER OF DESIGN ELEMENTS

It is always a nice feeling to have some relief after doing a complex design section. To eliminate one or more design sections, determine which wefts you will not be weaving with anymore, and either cut them with scissors, leaving a tail of about 2″, or taper the ends of the wefts and weave them into the design block.

If you cut the wefts, leave the excess tails hanging on the right-hand side of the design blocks. If you have finished your turnaround, the wefts should already be hanging at their starting positions. After weaving 2″ or 3″ above that point, it will be safe to cut the excess hanging wefts close to the face of the textile. If they are cut sooner, the blunt ends may work themselves out, and your textile will not look as neat.

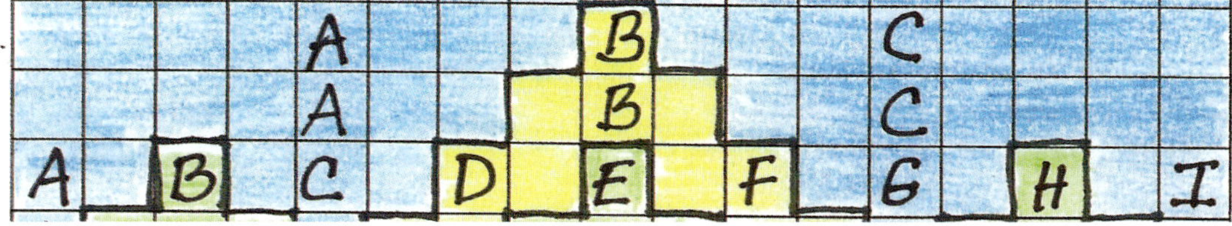

In our example, after the wefts you no longer need have been trimmed, you will be left again with Wefts A, B, and C.

Weft A on the far right is already in its starting position, so it does not need to be moved. Weft A will be woven across 14 warps. Weft B has a new starting position 2 warps to the left of its current position, and it will be woven across 6 warps. Weft C has a new starting position 2 warps to the right of its current position, and it will be woven across 14 warps.

As we advance the design and are ready to close up the step diamond, we will return to weaving a solid band of color across the entire width of the warp. At this point, you will trim every weft except for the one on the far right (Weft A), unless you want to make that solid band a different color from the original. If that is the case, Weft A will also be trimmed, and the tapered end of a new color weft will be anchored in at the left side in the male shed. (See "Weaving a Stripe or Band of Solid Color," page 92.)

HOW TO FIX MESSY INTERLOCK JOINS

Sometimes, the point where the wefts are interlocked looks "puffy." If that is the case, there are a couple of things you can try. First, when the batten is positioned in the female shed, before starting to weave the female row, grasp all of the hanging weft yarns at once. As you tug them gently but firmly, use a heavy comb to do a pack-down.

If that does not work, bring the whole design block up with your fingers or a needle. Take the blunt end of your curved needle, and beginning from the bottom of the design block, start slightly tightening a row at a time. Bring the excess weft to the top of the design block. Be careful not to pull it too hard. After the edges have been firmed up, use the needle or the weaving comb to pack the woven wefts back down.

WEAVING DESIGN BLOCKS: RECAP

(According to granddaughter Roxanne Lee, it's the Modern Fiber Warfare of Navajo Weaving.)

To review, there are four hard and fast rules pertaining to the weaving of design blocks. The most important rule is number 4.

1. With the batten inserted in the male shed, anchor the weft yarns in each design block section of the male shed. There are no exceptions! The anchoring process does not add to the turnaround count when the wefts hang loose on the right side of each design block.

2. With the batten inserted in the female shed, starting from the far-right block, take each weft to the left. Make interconnections of wefts for block design elements in the female shed. There are no exceptions! After that row is done, the weft yarns will hang on the left side. Each design block is connected only in the female shed.

3. With the batten inserted in the male shed, starting with the far-right design block, take the weft to the right. Each design block will not interconnect to the right. There are no exceptions!

4. The weaving sequence of design blocks always starts from the right-hand side of the loom. In both the female and the male sheds, start with the right-hand side of the design block. There are no exceptions!

Remember to include the selvage cords in the warp counts. The left-hand selvage is included as a female warp, and the right-hand selvage is included as a male warp.

APPROPRIATION

Cultural appropriation is a complicated and nuanced issue. In addressing it, we are trying to preserve the work of our ancestors, our cultural identity, and the traditions that belong to the Navajo people. This is a spiritual imperative. There is no easy answer that will address the damage done by past injustices or current wrongs. What we seek is to create an increased awareness and a change in many current attitudes.

Companies and individuals take designs that represent sometimes hundreds or even thousands of years of design tradition that belong to a group of people and, without permission, use them for their own commercial gain. Sometimes artisans don't know that their work has been appropriated or stolen. When an artist becomes aware, the fight to revoke the use of the copied design is often impossible, as large companies often have a slew of lawyers in place to stave off intellectual property suits. Protecting one's work is a constant battle.

The Indian Arts and Crafts Act (IACA) was created in 1935 and updated in 1990. It is a truth-in-advertising law that prohibits misrepresentation in marketing of American Indian or Alaska Native arts and crafts products within the United States. The law also created the Indian Arts and Crafts Board (IACB), an agency within the Department of the Interior whose mission is to "promote the economic development of American Indians and Alaska Natives through the expansion of the Indian arts and crafts market." This agency processes IACA violation complaints, sends warning letters to the accused, and distributes educational literature. Even with this agency, the amount of economic damage to Diné weavers is substantial.

Barbara and I have both had our design work stolen, reproduced by weavers outside this country, and sold for a fraction of what it's worth, exploiting us and the weavers who are made to weave the design for a pittance. Manufacturers skirt the law by marketing our designs as "tribal," "ethnic," or "native art" rather than labeling the products "Navajo." We are reluctant to post photographs of our textiles online for fear that our designs will show up on manufactured household products and clothing.

More than this, we are faced with the lack of respect for the Navajo woven tradition. The designs that exist within our culture represent our identity, the journey of our people, the suffering we have lived through over generations, our survival, and our sacred cosmology. As weavers, we are asking for respect for our traditional designs. We ask that they not be used for commercial gain.

The deciding factor for what constitutes Navajo weaving appropriation is the recognizable use of Navajo designs. It is not the use of Navajo looms, tools, or fiber. We have, on occasion, received pushback for teaching Navajo weaving to non-Navajos. However, we believe that education and sharing leads to survival and an open world. We want people to learn more about the Navajo people and Navajo weaving.

Many non-Navajo students come to our classes to learn about the weaving, our culture, and our traditions. Knowledge and instruction are freely given, but students are not being taught to be Navajo weavers. If a weaver isn't Navajo, then Navajo weaving is not their tradition. Students are being taught the techniques. They are being given a safe place to explore and learn about our cultural woven traditions. By teaching all who want to learn, we are cultivating a diverse community of allies.

Barbara and I deeply respect and guard our sacred traditions. We bring sample designs for our beginning weaving classes that are simple and designed to teach specific weaving techniques. We have discussions about what is appropriate for beginning Navajo students and what is appropriate for non-Navajo students. We encourage and assist the non-Navajo students to come up with a design that is meaningful for them within their design sense and/or their own cosmology. Barbara and I also encourage all students to expand their creative designs.

Here are some guidelines when a non-Navajo student participates in Navajo weaving: Do not label the weaving as "Navajo." Do not sell these weavings. Explore them, learn about them, give them as gifts, make them for personal use, but don't sell them. Never copy the weaving of an artist without permission.

There is an important distinction between appropriation and learning exploration. Art students often copy the work of masters in order to learn how the work was created and what techniques were used. We like to encourage our students to do this by taking elements of a design and experimenting with them. We discourage the express copying of a historical Navajo work, but if a weaver does such a reproduction, they should cite the name of the artist and title of the original work and also note that their intent was to learn.

Very importantly, we stress that you should never weave or create Yei or Sand Paintings in your textiles. These are sacred to the Navajo people. We have specific traditions and cultural protocols dedicated to who creates them and how and when they should be used. Only those who are Navajo understand this cosmology and who are part of the tradition should weave these designs. Diné weavers weave Sand Paintings and Yei rugs and market them, and there is no harm in buying one to decorate your home. Most often, these rugs are woven by seasoned Diné weavers who observe proper protocols and who are initiated into these ways.

Navajo students have the right, even the responsibility, to explore all aspects of Navajo weaving. Weaving for us also represents our very survival as a people and as a family. Many of our Navajo students have retrieved their heritage and support themselves and their families now through their weaving.

Navajo weaving students should know that there are protocols in place for weaving sacred designs that they should research, respect, and follow. Yei Bi Chei dancers and teachers, Navajo medicine people, and cultural interpreters have issued warnings to beginning Diné weavers to prevent them from harming themselves and their families by weaving sacred designs without making proper prayers or having an initiation into the seasonal ceremonial societies.

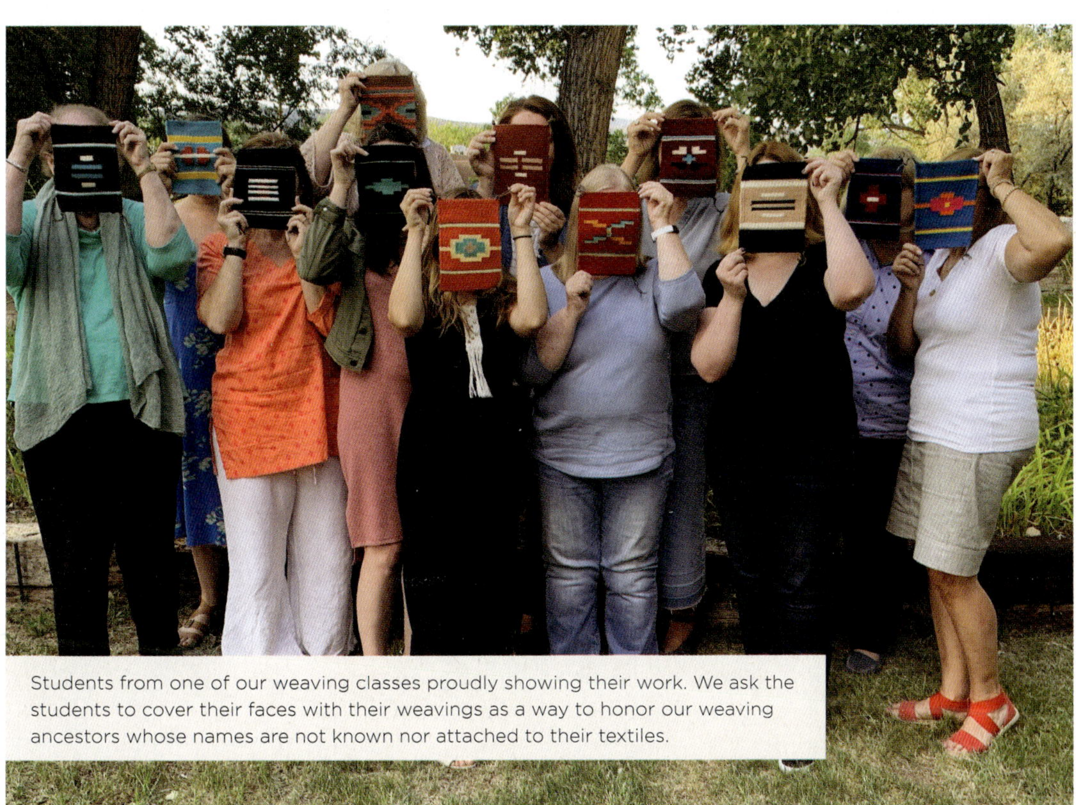

Students from one of our weaving classes proudly showing their work. We ask the students to cover their faces with their weavings as a way to honor our weaving ancestors whose names are not known nor attached to their textiles.

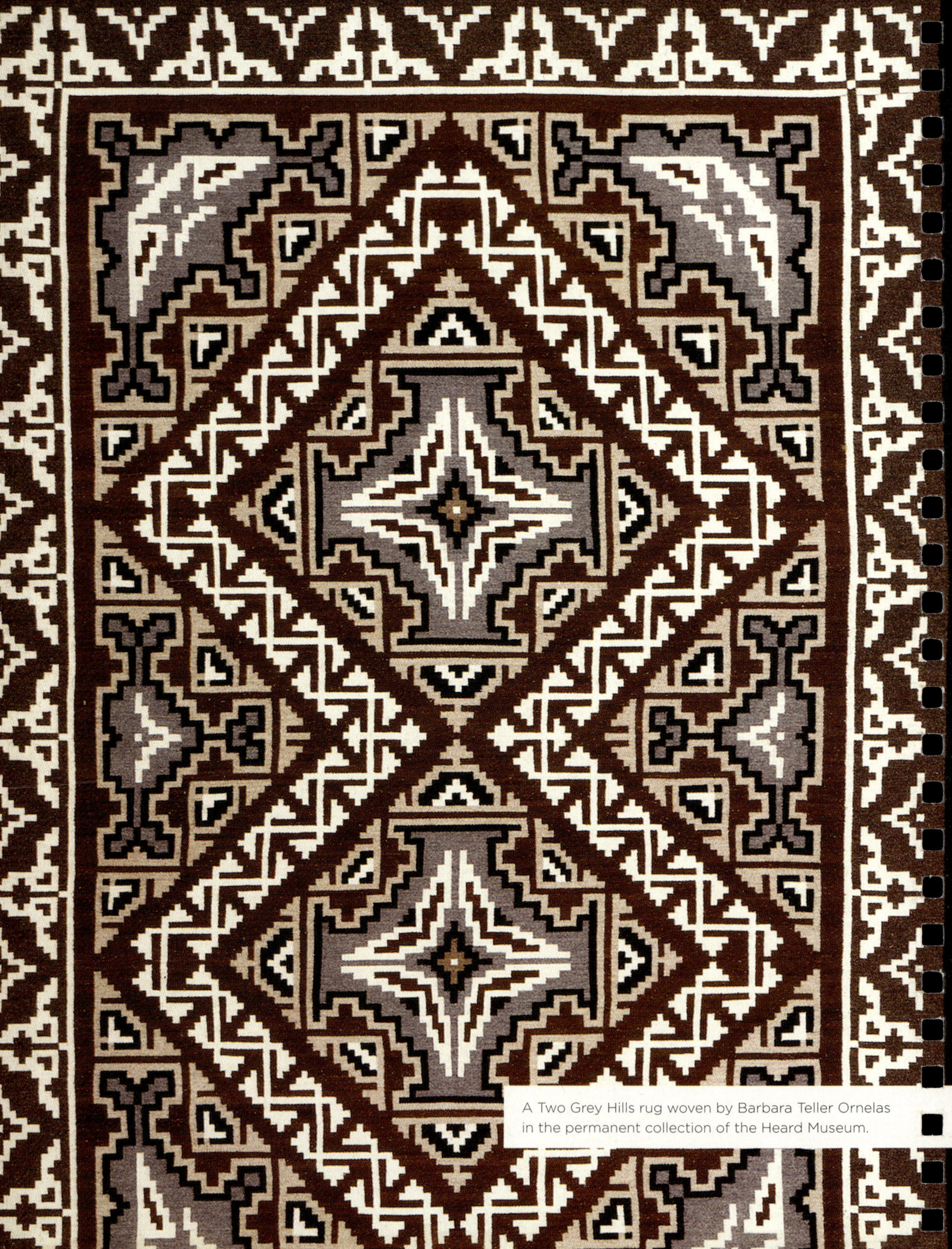

A Two Grey Hills rug woven by Barbara Teller Ornelas in the permanent collection of the Heard Museum.

CHAPTER

9

TROUBLESHOOTING

A miniature tapestry woven by Rosann Teller Lee.

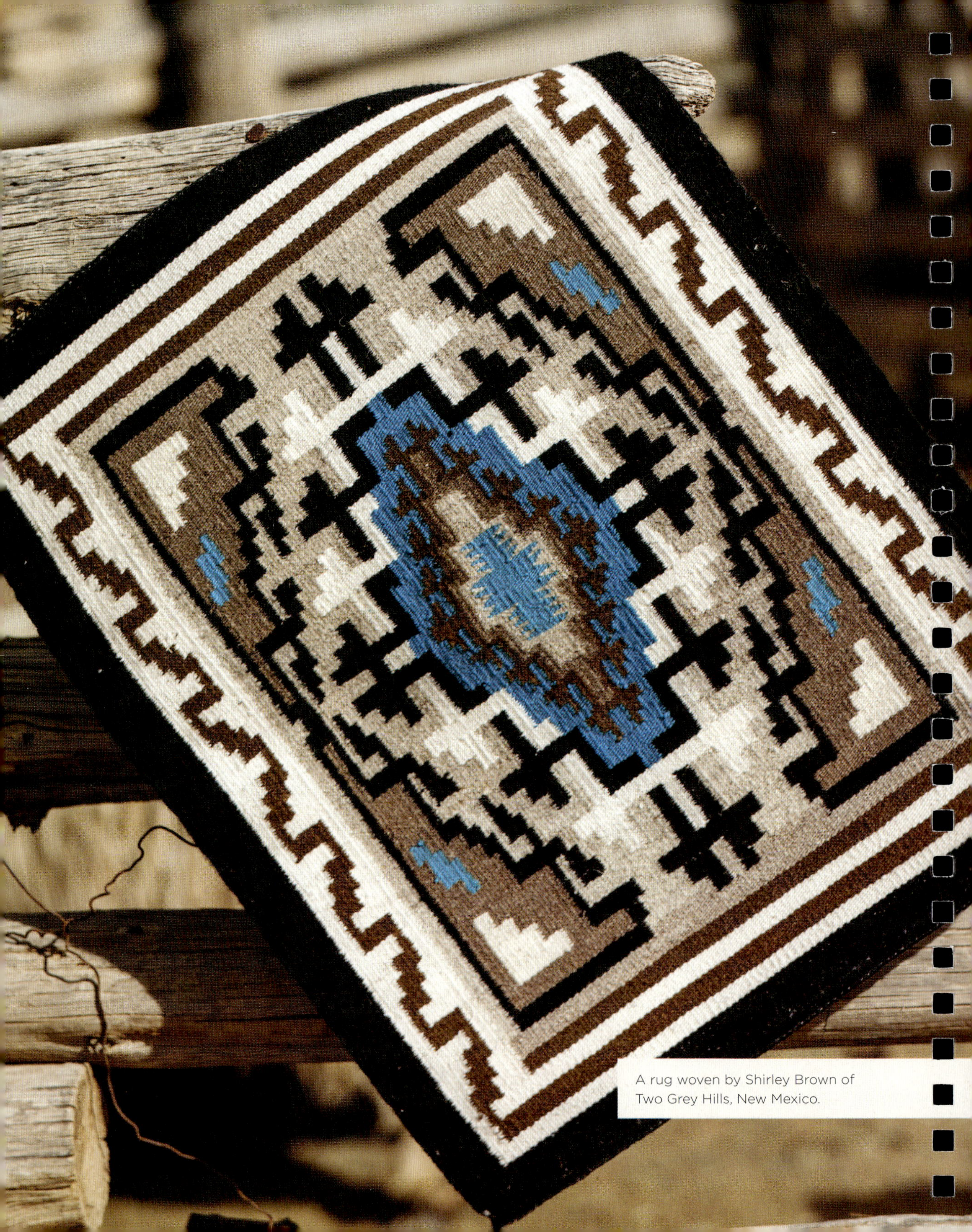
A rug woven by Shirley Brown of Two Grey Hills, New Mexico.

TROUBLESHOOTING — The not-so-glamorous side of Navajo weaving, and that is why we get the big bucks!

WEFT TENSION ISSUES: WHAT DO THEY LOOK LIKE?

THE HOURGLASS

If your weft tension is too tight, the warps will squeeze together, eventually resulting in a textile with an hourglass shape. Warps will gather closest together in the center and pull away from the edges. That will lead to the widening of the spacing between the warps at the edges. In areas where the warp spacing is narrower, the weft will not have enough room to pack down between the warps, so the warp threads will show through the weave no matter how hard you beat the weft down with the comb. In areas where the warp spacing is wider, the wefts will pack down too easily. The uneven spacing of the warp threads caused by tight weft tension will create high and low spots in your textile that filling in with short rows cannot remedy.

PREVENTION AND EARLY INTERVENTION. As you weave, lay the weft into the shed in sections approximately 3″ (12 warps) across and create tension arc bubbles. The middle arc should measure ½″ high. Keep an eye on your warp threads to make sure the intervals stay evenly spaced. Measure the width from edge to edge frequently to ensure that your textile stays within ¼″ of its original width. If it starts to get narrower, you know right away to loosen your weft tension. You can do that by making tension bubbles higher as you weave. The creation of tension breaks is also a good prevention technique. Tension breaks are especially helpful when weaving large solid-color blocks or stripes.

To create a tension break, complete three turnarounds. On the fourth turnaround, weave in the female shed to about the midpoint before changing direction and weaving back to the right side in the male shed. On the next turnaround, weave the entire female row. Change to the male shed and weave the weft to the point where the weft was woven in the prior half-woven female row. Weave back to the left side in the female shed. Then, change sheds again to weave in the male shed to complete the turnaround. If a tension break is created every fourth turnaround, you can fit approximately four tension breaks into a band measuring 1″ high.

BUCKLING OR RIPPLING

If you notice ripples forming in some sections of your woven textile, the weft tension in the section where the ripples appear is looser than in the surrounding woven areas.

TROUBLESHOOT. Lift the woven weft to the point where the ripples begin, and tighten it row by row with a sacking needle. Use your judgment. It may be easier to unweave and reweave the entire section.

DESIGN MISTAKES: CAN I FIX IT WITHOUT UNWEAVING ENTIRE ROWS?

WEAVING IN THE SAME SHED

If you have accidentally woven in the same shed for multiple rows, you will start to see the same warps exposed and you won't be able to cover them up with beating. If you catch the problem right away, it is not difficult to unweave the top rows and reweave them, remembering to switch to the correct shed when changing direction.

TROUBLESHOOT. There are circumstances in which it is not so easy to unweave and reweave to fix this issue. Perhaps the mistake occurred an inch or so below where you are currently weaving. Or the mistake happened toward the top of your project when the weaving got difficult because the space was smaller and the male and female rods had been removed.

You may find it easier to gently pull the woven wefts up above the mistake until the area of the mistake has been reached. Use two umbrella needles; thread the weft yarn on one umbrella needle and use the second one to go through the first layer of the same weft. This will separate the two wefts that are in the same shed. After picking up the opposite warps, let the needle stay in place as a batten. Take the first umbrella needle threaded with the weft yarn and insert it through the warps, leaving both ends of the weft hanging out. Use a sacking needle to gently push down each new weft into the alternating shed between the rows woven in the same shed. Take the next layer and do the same with a separate piece of yarn until you have successfully separated each weft row. Gently tug at each edge and trim the excess yarn. Make sure that the top layer of the corrected row is in the direction of the male shed to the right or the female shed to the left.

FIXING A BROKEN WARP YARN

Loosen the turnbuckles by a full turn. It is best to do a replacement of the whole pair, both male and female, where the break is. Using the warp yarn, measure a double vertical length. Thread this long piece of extra warp on a curved needle a b.

Take the first end of the warp and thread it between the twisted selvage at the top of the selvage binding and work the needle through the selvage and out the other end. This is the female warp. The back warp string will come forward and go through the female heddle loop. Take the needle off this end of the warp. The front side of the extra warp will be put behind the male shed rod; this is the male warp. Pull both warps down c.

Thread the back warp into the curved needle and on the left side of the warp path, work the needle down through the woven weft ½″. Take the needle out, rethread the other warp end, and work this end through the right side of the warp path through the woven weft for about ½″. The newly inserted warp pairs will be adjacent to each other in the weaving d e.

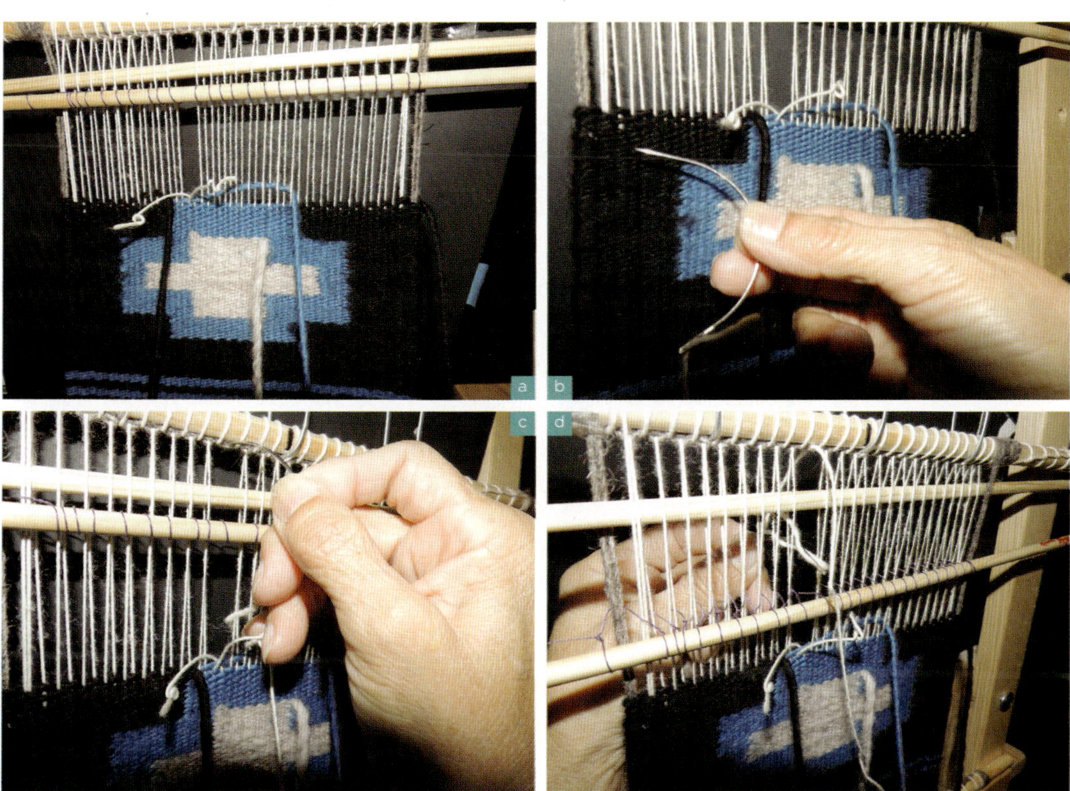

Tug both warp ends taut and tie the remaining broken strings to each of the new strings that you've added with square knots f g h i. Weave over the main break, leaving the ends of the knots out. Continue to weave past the main break for 1″ to 2″. Leave the excess warp there until the textile is finished, and then cut off all exposed knots and excess warps hanging out j.

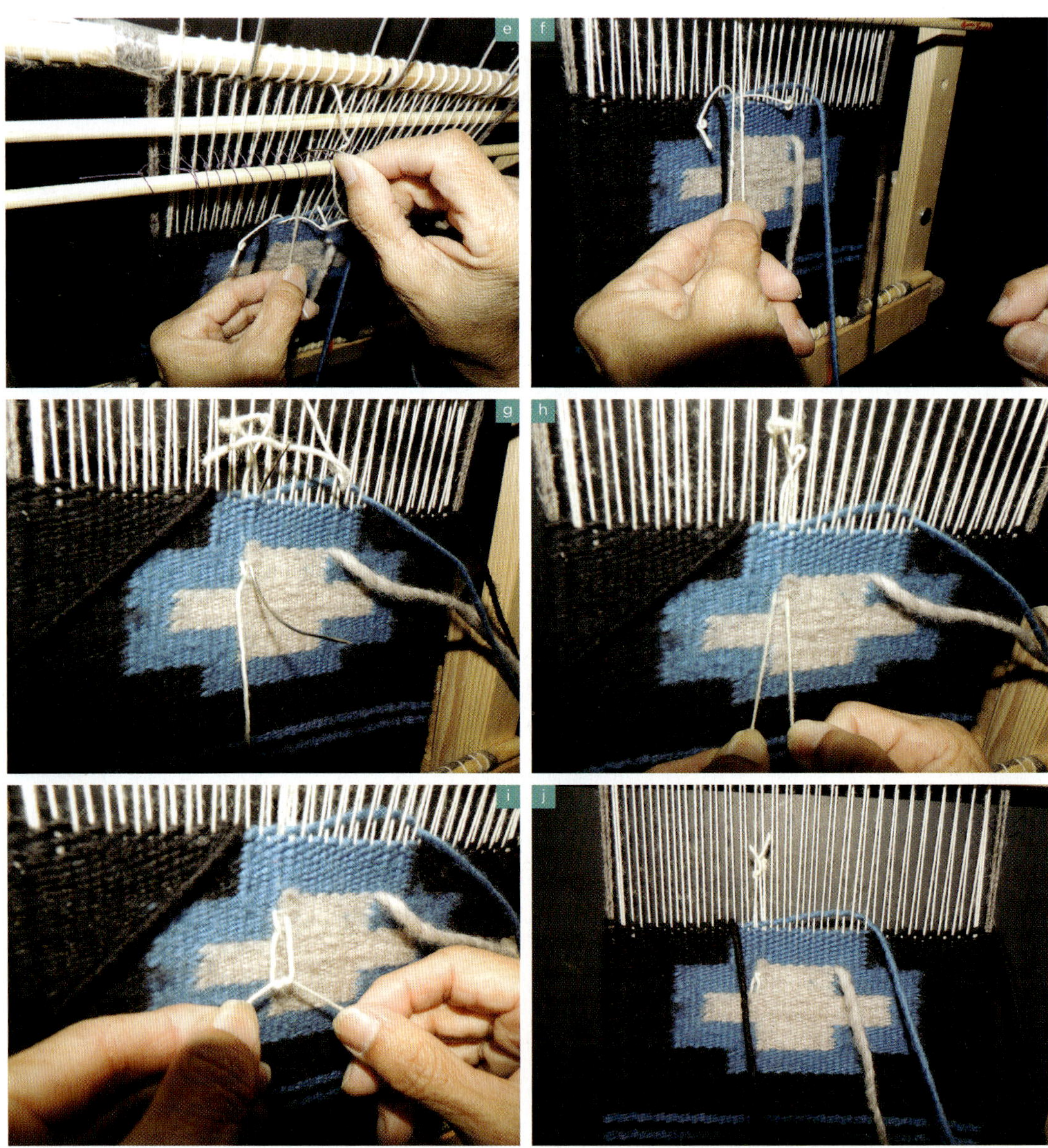

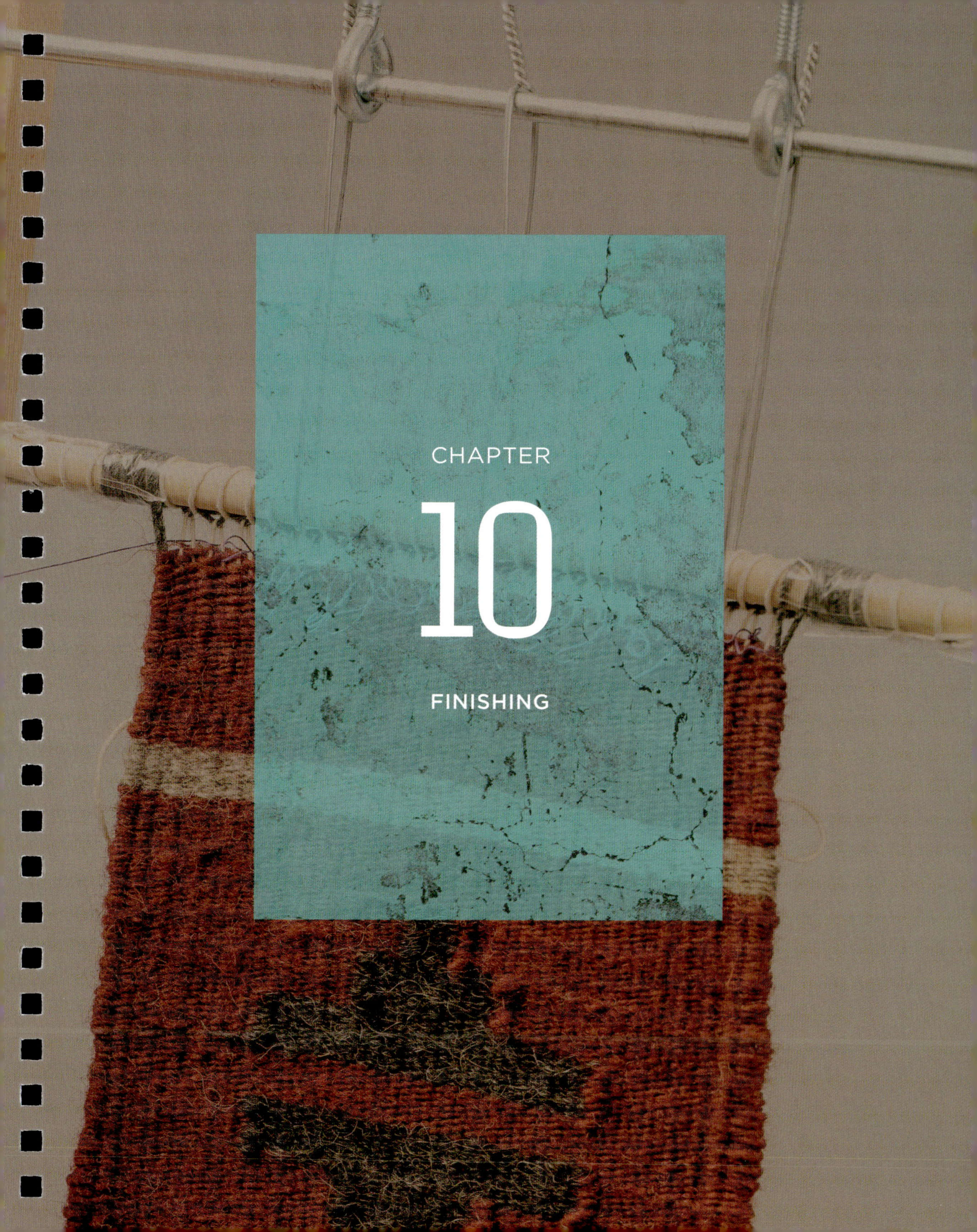

CHAPTER 10

FINISHING

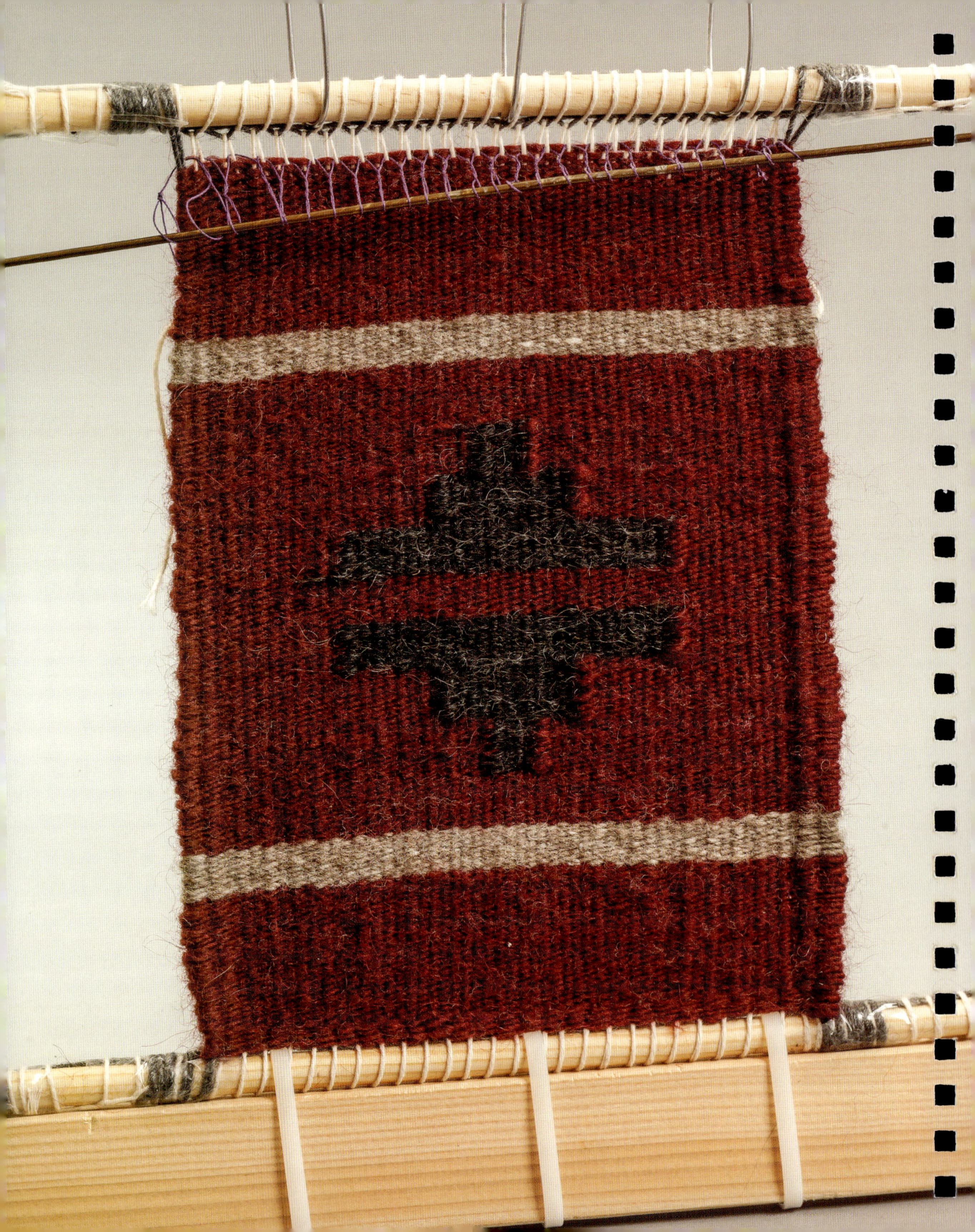

FINISHING — I am done. Am I done? If you still see daylight under the top selvage cords, you are not done.

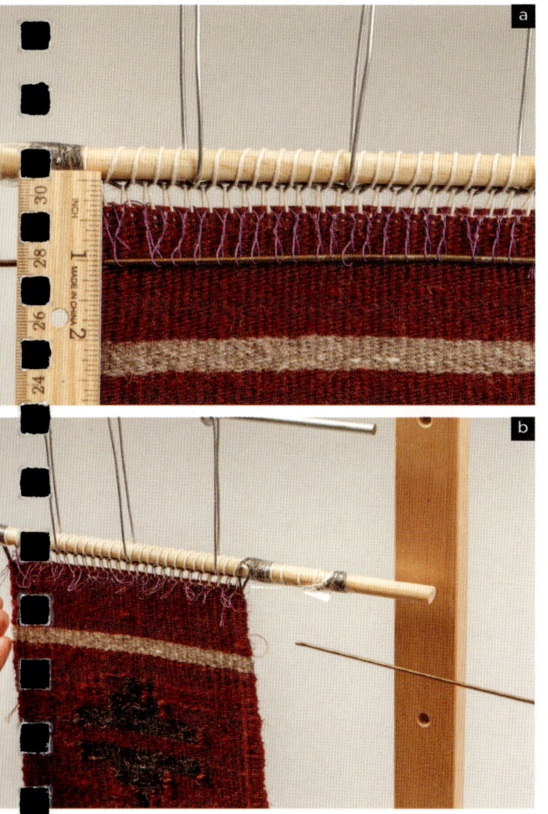

As you get closer to finishing the textile, you will start to run out of space to weave in a. The warps will get tighter. The female heddle rod and the male shed rod will become too big to be helpful, so they will have to be changed out for thinner, wire ones around the 2″ mark. Use those for as long as you can, but they too will soon become too wide as you continue to weave to the top b c.

About 1″ from the top, take out the female heddle rod altogether and replace the male shed rod with a string. At that point, you will not be able to fit any batten all the way through from one side to the other to separate the warps. Instead, you will be working with two needles. You may use a combination of umbrella needles, sacking needles, and curved needles. Use one needle as your batten and the other needle to feed the weft through the narrow shed. When separating the warps with the needle batten, be sure to lead with the blunt end to prevent the needle from piercing and weakening the warps.

Since the female heddle has now been removed, you will separate the female warps manually with the blunt end of your curved needle batten before feeding the weft through with the

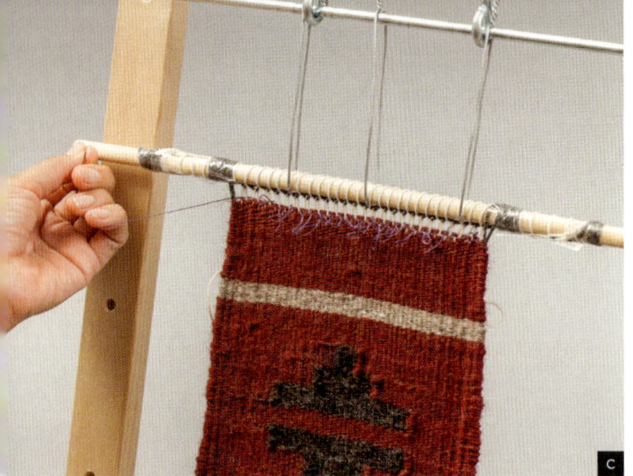

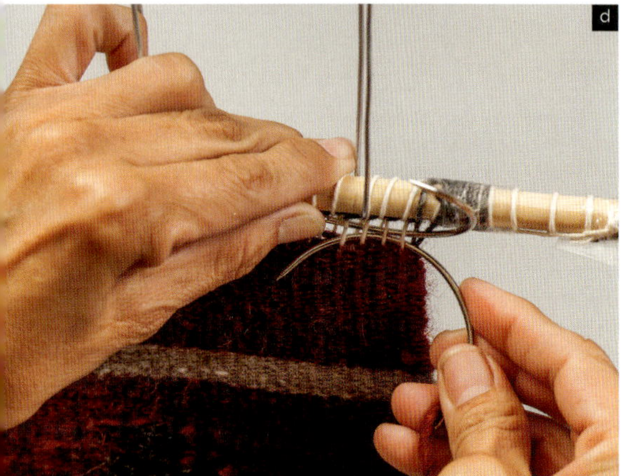

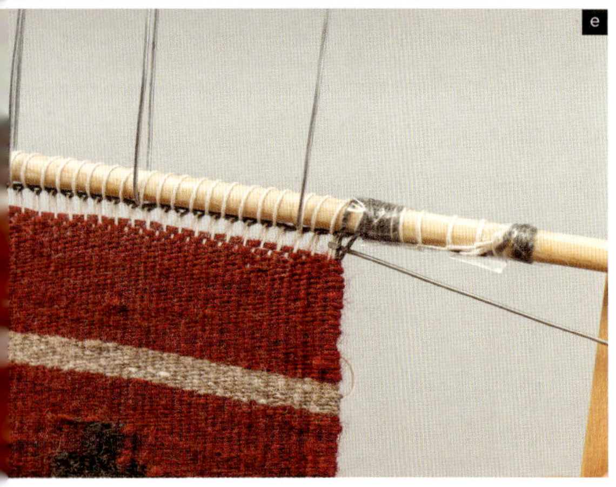

second needle d. As you weave with two needles, remember to create tension bubbles as you lay in the weft. If it is pulled through the warps without the arc of a tension bubble, the weft will be woven in too tightly, and the edges of your textile will be pulled in.

As you weave, the space you have to work in will continue to shrink. The needle you use for your batten will fit through a smaller number of warps until there are just two, and then one. It will no longer be needed as a batten at that point.

No matter how tedious this portion of the weaving may feel, do not try to shortcut the process by using only one needle to pull the weft through. Doing that will cause unnecessary abrasion to the warps, which will weaken and possibly break them. Continue to separate the male and female warps until you are about ⅛″ from the top of the selvage cord under the top wooden dowel.

Before beginning the final two-by-two weaving section, make sure to complete the current turnaround with the hanging weft on the right side of the warp resting behind the male side selvage. Bring the threaded weft around and in front of the side selvage cord. Then, pick up every other male or female pair of warps, beginning with the double warp inside the side selvage cord. Only pick up and weave through 2 or 3 warp pairs at a time. Gently pull the weft through and pack it down with the finishing comb. Do that until the weft is woven to the left-hand edge of the warp, where the weft should run behind the female side selvage cord.

Continue weaving the two by twos in the male direction, to the right side e f g. Start by bringing the threaded weft around and in front of the female selvage cord. Then pick up every

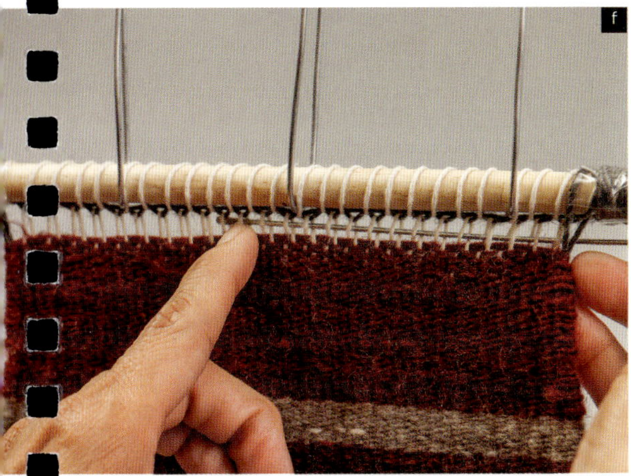

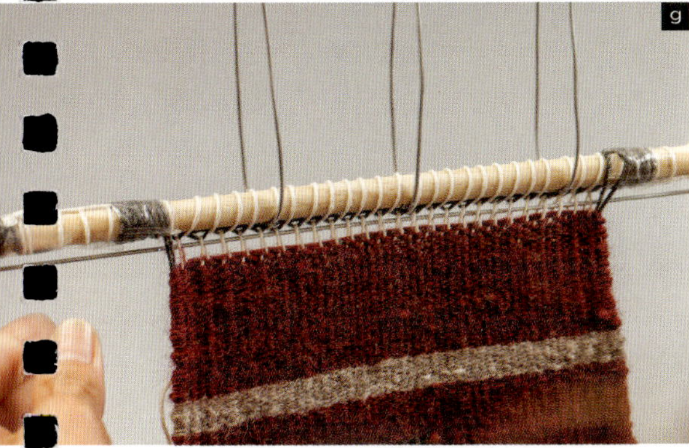

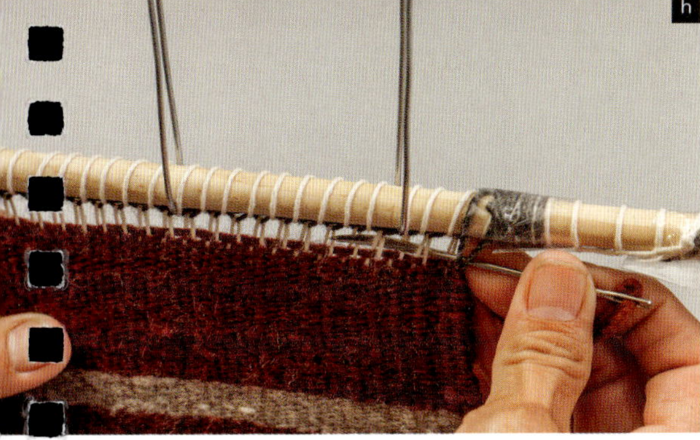

other male or female pair of warps (the opposite of what was picked up before), beginning with the double warp inside the side selvage cord. Gently pull the weft through and pack it down with the finishing comb. When the weft is woven to the right edge of the warp, it should run behind the male side selvage cord. You have completed one turnaround of weaving your two by twos h. There are just three more turnarounds to go!

At the end of the fourth turnaround of weaving the two by twos, the hanging weft should be resting behind the male side selvage cord on the right-hand side. Turn the weft around one last time and weave it in the female direction for a few warp pairs to secure the weft tail before cutting the excess as close to the face of the textile as you can. Doing that ensures that the weft end stays hidden and does not wiggle out as easily as it would if it were trimmed while hanging off the side.

Weavers like to say that the finishing part of a textile is the part that "makes or breaks" weavers. Now, you know why. Make sure to give yourself plenty of time. Listen to music, and rest and massage your hands and fingers often. If you feel frustrated or tense, take a break and work on the rug once harmony is restored. Treat your rug, your loom, and your weaving tools with respect at all times, and do not make disparaging remarks on how bad the rug looks. A rug is a wonderful production of your own individual creativity, and that is a very powerful thing. In the Navajo way, we believe that if you cut off your warp without finishing the rug, it is out of harmony, so we recommend that you finish weaving every textile that you start.

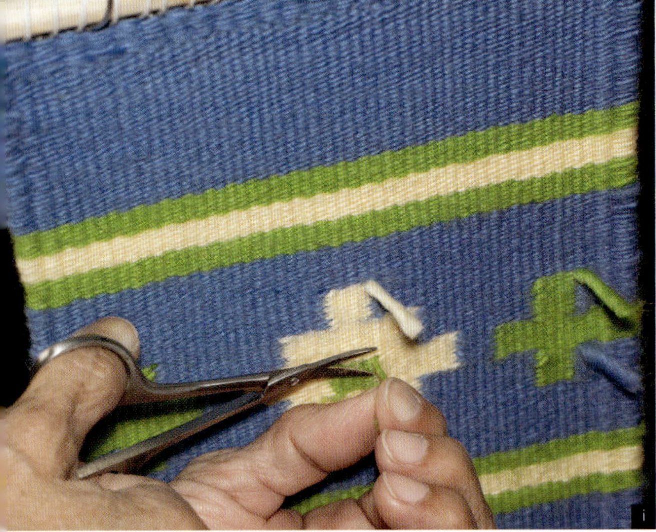

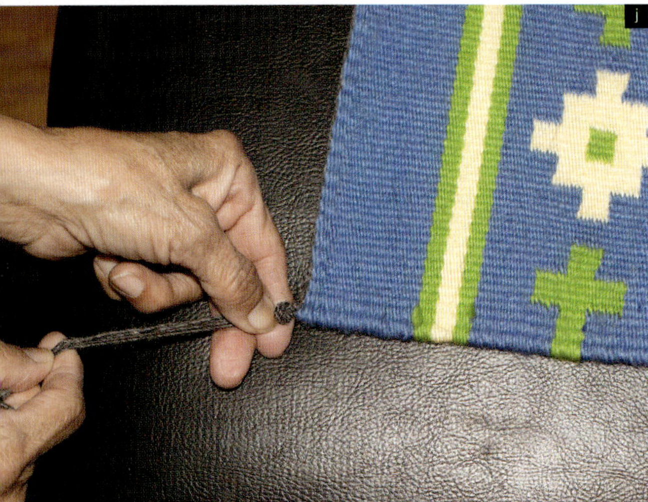

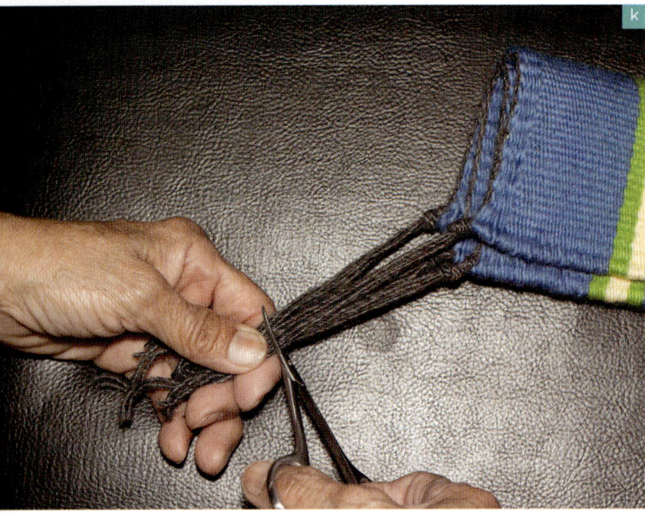

THE FINAL TAKE DOWN

While your finished textile is still stretched on the loom, use scissors to trim off all weft ends that are sticking out by gently tugging each weft end and snipping it as close to the face of the weave as you can i. Small curved scissors work best. You can also take this opportunity to use a curved needle to straighten up any stripes or vertical design blocks.

Loosen the metal turnbuckles or rope just enough to relax the textile, but keep it strung up and supported. Remove any tape from the ends of the top and bottom dowels at the four corners of the loom. Use a sacking needle if you cannot find the tape end.

Beginning at the center, snip the zip ties off the bottom of the loom with wire cutters. Once they are removed, you can free the top of the warp from the loom. Set the loom aside and lay the textile flat on a clean work surface with the bottom edge facing you as you prepare to begin removing the cotton string from the bottom dowel.

Lift the middle string with the curved needle and snip it with scissors. Then, use the needle to pick out and unlace the cotton string, alternating between working a little to the left and an equal amount to the right. Cut the excess string off when it gets long, taking care not to cut the selvage cord, the warps, or the wefts in the process. Once you have the entire bottom of the sewing removed and the textile is freed from the bottom dowel, repeat the process with the sewing at the top of the warp.

After both ends of the textile have been freed from the dowels, take a look at the corners of the textile, paying specific attention to the selvage cords and their hanging ends. There should be four cords at each corner—two side selvages and two top or bottom selvages. Untie any knots on the side selvage cords but leave the knots on the top and bottom twined selvage cords intact. When the side selvage knots are undone at one corner, pull all four selvage cords together and tie them in an overhand knot. Tighten the knot and push it close to but not into the corner of the woven piece j. Repeat on the remaining three corners.

Fold the weaving into quarters so that all sixteen of the selvage cords meet at one corner together. Hold all of the selvage cords together and cut the ends an even length, 2″ to 3″ long, to form tassels k.

CONGRATULATIONS. IN BEAUTY, YOUR WEAVING IS COMPLETE.

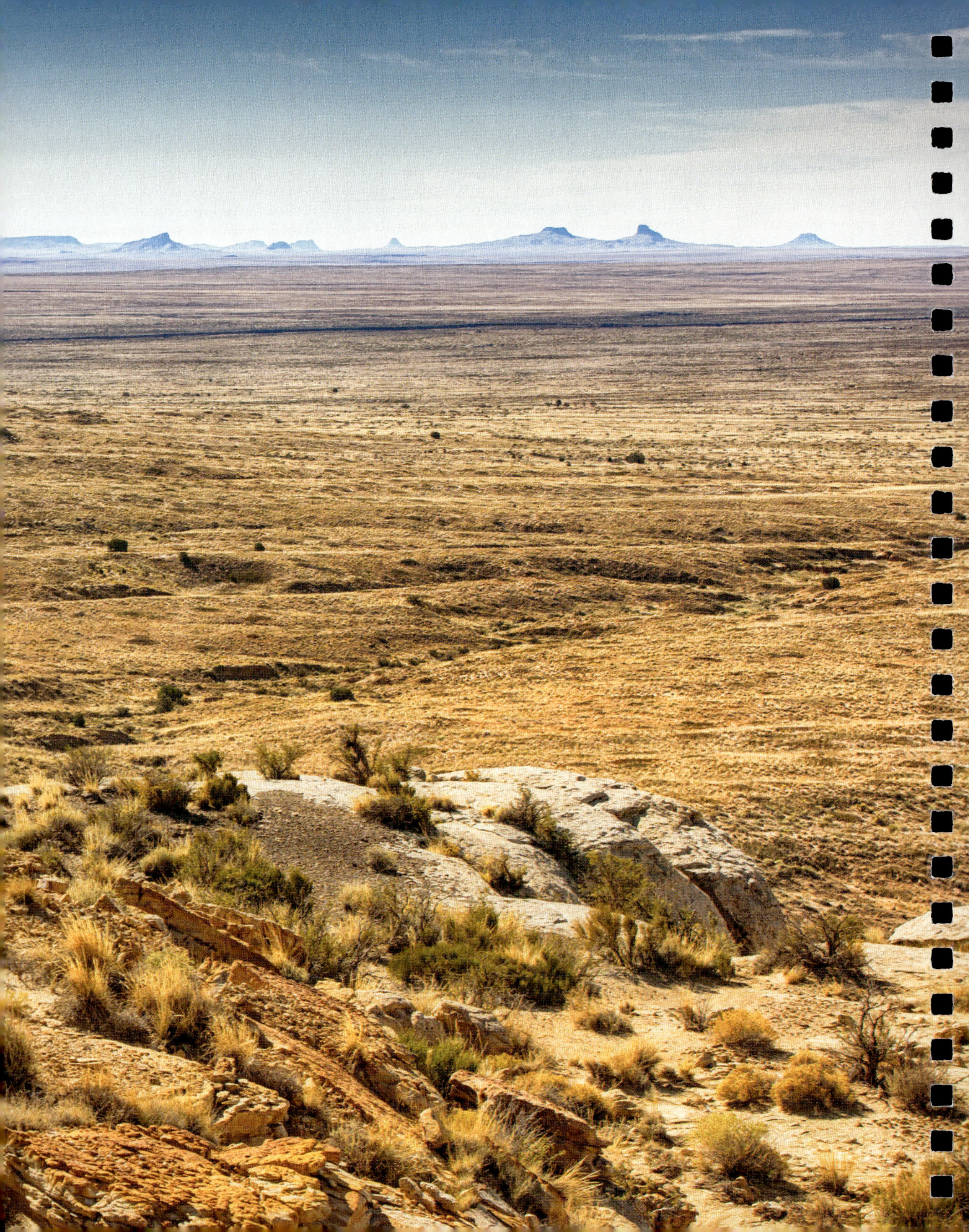

RESOURCES

NAVAJO WEAVING TOOL AND LOOM MAKERS

Arquilino Aragon

#27 RD 5777, Farmington, NM 87401 | (505) 360-6037

Weaving tools, looms, and spindles. Uses native wood for weavers, provides custom orders, and does bulk orders for classes using commercial wood.

Belvin Pete

2142 Irving St., Denver, CO 80211 | (303) 548-5951
Belvin.pete@gmail.com | www.NavajoRugWeavers.com

Weaving tools, metal umbrella needles, warping kits, looms from miniatures to extra-large sizes, warping frames, spindles, custom made to height and hand size, and custom engineering on all items plus adaptability for physically challenged weavers. Uses native woods, exotic woods, and commercial woods for all budgets.

Peter Russell

PO Box 1661, Shiprock, NM 87420 | (505) 406-1396

Weaving tools for rugs and sash belts; metal wire needles.
Specializes in finishing tools.

TEXTILE REPAIRS, RESTORATION, CONSERVATION

Robert Mann Rugs
Robert Mann | 2151 W. 56th Ave., Denver, CO 80221
(303) 292-2522 | MannRugs.com

Navajo Rug Restorations
Marie Lynn Hunken | Tucson, AZ
(520) 797-4735 | MarieLynnH@yahoo.com

ORGANIZATIONS

Navajo Cultural Arts Program
Diné College | 1 Circle Drive, Tsaile, AZ 86556
Navajoculturalartsprogram.org | (928) 724-6616

The Navajo Cultural Arts Program (NCAP) intends to enhance and revitalize traditional Navajo cultural arts practices.

Diné Be'iiná Inc.
PO Box 2684, Shiprock, NM 87420 | Navajolifeway.org | (505) 406-7428

This nonprofit seeks to preserve, protect, and promote the Navajo way of life; to encourage the participation and cooperation of the Navajo people among themselves and with other people and organizations; and to engage in research, education, and development.

GALLERIES, FIBER CENTERS, TRADING POSTS & ART CENTERS

Toh-Atin Gallery
145 W. 9th St., Durango, CO 81301 | (970) 247-8277 | toh-atin.com

Bahti Indian Arts
4330 N. Campbell Ave., Tucson, AZ 85718 | (520) 577-0290 | Bahti.com

Heard Museum Shop
2301 N. Central Ave., Phoenix, AZ 85004 | (602) 252-8848 | Heard.org

Tanner's Indian Arts
237 W. Coal Ave., Gallup, NM 87301 | (505) 863-6017 | Tannersindianarts.com

Two Grey Hills Trading Post
Two Grey Hills, P.O. Box 2639, Farmington, NM 87499
(505) 860-5553 | Twogreyhills.com

Harrisville Designs, Retail Shop & Studio
PO Box 806, Harrisville, NH 03450 | (800) 338-9415 | Harrisville.com

R.B. Burnham and Company
Hwy 191 South, Sanders, AZ 86512
(928) 688-2777 | Rbburnhamtrading.com

Navajo Arts and Crafts Enterprise
PO Box 160, Window Rock, AZ 86515 | (928) 871-4090 | Gonavajo.com
Several locations throughout Arizona and New Mexico

Weaving in Beauty
233 W. Coal, Gallup, NM 87301 | (505) 297-6343

Grandma's Spinning Wheel
6544 E. Tanque Verde Rd., Tucson, AZ 85715
(520) 290-3738 | Grandmasspinningwheel.com

Hubbell Trading Post Historic Site
Hwy 191, Ganado, AZ 86505 | NPS.gov/hutr/index.htm

Idyllwild Arts Academy & Summer Program
PO Box 38, 52500 Temecula Road, Idyllwild, CA 92549
(951) 659-2171 | Idyllwildarts.org

New Mexico Fiber Arts Center
325 N. Paseo de Oñate, Española, NM 87532 | (505) 747-3577 | Evfac.org

The Natural Twist
Albuquerque, NM | (505) 453-2277 | Thenaturaltwist.com | Online only

Griswold Trading Post
1591 Highway 264, Tse Bonito, NM 87301 | (505) 371-5393 | Griswoldpawn.com

Foutz Trading Post
PO Box 1904, Shiprock, NM 87420 | (800) 383-0615 | Foutztrade.com
Several locations throughout New Mexico

FIBER ARTS FESTIVALS AND EVENTS FEATURING NAVAJO FIBER AND WEAVING

Albuquerque Fiber Arts Fiesta
Albuquerque, NM | Fiberartsfiesta.org

Estes Park Wool Market
Estes Park, CO | Estesparkeventscomplex.com/wool-market.html

Heard Museum Indian Fair and Market
Phoenix, AZ | Heard.org/fair/

Intermountain Weavers Conference
Durango, CO | Intermountainweavers.org

Salida Fiber Festival
Salida, CO | Salidafiberfestival.com

Santa Fe Indian Market
Santa Fe, NM | SWAIA.org

***Spin Off* Autumn Retreat**
Boulder, CO | Longthreadmedia.com

Taos Wool Festival
Taos, NM | Taoswoolfestival.org

A BUYER'S GUIDE TO NAVAJO WEAVING

In every class we teach, students ask us from whom they can buy a Navajo blanket, rug, or tapestry. The list below provides contact information and design styles for current Navajo weavers who sell their work and accept commissions.

Our ancestors' weaving had to follow the marketing directives of the Trading Posts, but today, weavers often design and innovate without too much attachment to the Trading Post styles. These weavers provide a glimpse into the future of Navajo weaving.

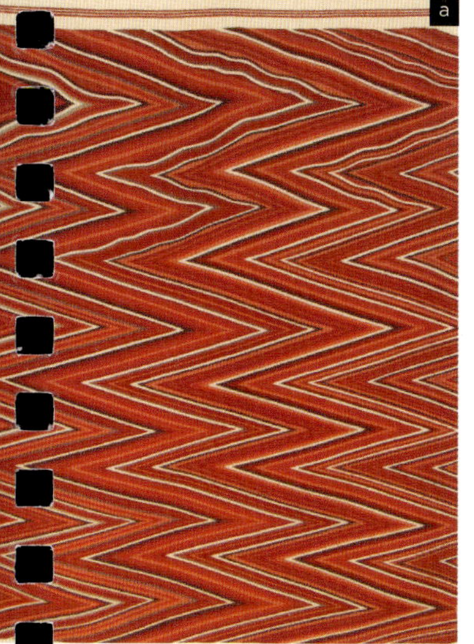

Venancio Aragon
Germantown Tuft
Albuquerque, New Mexico
Venancio_aragon@hotmail.com

Kevin Aspaas a
Wedge Weave
Shiprock, New Mexico
wolachii10@gmail.com | (505) 716-0972

Berdine Y. Begay
Contemporary, Pictorial
Tselani, Arizona
berdinebegay@yahoo.com | (918) 431-4342

D.Y. Begay
Contemporary, Landscapes, and Pictorial
Tselani, Arizona | dybegay@gmail.com
www.navajo-indian.com | (602) 538-5339

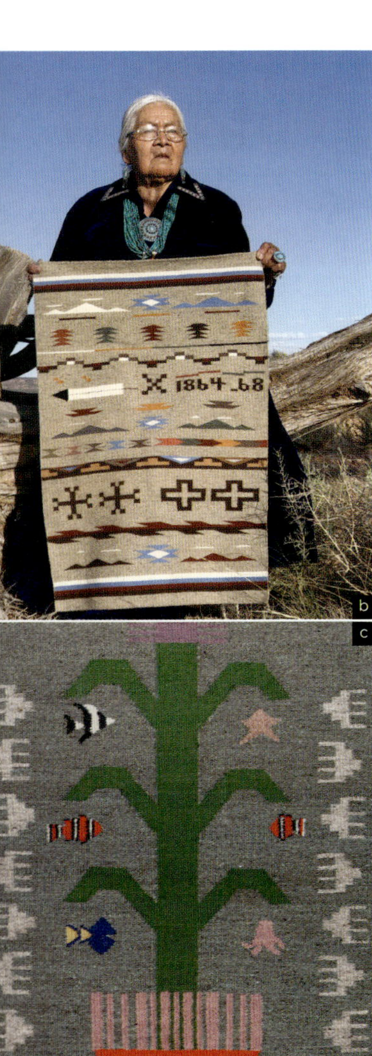

Gerard Begay
Clothing, Rug Dresses, Chief's Blankets, and Twill
Phoenix, Arizona
gerardbegay@yahoo.com | (480) 843-2385

Mary H. Begay b
Burnt Water
Ganado, Arizona | gloriajeantextiles@gmail.com

Sue Begay
Geometrics
Dennehotso, Arizona
Suevbegay@yahoo.com | (928) 429-4890

Chris Brown
Twill
Chandler, Arizona
brown.christian.n@gmail.com | (480) 201-8803

Berdina Y. Charley
Contemporary, Pictorial
Tselani, Arizona
berdinebegay@yahoo.com | (918) 431-4342

May Clark
Pictorial, Rug Dresses
Navajo and Hopi Indian Relocation Area
I_weave@yahoo.com | (928) 245-2841

Titus Steiner Cody
Pictorial
Pine Hill, New Mexico | boomanc6@gmail.com

Velma Kee Craig c
Pictorial
Phoenix, Arizona
velmakc@gmail.com | (480) 524-1280

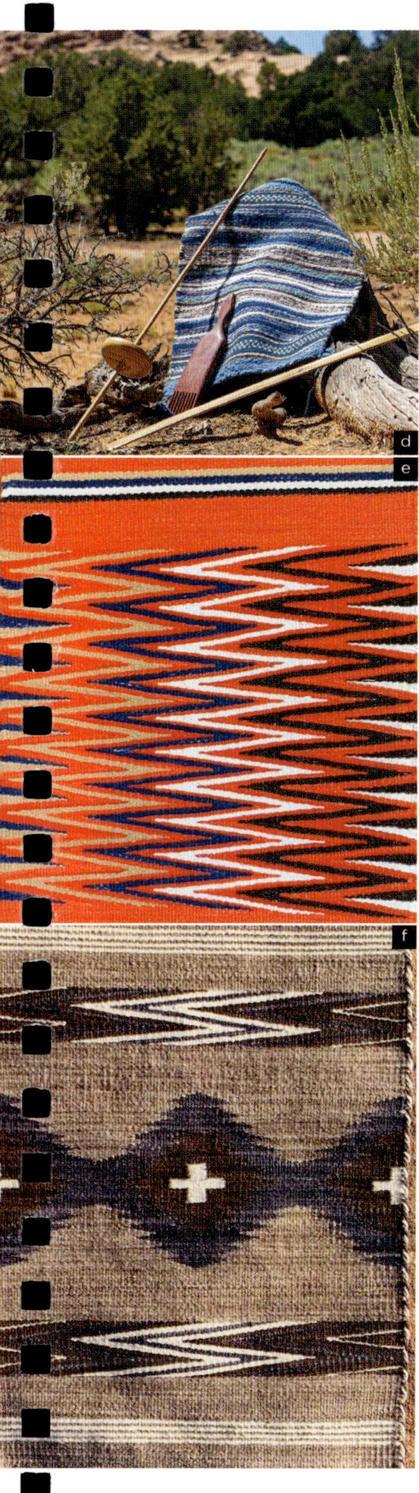

Eliseo Curley
Chief Blankets
Shiprock, New Mexico
elicurley53@gmail.com | (505) 635-9255

Gloria Fain
Ganado
Phoenix, Arizona | gloriajeantextiles@gmail.com

Vigie Fausto
Two Grey Hills
Phoenix, Arizona | Vigiefausto7@gmail.com

Jackie Frank d
Pictorial
Echo Springs, Arizona
rezboy.jf@gmail.com | (928) 380-0341

Naiomi Glasses e
Wedge Weave, Chief's Blanket, and Woven Purses
naiomiglasses@gmail.com | (928) 429-5905

Tyler Glasses f
Sampler, Transitional, Wedge Weave, Germantown
t_glasses@yahoo.com | (928) 209-7016

Genevieve Hardy
Dresses, Table Runners
Fort Defiance, Arizona
jus.weaving@yahoo.com

Nathan Harry
Storm, Two Grey Hills, Chief's Blankets
Shiprock, New Mexico
n2navajo_rugs@yahoo.com | (505) 516-7026

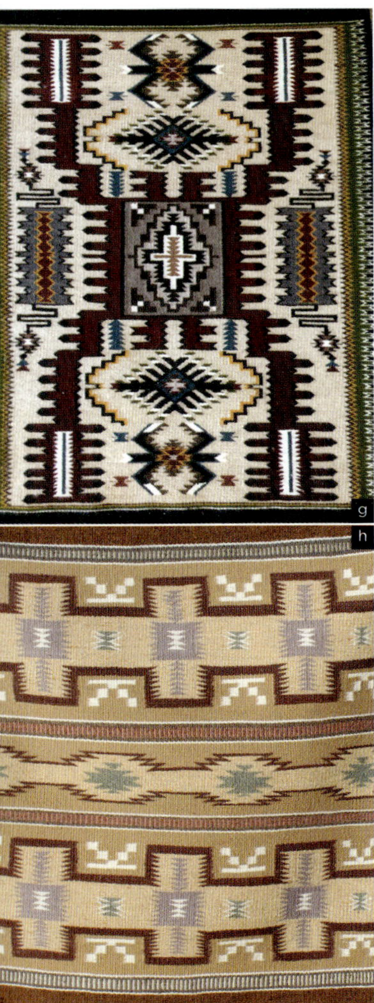

Erma Horseherder-Nells
Storm Pattern, Pictorial, and Sampler
Big Mountain, Arizona
ermajnells@yahoo.com

Daniel Keams, Jr g
Storm Pattern
jrkeams@gmail.com | (928) 380-5790

TahNibaa Naataanii
Old Style Period Pieces, Shawls, and Serapes
Table Mesa, New Mexico
weavinginbeauty@yahoo.com | (505) 809-0721

Florence Riggs
Rug Dresses, Pictorial
Tuba City, Arizona
Riggs.florence2015@icloud.com | (928) 707-0978

Rosalita Teller h
Chinle
Chinle, Arizona
roseyteller@ymail.com | (928) 781-5672

Brenda Spencer
Wide Ruins
Wide Ruins, Arizona
brnspncr99@yahoo.com | (928) 551-2719

Ephraim "Zefren" Anderson
Whitehouse Revival II
Shiprock, New Mexico
raidex82@gmail.com | (505) 320-1115

GLOSSARY OF NAVAJO TEXTILE TERMS

DINÉ (Navajo)

NA'ASHJÉ'II ASDZĄ́Ą́ (Spider Woman)

NA'ESHJÉ'II HASTĮĮ (Spider Man)

ASDZĄ́Ą́ NÁDLEEHÉ (Changing Woman)

BEE'ADIZÍ (spindle)

BEE AK'ÍNÍLTŁISH (batten)

NANOOLZHEE' (weft)

DIBÉ (sheep)

DIBÉ BIGHAA' (sheep's wool)

HA'NILCHAAD (carded wool)

DAH'IISTŁ'Ǫ́ (loom)

DIYOGÍ (rug)

BILAGÁANA (Caucasian)

NIZHÓNÍ (beautiful)

HOZHÓ (harmony)

YÁBITŁ'ÓÓL - top heddle rod

NI'BITŁ'ÓÓL - bottom heddle rod

NIZHÓNÍ DÓÓ AHXÉHEE'

YISHTL'Ó (Plain weave)

YISHBÍZ (braided twill)

I'ÍMÁS (twill design)

DIYÓGI - Woven with wide spaced warps and loose weft

AŁNÉ'ĘSTŁÓNI - Two Sided woven

BEEL'DLÉH + (how it's woven) - (means it is used as a blanket)

TŁ'ÓH BEÉSHTŁÓNI - (woven with yarn of new technology) Germantown or Aniline dyed yarns

PHOTOGRAPHY CREDITS

JOE COCA:
pp. iv, x, 1–2, 6, 19–24, 27–28, 32–33, 36, 38–41, 46–52, 54–55, 60–61, 63–69, 72, 75–76, 78, 81, 83, 113–114, 126

BELVIN PETE:
5, 9, 15, 16, 30, 42, 62, 71, 77, 79, 84, 87, 89, 90, 92, 95–99, 101–105, 117–124

LYLE HARVEY: 18

INDEX